Money, Culture, Beauty. The Botti Family

Angela Orlandi

Money, Culture, Beauty. The Botti Family

Merchant-Bankers in Renaissance

Springer

Angela Orlandi
Department of Economics and Management
'F. Datini' International Institute of Economic History Foundation
Prato, Italy

ISBN 978-3-032-00452-9 ISBN 978-3-032-00453-6 (eBook)
https://doi.org/10.1007/978-3-032-00453-6

This Springer imprint is published by the registered company Springer Nature Switzerland AG
The registered company address is: Gewerbestrasse 11, 6330 Cham, Switzerland

Acknowledgements

I first began studying the activity of Simone Botti's sons many years ago, searching for them in archives in Italy and abroad. In Florence, of course, but also in Cádiz, Seville and Sanlúcar de Barrameda, among the papers of the Guzman family, dukes of Medina Sidonia and the undisputed lords of sixteenth-century Andalusia. Documents of every kind allowed me to enter their lives. Curious and rich attestations of the activity of men ready for adventure, stories of merchants able to 'manage ... goods and money with steadfast orderliness aimed towards their purpose'[1] and stories of great merchants who, while trying to limit the lavishness of their lifestyle, chose to use their wealth to help artists and build art collections. They were the main characters of these stories, who worked knowing, to cite Antonio Maria Venusti, that divine Trade brought 'much convenience, much honour and much glory',[2] without forgetting, however, that 'sumptuous dress, a fine appearance and grand banquets [...] are not a merchant's lot'.[3]

And so, I have tried to recount the interweaving of money, culture and beauty that characterised the activity of the Botti brothers, merchants and bankers of Renaissance Florence.

If this volume has seen the light of day, I have many people to thank. It is with infinite gratitude and affection that I would like to thank José Jesús Hernández Palomo, researcher at the CSIC, who introduced me to the secrets of the Andalusian archives with immense expertise and tireless willingness to help when I arrived at the Escuela de Estudios Hispano-Americanos in Seville. Pepe is no longer with us, and this volume is dedicated to him.

[1] B. Cotrugli, *Il libro dell'arte di mercatura*, ed. Ugo Tucci, Arsenale Editrice, Venice 1990 p. 158.

[2] A.M. Venusti, *Discorso d'intorno alla mercantia*, 1561 pp. 13–14, cited in Ph. Braunstein, F. Franceschi, '«Saperssi governar». Pratica mercantile e arte del vivere', in *Il Rinascimento italiano e l'Europa. Commercio e cultura mercantile*, vol. IV, Colla Editore, Vicenza 2007 pp. 655–677.

[3] ASF, *Miscellanea*, 107 fascicolo 3, Florence-Valladolid, Matteo Botti to Giovanbattista Botti (personal), 25 May 1542 c. 184v.

I would also like to thank Francesco Ammannati, Enrico Basso, Laura Bruschetini, Hilario Casado Alonso, Simonetta Cavaciocchi, Daniela Degl'Innocenti, Giuliano Doria, Giovanni Falaschi, Letizia Finocchiaro, Franco Franceschi, Cristiano Giometti, David Igual Luis, Heinrich Lang, Federica Nigro and Pinuccia Franca Simbula; all of them contributed to improving my work, each in their own way. Whether pointing out useful historiographic and archival references, taking on the laborious reading of an early draft or offering invaluable suggestions. Giampiero Nigro remains my guide.

Contents

List of Cards

List of Figures

List of Tables

Chapter 1
Introduction

A family biography, but above all the history of a Florentine corporate group, this volume tells the story of the Botti family, which was active in the leading economic markets in the first half of the sixteenth century. Florence, Pisa, Cádiz, Seville, Venice, Valladolid, Rome, Antwerp and Lyon were the cities where our merchants carried out their financial and trade activity, in the form of opening companies and prolonged stays.

This study, which draws mainly on the extraordinary documentary sources left by the Botti family, touches on several historiographic themes. The first is that of migration in Europe during the Middle Ages and early modern period. The second, research on the families of Renaissance Florence. The third, more rarely explored, intercultural trade.

A. Orlandi, *Money, Culture, Beauty. The Botti Family*,
https://doi.org/10.1007/978-3-032-00453-6_1

As for the presence of merchants abroad, the literature on this subject is vast and will not be our focus here.[1] We will limit ourselves to noting that the topic has

[1] Without claiming to be exhaustive, we will try to outline the main points. After the early studies by Federigo Melis and Armando Sapori on Florence, Edoardo Grendi on Genoa and Frederic Lane on Venice, the theme of foreigners abroad was revived in the mid 1970s by Fernand Braudel in his book *Out of Italy.* A decade later, at a meeting of the Gruppo Interuniversitario per la Storia dell'Europa Mediterranea (GISEM) in Venice, interest in the topic was rekindled, with research oriented in two directions: the international elites and relationship systems. In the 20 years that followed, seminars and conferences were organised on the circulation of political and economic elites, migration, rejection and embrace and the status of foreigners. Braudel and Melis, as well as the members of GISEM, introduced interesting new elements, arguing that the expansion of the medieval and early modern Mediterranean was rooted in the circulation of people and goods. Within this framework, an important role was played by a diverse range of merchant groups, often organised by geographic provenance, that controlled the networks they created. The two historians explained their success in terms of the economic rationality they subscribed to, a rationality expressed in companies, business methods and innovation. Their success was also due to a shared origin, which ensured close connections, reciprocal support and frequent information exchange. In the wake of these interpretations, and increased attention to exchange and intercultural relationships, the theme of traders abroad was explored later in research on merchant communities and networks across Europe and beyond. Italian, French, English, Spanish and Portuguese groups were analysed, as well as communities in the Indian Ocean. This research, which touched on behaviour, methods, procedures and hierarchies, turned more attention to the informal rules (trust, information, reciprocity, friendship, reputation) that supported links between traders based in different political and cultural areas. See B. Bailyn, *The New England Merchants in the Seventeenth Century*, Harvard University Press, Cambridge 1955; F. Braudel, *L'Italia fuori d'Italia. Due secoli e tre Italie*, in *Storia d'Italia. Dalla Caduta dell'Impero Romano al secolo XVIII. L'economia delle tre Italie*, eds. R. Romano and C. Vivanti, Giulio Einaudi editore, Turin 1974, pp. 2092–2248; Ph. Braunstein, 'Réseaux familiaux, réseaux d'affaires en pays d'Empire: les facteurs des société Fugger (1380–1520)', in *Le négoce international, XIIIe-XXe siècle*, ed. F. Crouzet, Economica, Paris 1989, pp. 23–34; K.N. Chauduri, *Trade and Civilisation in the Indian Ocean. An Economic History from the Rise of Islam to 1750*, Cambridge University Press, Cambridge 1985; *Dentro la città. Stranieri e realtà urbane nell'Europa dei secoli XII-XV*, ed. G. Rossetti, GISEM, Liguori, Naples 1989; M. Fusaro, 'Cooperating mercantile networks in the early modern Mediterranean', *Economic History Review*, 65, 2, 2012, pp. 701–718; M. Fusaro, 'Les Anglais et les Grecs. Un réseau de coopération commerciale en Méditerranée vénitienne', *Annales. Histoire, Sciences Sociales*, 58, 3, 2003, pp. 605–625; M. Fusaro, 'The Greeks of Venice, 1498–1600: Immigration, Settlement, and Integration', *Renaissance Quarterly*, 71, 2, 2018, pp. 716–717; J. Gentil da Silva, *Stratégie des affaires à Lisbonne entra 1595 et 1607. Lettres marchandes des Rodrigues d'Evora et Veiga*, A. Colin, Paris 1956; A. Greif, 'The Organisation of Long-Distance Trade: Reputation and Coalitions in the Geniza Documents During the Eleventh and Twelfth Centuries', *The Journal of Economic History*, 49:4 (1989), pp. 847–882; E. Grendi, 'Traffico portuale, naviglio mercantile e consolati genovesi nel Cinquecento', in *Rivista Storica Italiana*, LXXX, 1968, pp. 593–629; F. Lane, *Venice. A Maritime republic*, The Johns Hopkins University Press, Baltimore 1973; H. Lapeyre, *Simon Ruiz et les «asientos» de Philippe II*, A. Colin, Paris 1953; H. Lapeyre, *Une famille de marchands, les Ruiz. Contribution à l'étude du commerce entre la France et l'Espagne*, A. Colin, Paris 1955; V. Magalhães Godinho, *L'économie de l'empire portugais aux XVe et XVIe siècles*, SEVPEN, Paris 1969; F. Melis, *I mercanti italiani nell'Europa medievale e rinascimentale*, ed. L. Frangioni, Istituto Internazionale di Storia Economica "F. Datini" - Prato, Le Monnier, Florence 1990; A. Molho, D. Ramanda Curto, Les réseaux marchands à l'époque moderne', *Annales. Histoire, Sciences Sociales*, 58, 3, 2003, pp. 569–580; J. Poettering, *Migrating Merchants: Trade, Nation, and Religion in Seventeenth-Century*

recently been freshly explored in terms of capitalistic development.[2]

The Botti family's strongest ties were with Spanish markets. This was a period during which Andalusia's appeal increased considerably. A border region between the Mediterranean and the Atlantic, foreign businessmen flocked to the area ready to exploit the trade opportunities offered by the discovery of the New World. This is a wide-ranging topic that was recently brought further to the fore by five conferences in Seville that offered rich analysis of issues linked to early globalisation, the role of trade in its development and exchange between cities and ports.[3]

Cádiz and Seville became cosmopolitan markets. Cádiz, located on the Atlantic Ocean, saw its port fill with ships. Seville was transformed, its quarters and streets flooding with people looking for business and adventure: sailors, vagabonds and

---

Hamburg and Portugal, De Gruyter Oldenbourg, Berlin 2019; *Sistema di rapporti ed élites economiche in Europa (secoli XII-XVII)*, ed. M. Del Treppo, GISEM, Liguori, Naples 1994; *Strutture del potere ed élites economiche nelle città europee dei secoli XII-XVI*, ed. G. Petti Balbi, GISEM, Liguori, Naples 1996; D. Studnicki-Gizbert, 'La "nation" portugaise. Réseaux marchands dans l'espace atlantique à l'époque moderne', *Annales. Histoire, Sciences Sociales*, 58, 3, 2003, pp. 627–648.

[2] B. Figliuolo, 'Mercanti fiorentini e il loro spazio economico: un modello di organizzazione capitalistica', *Archivio Storico Italiano*, 638, 2013, pp. 639–664. I have also researched this theme through the lens of Social Network Analysis and application of different theories of management: A. Orlandi, 'Le prestazioni di una holding tardo medievale rilette attraverso alcune teorie di management e la Social Network Analysis', in *Innovare nella Storia Economica: Temi, Metodi, Fonti*, Rome 10–11 October 2014, Fondazione Istituto Internazionale di Storia Economica "F. Datini" - Prato, Prato 2016, pp. 117–148; A. Orlandi, 'Networks and Models of the Commercial Penetration of the Late Medieval Mediterranean. Revisiting the Case of Datini', *in Commercial Networks and European Cities, 1400–1800*, eds. A. Caracausi and C. Jeggle, Pickering & Chatto Publishers Ltd., London 2014, pp. 81–106.

[3] See *Ciudades atlánticas del sur de España. La construcción de un mundo nuevo (siglos XVI-XVIII)*, eds. J.J. Iglesias Rodríguez, J.J. García Bernal, I.M. Melero Muñoz, Universidad de Sevilla, Seville 2021; *Ciudades y puertos de Andalucía en un Atlántico global, siglos XVI-XVIII*, eds. J.J. Iglesias Rodríguez, J.J. García Bernal, I.M. Melero Muñoz, Universidad de Sevilla, Seville 2022; *En torno a la primera globalización: circulaciones y conexiones entre el Atlántico y el Mediterráneo (1492–1824)*, eds. J.J. Iglesia Rodríguez et al., Universidad de Sevilla, Seville 2022; *Mercaderes y redes mercantiles en la Península Ibérica. Siglos XV-XVIII*, eds. M.F. Fernández Chaves et al., Universidad de Sevilla, Seville 2019; *Trata atlántica y esclavitud en Sevilla (ca. 1500–1650)*, ed. E. Corona Pérez, Universidad de Sevilla, Seville 2022. On the role of the 'multi-risk' merchants active in trade between the Mediterranean and the Atlantic, see the research proposal in 'Del Mediterráneo al Atlántico. Mercaderes en las urbes (Siglos XVI-XVII)', eds. J.J. García Bernal, A. Guillaume Alonso, B. Pérez, M. Zerari-Penin, *Studia historica. Historia moderna*, 42, 2, 2020, pp. 13–19. For essays with a broader scope, looking at the whole Iberian Peninsula, see: *Globalization and Enlightenment, 1500–1800*, Part Two of *An Economic History of the Iberian Peninsula, 700–2000*, eds. L. Freire Costa, R. Grafe, A. Herranz-Locán, D. Igual Luis, H. Vasconcelos Vilar, Cambridge University Press, Cambridge 2024. With specific relevance to our subject, see C. Antunes, R. Grafe, X. Lamikiz, 'Trade and the Colonial Economies', 1500–1828, in *An Economic History*, pp. 409–442 and B. Yun Casalilla, 'The Economic History of Iberia in a Wider Context, 1500–1800', in *An Economic History*, pp. 443–470; B. Yun Casalilla, 'The Peninsular Economies and the Impact of Globalisation (ca. 1494–1700)', in *The Iberian World, 1450–1820*, eds. F. Bouza, P. Cardim, A. Feros Carrasco, Routledge, London 2019, pp. 189–210.

artists, but most importantly bankers and merchants. The city filled with the Portuguese, French, Germans, English, Italians and Flemings, becoming an international hub.[4]

The presence of Florentines in Andalusia and their role in trade with the West has been amply discussed. A few historians argued in the past that their activity after the discovery of the New World was fairly limited.[5] According to their research, the number of Tuscan companies increased in the first quarter of the sixteenth century, but they played a middling economic role in terms of innovation and the quantity and value of the goods traded. More recent literature has shown that the activity of those merchants was actually significant and not held back by mediocre routine.[6] The Botti family is an exemplary case in point.

The second historiographic current concerns research on the major merchant families of Renaissance Florence. There is a rich body of literature on this subject that starts with the pioneering work of Richard Goldthwaite and Paolo Malanima[7] and it has never stopped drawing scholars' attention, although they have often

---

[4] In addition to the more recent literature listed in Footnote 3, see the classic studies B AND L. BENASSAR, *1492 ¿Un mundo nuevo?*, Nerea, Madrid 1992; A.M. BERNAL RODRÍGUEZ, A. COLLANTES DE TERÁN, A. GARCÍA-BAQUERO, *Sevilla, de los gremios a la indstrialización*, Ayuntamiento de Sevilla, Seville 2008; R. CARANDE, *Carlo V e i suoi banchieri*, Marietti, Genoa 1987; J.H. Elliot, *La Spagna imperiale: 1469–1716*, Il Mulino, Bologna 1982; A. GARCÍA-BAQUERO, *Comercio y burguesía mercantil en el Cádiz de la Carrera de Indias*, Diputación Provincial de Huelva, Cádiz 1991; F. MORALES PADRÓN, *Historia de Sevilla. Las ciudad de Quinientos*, Universisad de Sevilla, Seville 1989; E. DE ORY LOZANO, Colón, Cádiz y el descubrimiento de América, S.L. Rústica Editorial, Cádiz 1993; J. LYNCH, *España bajo los Asturias/1. Imperio y absolutismo (1516–1598)*, Ediciones Península, Barcellona 1989; A. Rumeu De Armas, *Cádiz, metrópoli del comercio con África en los siglos XV y XVI*, Dante, Cádiz 1976.

[5] J. GIL, *Los mercaderes florentinos en Sevilla*, in *Mundus Novus. Amerigo Vespucci e i metodi della ricerca storico-geografica, Atti del Convegno Internazionale di Studi, Roma-Firenze 27–30 novembre 2002*, ed. A. D'Ascenzo, Società Geografica Italiana, Rome 2004, pp. 101–141; C. VARELA, *Colombo e i fiorentini*, Vallecchi, Florence 1991, pp. 15–35; C. VARELA, 'Vida cotidiana de los florentinos en la Sevilla del descubrimiento, in Presencia italiana en Andalucía siglos XIV-XVII, Actas del III Coloquio Hispano-Italiano', Escuela de Estudios Hispano-Americanos de Sevilla, Seville 1989, pp. 11–22.

[6] A. ORLANDI, 'Dall'Andalusia al Nuovo Mondo: affari e viaggi di mercanti toscani nel Cinquecento', in *Vespucci, Firenze e le Americhe.* Atti del Convegno Internazionale, Firenze 22–24 novembre 2012, eds. G. Pinto, L. Rombai, C. Tripodi, Olschki, Florence 2014, pp. 63–86; A. ORLANDI, 'Fiorentini alla ricerca del Nuovo Mondo', in *Amerigo Vespucci e i mercanti viaggiatori fiorentini del Cinquecento*, eds. M. Azzari amd L. Rombai, Firenze University Press, Florence 2013, pp. 131–156; A. ORLANDI, 'Tuscan Merchants in Andalusia: A Historiographical Debate', in *Italian Merchants in the Early-Modern Spanish Monarchy*: Business Relations, Identities and Political Resources, eds. C. Brilli, M. Herrero Sánchez, Routledge, London 2017, pp. 13–32.

[7] R.A. GOLDTHWAITE, *Private Wealth in Renaissance Florence: A Study of Four Families*, Princeton University Press, Princeton 1968; R.A. GOLDTHWAITE, *La costruzione della Firenze rinascimentale. Una storia economica e sociale*, Il Mulino, Bologna 1984; P. MALANIMA, *I Riccardi di Firenze. Una famiglia e un patrimonio nella Toscana dei Medici*, Olschki, Florence 1977.

limited themselves to particular aspects of the families' activity.[8] What are missing are studies that reconstruct the contemporary activity of companies in different European economic contexts in the sixteenth century.

The third major research direction is concentrated on how trade diasporas, long sojourns and the intensity of economic relationships facilitated the intersection of different cultures.[9]

This book concentrates in particular on the latter two threads. The aim is to demonstrate the prolonged activity of Tuscan traders in European markets, their

---

[8] Among the numerous studies, we will list just the more recent ones here: G. Battista, *Le avventure di una famiglia di mercanti-banchieri fiorentini. Storia documentata dei Rinieri del Vaio di San Giovanni*, Aska Edizioni, Montevarchi 2024; I. Chabod, *Ricostruzione di una famiglia. I Ciurianni di Firenze tra XII e XV secolo, con l'edizione critica del «Libro propio» di Lapo di Valore Ciurianni e successori (1326–1429)*, Le Lettere, Florence 2012; G. Ciappelli, *Una famiglia e le ricordanze; i Castellani di Firenze nel Tre-Quattrocento*, Olschki, Florence 1995; A. Crabb, *The Strozzi of Florence: Widowhood and Family Solidarity in the Renaissance*, University of Michigan Press, Ann Arbor 2000; F. Guidi Bruscoli, *Bartolomeo Marchionni, «Homem de grossa fazenda» (ca. 1450–1530). Un mercante fiorentino a Lisbona e l'impero portoghese*, Olschki, Florence 2014; F. Guidi Bruscoli, *Benvenuto Olivieri. I «mercatores» fiorentini e la Camera apostolica nella Roma di Paolo III Farnese (1534–1549)*, Olschki, Florence 2000; P. Jacks, W. Caferro, *The Spinelli of Florence. Fortune of a Renaissance Merchant Family*, The Pennsylvania State University Press, University Park 2001; E. Plebani, *I Tornabuoni. Una famiglia fiorentina alla fine del Medioevo*, Franco Angeli, Milan 2002; S. Tognetti, *Da Figline a Firenze. Ascesa economica e politica della famiglia Serristori (secoli XIV-XVI)*, Opus libri, Florence 2003; S. Tognetti, *I Gondi di Lione. Una banca d'affari fiorentina nella Francia del primo Cinquecento*, Olschki, Florence 2013; S. Tognetti, *Il banco Cambini. Affari e mercati di una compagnia mercantile-bancaria nella Firenze del Quattrocento*, Olschki, Florence 1999; C. Tripodi, *Gli Spini tra XIV e XV secolo. Il declino di un antico casato fiorentino*, Olschki, Florence 2013; C. Tripodi, *Prima di Amerigo. I Vespucci da Peretola a Firenze alle Americhe*, Viella, Rome 2018; A.M. Zandri, *Famiglie storiche toscane. I Capponi*, Polistampa, Florence, 2004.

[9] With his introduction of the concept of 'trade diaspora' in 1984, Philip Curtin initiated reflection on the role of merchants in cultural intermediation. See P.D. Curtin, *Cross-Cultural Trade in World History*, Cambridge University Press, Cambridge-New York 1984. Also see L.U. Afonso, 'Patterns of Artistic Hybridization in the Early Protoglobalization Period', *Journal of World History*, XXVII/2, 2016, pp. 215–53; M. Ajmar-Wollheim, L. Molà, 'The Global Renaissance: Cross-Cultural Objects in the Early Modern Period', in *Global Design History*, eds. G. Adamson et al., Routledge, London 2011, pp. 11–20; A Grafton, 'Introduction: Notes from Underground on Cultural Transmission', in *The Transmission of Culture in Early Modern Europe*, eds. A. Grafton, A. Blair, University of Pennsylvania Press, Philadelphia 1990, pp. 1–7. Francesca Trivellato has studied these issues, including in more general terms, focusing on contact between Renaissance Italy and the Jewish and Muslim worlds: F. Trivellato, 'Renaissance Italy and the Muslim Mediterranean in Recent Historical Work', *The Journal of Modern History*, LXXXII, 2010, pp. 127–155. Also see F. Trivellato, 'Juifs de Livourne, Italiens de Lisbonne, Hindous de Goa. Réseaux marchands et échanges interculturels à l'époque moderne', *Annales. Histoire, Sciences Sociales*, 58, 3, 2003, pp. 581–603; F. Trivellato, *The Familiarity of Strangers. The Sephardic Diaspora, Livorno and Cross-Cultural Trade in the Early Modern Period*, Yale University Press, New Haven-London 2009; B. Yun Casalilla, 'The Spanish Empire, Globalization, and Cross-Cultural Consumption in a World Context, c. 1400-c. 1750', in *Global Goods and the Spanish Empire, 1492–1824. Circulation, Resistance and Diversity*, eds. B. Aram, B. Yun Casalilla, Palgrave, London 2014, pp. 277–306.

pervasiveness and how they set into motion an intercultural trading network driven by reciprocal processes of cross-fertilization. In short, we will use the Botti documents to try to reconstruct the role of international trade in shaping the taste of Florentine artisans and to show how the city's merchants managed to circulate the goods that came out of its workshops in even radically different contexts. In other words, we will try to understand the interaction between the wealth of those men and their culture.

The archival documentation upon which this analysis is based is preserved in the Archivio di Stato, Florence in the Libri di commercio e di famiglia, Miscellanea Medicea and Carte Strozziane collections. The Libri di commercio e di famiglia collection contains ten letter books, three account books, a memoir, an asset management book and documents relative to division of property.[10] In the Miscellanea Medicea collection, we find three letter books and some loose letters.[11] And lastly, the Carte Strozziane collection preserves an account statement relative to the family's insurance proceedings.[12] All of this material dates to the period between 1524 and 1566.[13]

The special nature of the documentation used for this research encourages resuming reflection on this type of source, justifying its selection and specifying its strengths, informative possibilities, limits and inadequacies. Account books, which record the movement of goods and cash, were used to monitor the development of company wealth. Although they may be difficult to interpret in some ways, when available they make it possible to quantitatively reconstruct different aspects of a business. In particular, they make it possible to value turnover and the relative weight of the company's different activities. They offer insight on transactional procedures and business and financial methods. In the present case, most of the accounts are missing, considerably reducing the possibilities for this type of reconstruction.

Unlike account books, letters provide information about events, through careful description and analysis. The Florentines were particularly attentive to written correspondence and their letters inform us about internal matters, the type of business

---

[10] Archivio di Stato, Florence, Libri di commercio e di famiglia (henceforth ASF, Libri di commercio), 710, 711, 712, 713, 714, 715, 716, 721, 723, 724, 725, 726, 727, 734, 742, 743. One of the letter books was kept in Pisa, one in Lyon and eight in Florence. Towards the end, number 743 becomes a kind of notebook of exchanges in which Simone Botti, during a period in Rome (1546–1548), makes detailed note of drafts and remittances made on his behalf and that of his siblings. Of the three account books (numbers 724, 725 and 734), two were written up in Lyon and one in Venice.

[11] ASF, *Miscellanea Medicea* (henceforth *Miscellanea*), 107, fascicolo 2, fascicolo 3, fascicolo 4, fascicolo 5.

[12] ASF, *Carte Strozziane, V Serie* (henceforth *CSVS*), 1090. In addition to this main group, there are many other documents that we will cite ad hoc.

[13] There is some discontinuity in the documentation from this period. In letter book 712, pages are missing and the numbering is interrupted for the years 1529 and 1530, while the years between 1535 and 1539 and between 1548 and 1551 are entirely undocumented. For the period from 1555 to 1566, the manuscripts are less rich and the letters are thinner and most importantly of limited interest for our purposes.

carried out between correspondents and the context in which they worked. They therefore often provide evidence of the complexity of trade, the structure of the companies and the development of the mercantile mentality.

The reliability of this material is intrinsic to the reasons for the correspondence. Letters needed to provide timely knowledge of economic matters and markets so that it would be possible to quickly formulate predictions and make decisions. And so, if these materials are studied critically, keeping in mind that the information they provide is limited to the sphere of the person who wrote the letters, they open the way for broad analysis.[14] Unfortunately, we have no correspondence from Cádiz, Seville or Valladolid and so our study lacks, with very few exceptions, the Spanish perspective. The task of describing the Botti family's activity in Castile therefore falls to the Tuscan sources. To make up for this lack of material, the Italian documentation has been supplemented by Spanish documents in the Archivo General de Indias, the Archivo General de Simancas, the Archivo Histórico Provincial de Sevilla and the Archivo Histórico Provincial de Cádiz. Among the published material, we have analysed the records published in the Catálogo de los Fondos Americanos del Archivo de Protocolos, Seville.

[14] A. ORLANDI, *Mercanzie e denaro: la corrispondenza datiniana tra Valenza e Maiorca (1395–1398)*, Universitat de València, Valencia 2008.

Chapter 2
The Strength of Florentine Capitalism

In addition to trade, upon which the city of Florence was in truth founded, painting, sculpture and architecture, three highly noble arts, were always considered great and wise.

(Benedetto Varchi) ('Oltrachè nella mercatura, sopra la quale in verità è fondata la città di Firenze, furono sempre [...] grandi e accorti reputati, la pittura, la scoltura e l'architettura tre nobilissime arti'. B. Varchi, Storia fiorentina, Soc. Tipografica de' Classici Italiani, Milan 1803 https://www.digitale-sammlungen.de/en/view/bsb10754828?page=128,129 accessed 1 June 2024.)

2.1 The 'Florence Factor'

In his celebrated book *L'Italia fuori dall'Italia*, Fernand Braudel argued that Europe was schooled by the Italian Renaissance. The French historian observed that this cultural imperialism corresponded to the vitality of the peninsula's manufacturing activity. Countless luxury products circulated in Europe and with them the image of the artisans who made them. This phenomenon intensified in the sixteenth century, when, according to Braudel, Italian taste became a model for the figurative arts, architecture and literature as well as for the world of workshops that produced rich, refined goods.[1]

[1] F. Braudel, *L'Italia fuori dall'Italia*, pp. 2142–2146; M. Belfanti, 'Renaissance et made in Italy: l'invention d'une identité culturelle pour l'industrie de la mode', in *La gloire de l'Industrie, XVIIe-XIXe siècle. Faire de l'histoire avec Gérard Gayot*, eds. P. Minard, C. Maitte, M. de Olivera, Presses Universitiares de Rennes, Rennes 2012, pp. 145–162; F. Braudel, *Le modèle italien*, Arthaud, Paris 1989; E. Pommier, *L'invention de l'art dans l'Italie de la Renaissance*, Gallinard, Paris 2006. On the circulation of Italian art in particular, see, among others, P. Burke, L. Clossey, F. Fernández-Armesto, 'The Global Renaissance', *Journal of World History*, XXVIII, 1, 2017, pp. 1–30; T. DaCosta Kaufmann, *Court, Cloister, City. The Art and Culture of Central Europe, 1450–1800*, University of Chicago Press, Chicago 1995, pp. 23–49; J.-B. Delzant, 'Per l'onore della città, per l'onore del signore. Circolazione di modelli politici e di artisti tra le signorie cittadine dell'Italia centrale (secolo XV)', in *Civiltà urbana e committenze artistiche al tempo del*

A. Orlandi, *Money, Culture, Beauty. The Botti Family*,
https://doi.org/10.1007/978-3-032-00453-6_2

This interpretation, which dates to the 1970s, inspired further reflection, looking at the underlying economic phenomena. For example, Paolo Malanima, in a quantitative analysis of the economy of central and northern Italy between 1350 and 1550, noted that Florence also went through two phases during that period. The first, which concluded at the end of the fifteenth century, was marked by a higher standard of living than would be enjoyed in the subsequent decades, thanks to the trend in wages, prices and the average GDP per capita. He concluded that 'Improvement in material conditions alone may not have been sufficient to promote the new approach to culture, politics, and art portrayed by Burckhardt more than 150 years ago, but it was certainly a prerequisite'.[2] A prerequisite with a specific economic, social and cultural profile and that can be summarised as the 'Florence factor'.[3] Considered a precedent to the 'Italy factor', it corresponded to a capitalistic model that combined risk culture, optimization of human capital and a fertile mix of training, aesthetic sensibility and environmental quality. The economic strength of the city between the fourteenth and sixteenth centuries was rooted in this complex system of values and relationships.[4]

2.1.1 The Economic Model

At the end of the fourteenth century, Florence and Tuscany were already benefiting from various forms of wealth diversification and the gradual expansion of the segment of the population working in trade, craft production and services.

Florentine businessmen created a highly effective capitalistic model. In the areas of managerial organisation and invested capital, entrepreneurs created complex companies managed by capital associations or individual businesses. Among the different company types, Federigo Melis identified a precursor to the holding

Maestro di Offida (secoli XIV–XV). Atti del convegno (Ascoli Piceno, Palazzo dei Capitani, 1–3 dicembre 2011), eds. I. Lori Sanfilippo, S. Maddalo, Istituto Storico per il Medioevo, Rome 2013, pp. 13–37; B.M. Greer, 'The Turning Tide. The Last Significant Influence from the Netherlands: Hugo van der Goes and the Florentine Painters Ghirlandaio and Botticelli', *Fifteenth Century Studies*, VII, 1983, pp. 121–177; P. Nuttall, *From Flanders to Florence. The Impact of Netherlandish Painting, 1400–1500*, Yale University Press, New Haven 2004; D. Wolfthal, 'Florentine Bankers, Flemish Friars, and the Patronage of the Portinari Altarpiece', in *Cultural Exchange between the Low Countries and Italy (1400–1600)*, ed. I. Alexander-Skipnes, Brepols, Turnhout 2007, pp. 1–21.

[2] P. Malanima, 'Italy in the Renaissance: A Leading Economy in the European Context, 1350–1550', *Economic History Review*, 71, 1, 2018, pp. 3–30. Paolo Malanima was referring to J. Burckhardt, *Die Kultur der Renaissance in Italien*, Schweighauser'schen Verlagsbuchhandlung, Basel 1860.

[3] G. Nigro, 'Alle origini del fattore Italia: lavoro e produzione nelle botteghe fiorentine del Rinascimento', in *En torno a la economía mediterránea medieval. Estudios dedicados a Paulino Iradiel*, ed. A Furió, PUV, Valencia 2020, pp. 41–51, p. 41.

[4] Ibid.

company, which he called a 'system of partnerships'.[5] It was often based on individual companies based in different geographical locations but all directly or indirectly controlled by a majority partner. This was an important innovation and a rational response to the tragedy of the major company failures in the first half of the fourteenth century.

Another important aspect was the gradual replacement of the traditional thirteenth-century family business with the founding of companies opened to outsiders.[6] This was due to economic growth and the consequential need for bigger investment, requiring people to look for financing outside the family. It was also due to the spread of the mechanism of trust, resulting from interpersonal relations, which facilitated exchange. There were also many small businesses. They have always been undervalued in the literature, but the economic activity of the larger entrepreneurial groups would not have been so incisive without their support and their innovative mentality.[7]

Many of these companies were a manifestation of the bourgeois middle class, the new rich, merchants and artisans especially active in Tuscany who, at least between

---

[5] F. Melis, 'Le società commerciali a Firenze dalla seconda metà del XIV al XVI secolo', in F. Melis, *L'azienda nel Medioevo*, ed. M. Spallanzani, Istituto Internazionale di Storia Economica "F. Datini" Prato, Florence, Le Monnier 1991, pp. 161–178, p. 166.

[6] The subject of the family in the medieval and early modern periods has been researched by scholars from a range of different perspectives and using varied methods, including legal/institutional and socio-anthropological. Among the numerous studies, we will concentrate here on those that mark the development of the historiographic debate. Through the study of a few major Florentine families, Richard Goldthwaite and Gene Brucker used international growth to explain the replacement of the expanded family with a nuclear model that integrated the economic support of family members with external capital. Within this framework, the two historians also mapped out the figure of a solitary entrepreneur. In their research on Tuscan families, Francis William Kent, David Herlihy and Christiane Klapisch-Zuber came to different conclusions, finding the continued existence of large Florentine families in the fifteenth century. Then, John Padgett sought to synthesise the two positions, noting that the social mobility of the elite in contemporary Florence was real, despite the tendency to perpetuate the identity of the lineage through marriage and other strategies. That said, Padgett perceived a gradual change in the function of lineage, which became less important in the economy but more incisive in politics. G.A. Brucker, *A Florentine Politics and Society, 1343–1378*, Princeton University Press, Princeton 1962; G.A. Brucker, *Renaissance Florence*, University of California Press, Berkeley 1969; R.A. Goldthwaite, *La costruzione*; R.A. Goldthwaite, *L'economia della Firenze rinascimentale*, Il Mulino, Bologna 2013; R.A. Goldthwaite, *Private Wealth*, p. 254; D. Herlihy, C. Klapisch-Zuber, *I toscani e le loro famiglie. Uno studio sul catasto fiorentino del 1427*, Il Mulino, Bologna 1988; F.W. Kent, *Household and Lineage in Renaissance Florence. The Family Life of the Capponi, Ginori and Rucellai*, Princeton University Press, Princeton 1977; J.F. Padgett, 'Open Elite? Social Mobility, Marriage and Family in Florence, 1282–1494', *Renaissance Quarterly*, 63 (2010), pp. 357–411. On professional knowledge as a factor in social mobility, see *La mobilità sociale nel Medioevo italiano. Competenze, conoscenze e saperi tra professioni e ruoli sociali (secc. XII-XV)*, eds. L. Tanzini, S. Tognetti, Viella, Rome 2016.

[7] Even just looking at the names of the senders and recipients in Francesco Datini's thick correspondence reveals the presence of a healthy number of small and medium businesses in the places where his correspondents were based. A. Orlandi, 'Tradizione e innovazione nel capitalismo toscano tardo trecentesco', *Storia Economica* 20, 2, 2017, pp. 395–410.

the fourteenth and fifteenth centuries, favoured economic practices. Individuals who also knew how to climb the social ladder in a different way, through wealth, and were the main drivers of technical and economic innovation in the decades around the turn of the fourteenth century.

This capitalistic model made up of commercial and manufacturing enterprises guaranteed flourishing, high-quality production, quickened by the rich wool and silk industries, merchant warehouses and bankers, big and small.

Put another way, manufacturing activity was guaranteed, even more so than trade, by the strong formulation and diversity of specialisation. The function of the classic artisan was of major importance.[8] Although they benefited from autonomous power in relation to the market, they owed their success to their strong tie to distribution companies. Their workshops produced everyday objects such as shoes, hats, gloves, dishes and cookware, furnishings like beds, coffers, chests and chairs and tools such as scissors, needles, ploughs and knives, but also refined wood and ivory combs, splendidly painted wedding chests, birth trays, jewellery and religious images for ex votos. The study of ex votos in particular allows us to reconstruct the artisan world in Florence during those centuries. Alongside the images on paper sold by street traders, life-size wax sculptures were made by the Benintendi (nicknamed *Fallimmàgini*, meaning image makers) in late fourteenth century Florence, commissioned to express gratitude for having escaped danger. They were displayed in the churches and, when they became too cumbersome, hung from the ceiling.[9] The most popular church for these works was Santissima Annunziata. To take one example, in the middle of the fifteenth century, Todero da Lecce, a soldier injured in the chest during the Battle of Anghiari, went to Florence after he recovered to repair the cuirass that had saved his life. While there, he took the opportunity to thank the Virgin, spending two florins 'to have an image made' to offer her. In another case, Cristofano da Cremona spent more than 12 florins for 'a silver head of his wife stuck through with a bolt': his wife had miraculously survived being hit by a crossbow bolt.[10]

There is no need to stress that this context also included numerous artist/artisans, such as Donatello and Benvenuto Cellini, always waiting for wealthy clients. But they did not limit themselves to just satisfying their clients; they were true entrepreneurs. For example, on 30 June 1568, Benvenuto Cellini contributed 450 florins to join a limited partnership in the city with the goldsmiths Antonio and Guido da Fossombrone.[11]

---

[8] For a concrete example of this artisan model, see F. Ammannati, 'Un calzolaio del Quattrocento: Girolamo Talducci e la sua bottega in Porta Santa Trinita', *Prato Storia e Arte*, 113, 2013, pp. 143–155.

[9] G. Nigro, 'L'economia', in *Eccellenza, Innovazione, Creatività nella Storia della Toscana*, ed. V. Baldacci, Edizioni dell'Assemblea, Florence 2008, pp. 25–38.

[10] A. Orlandi, 'Il costo della guerra. La compagnia di Michele Attendolo da Cotignola ad Anghiari', in *Il prezzo della guerra. Italia e Penisola iberica nei secoli XIII-XVI*, Associazione Culturale Antonella Salvatico. Centro Internazionale di Ricerca sui Beni Culturali, La Morra 2018, pp. 135–162.

[11] ASF, *Mercanzia*, Libri delle accomandite, 10832, c. 203v.

Between Weaving and Art: Making Tapestries in Florence

One of the most fashionable furnishings in the sixteenth century was the tapestry. Flemish masters were the undisputed authorities and were called to work in all the European courts. The tapestry workshop that Francis I opened at Fontainebleau was especially famous, but Italy also had important manufacturing centres. Two were the courts at Ferrara and Mantua, where two Flemings worked, Janni Rost and Nicolas Karcher, both of whom Cosimo de' Medici wanted in Florence. Rost arrived in September 1545; Karcher in October of the same year. The Grand Duke wished not only to decorate Palazzo Vecchio but also to introduce the secrets of this new manufacturing activity into the city, as emerges from the following clause in the contract with Rost:

'Said Master Giovanni is required to teach and have those young men taught said craft of making tapestries and dying, and dying in every colour opportune and necessary for that art, and doing every type of work and dying and every thing and revealing the secrets of that craft, with all possible promptitude and diligence. And this such that the effect is that before the end of this contract and its extension, said art and craft of tapestry weaver, with all the secrets of dying as well, will have been learned, acquired and established in the city of Florence, such that one can practice said art perfectly in the city of Florence and in the State of said young Florentines without the help of or training by any foreigner whatsoever'.[12]

This was the origin of what became the Medici Tapestry Workshop, which produced thousands of works between 1546 and 1738, marked with the lily between two Fs and the Medici coat of arms. In the second half of the sixteenth century, numerous workshops began to crop up in via degli Arazzieri, via dei Cimatori, via della Ninna, via di San Gallo and via dei Servi.

The two Flemish artisans were paid a generous 600 scudi per year. They had large work spaces and twenty-four looms, a high number even by Brussels standards. The designs were commissioned from great artists like Bronzino, Pontormo, Bacchiacca, Salviati and Allori. The designs were paid for by the grand duke, while the cartoons remained the property of the weavers, who could reproduce them freely.

These splendid tapestries, which decorated city residences and country houses, were used on festive occasions like the feast of St John or Corpus Domini to embellish the streets and piazzas along with other textiles and choreographed entertainment, the enviable fruit of collaboration between art and manufacturing.[13]

When talking about the Florentine economic model, our thoughts turn most of all to merchants and traders working in the textile industry. The textiles were made by the famous companies of the Wool Guild using prized fibres from England, the Balearics, Maestrazgo and Castile. Expertly dyed and finished, they were the pride

[12] 'A' quali putti o giovani, detto Maestro Giovanni si obliga ad insegnare et fare insegna re detto mestiero di fare arazzerie et tintura, et tingere d'ogni sorte colore opportuno et necessario a tale arte, e fare d'ogni sorte lavoro e tintura et ogni altra cosa et segreto, a tale mestiero et tintura attenente, con ogni prestezza et diligenza possibile, et questo sì et in tal modo che lo effetto sia che avanti che finisca il tempo della presente convenzione et proroga, detta arte et mestiero di arazziere, con tutti i segreti ancora della tintura, si sia imparata, acquistata et ferma nella città di Firenze, sì et in tale modo che senza appoggio, amminiculo o ammaestramento alcuno, di qualsivoglia persona forestiera, decta arte et tintura si potrà fare et esercitare nella città di Firenze perfettamente, da decti putti et giovani fiorentini, o dello Stato'.

[13] C. Andelson, 'Cosimo I de' Medici and the foundation of tapestry production in Florence', in *Firenze e la Toscana dei Medici nell'Europa del '500, III Relazioni artistiche.* Il linguaggio architettonico europeo, Olschki, Florence 1983, pp. 899–924; *La Galleria degli arazzi. Fragilità della bellezza*, ed. G. Giusti, Giunti, Florence 2014, *Meraviglie tessute della Galleria degli Uffizi. Il restauro di tre arazzi medicei*, ed. C. Innocenti, Edifir, Florence 2000.

of the city's manufacturing activity. Frieze, embellished with tassels, flooded the fairs in Lyon, reaching Northern Europe and the rich Andalusian markets that formed the centre of the Carrera de Indias.

The silk producers were also of great importance, with a long history begun in the fourteenth century when their silks circulated along with those from Lucca and Venice.[14] These fabrics were of good quality but could not match the refined weaves that were made in the East and arrived in Italy via Constantinople. Over time, the quality and value of the Florentine textiles increased. Indeed, at the end of the fifteenth century, Bonsignore Bonsignori wrote from Bursa, an important Turkish silk centre, that far more silks were made in that city than in Italy, 'but they are not as beautiful'.[15] Florentine silk weavers and gold beaters were gaining supremacy even in those parts of the world the production of which they had initially imitated.[16]

The increase in manufacturing activity was accompanied by improvements in technique and taste, with the artisans, influenced by their sensitive, discerning clients, creating increasingly refined objects. These phenomena, along with the contradictory demographic growth and social mobility of a few segments of the population, continued in the fifteenth and sixteenth centuries, ensuring the businessmen an important role in the global economic system for at least a good part of the sixteenth century.

That said, demand in the territories of the Florentine state could not absorb its rich internal production. Its merchants were therefore chiefly occupied with intermediation on a vast scale and their economic strength came from the effectiveness of their relationships with different markets through their companies. They were active in the most important trading centres of the time. From the markets of Mediterranean Africa, including the Atlantic islands (the Canaries and Madeira), to Europe all the way to London and Lübeck, and the Eastern markets up to Adrianople (now Edirne) and Constantinople.[17]

---

[14] I. Del Punta, *Lucca e il commercio della seta nel Medioevo*, Pacini, Pisa 2011; F. Edler De Roover, *Le sete lucchesi*, Istituto Storico Lucchese, Lucca 1993; G. Livi, 'I mercanti di seta lucchesi in Bologna', in *Archivio Storico Italiano*, IV, 7, 1882, pp. 29–55. For a complete, relatively recent, survey of silk production in Lucca, see I. Del Punta, M.L. Rosati, *Lucca una città di seta. Produzione, commercio e diffusione dei tessuti lucchesi nel tardo Medioevo*, Pacini-Fazzi, Pisa 2017.

[15] A. Orlandi, 'Oro e monete da Costantinopoli a Firenze in alcuni documenti toscani (secoli XV-XVI)', in *Relazioni economiche tra Europa e Mondo Islamico. Secc. XIII-XVIII, Europe's Economic relations With The Islamic World 13th–18th Centuries*, Atti della "Trentottesima Settimana di Studi", 1–5 May 2006, ed. S. Cavaciocchi, Istituto Internazionale di Storia Economica "F. Datini" Prato, Le Monnier, Florence 2007, pp. 981–1004, p. 985.

[16] F. Guidi Bruscoli, M. Spallanzani, *Tessuti di seta tra Firenze e il Levante (ca. 1350–1550). Le fonti*, FUP, Florence 2023 analyses Florentine silk textiles and the increasing popularity of and demand for these fabrics in the East.

[17] Much has been written on Florentine merchants outside Florence. Setting aside the research on their presence on the Italian peninsula, this list includes a few edited volumes that concentrate on the subject and other texts that significantly update or add to the former: 'Hermanas. Relaciones entre la península ibérica y la península itálica, de la Edad Media a la Moderna', *eHumanista: Journal of Iberian Studies*, ed. González Arévalo, R., 38, 2018; *«Mercatura è arte». Uomini d'affari*

Their presence was so pervasive that, in the fifteenth century, people used to say: 'There are sparrows and Florentines in every corner of the world'.[18]

Between 1300 and 1500, they introduced a penetrative model rooted in managerial and financial strategies. Generally speaking, a merchant's decision to frequent a particular area and possibly set up shop there could have been motivated by many different reasons: political, religious, demographic, economic. For the Florentines, economic reasons were most important. They moved to the places that offered the greatest opportunities for profit, but without ever losing their ties to Florence. Their direct presence in those locations lowered the costs of intermediation and allowed them to personally chose the goods to buy. From this point of view, the organisational model of the 'system of partnerships' and the holding company worked perfectly.

---

toscani in Europa e nel Mediterraneo tardomedievale, eds. L. Tanzini, S. Tognetti, Viella, Rome 2012; A. Fábregas García, 'Estrategía de los mercaderes toscanos y genoveses en el Reino de Granada a través de la correspondencia Datini', *Serta Antiqua e Mediaevalia*, 5, 2001, pp. 259–302; R. González Arévalo, 'Florentinos entre Cádiz y Sevilla en los siglos XIV y XV', in *De mar a mar. Los puertos castellanos en la Baja Edad Media*, eds. E. Aznar Vallejo y R.J. González Zalacaín, Universidad de La Laguna, La Laguna 2010, pp. 273–307; R. González Arévalo, 'Privilegios, franquicias y consulados. Naciones italianas y diplomacia mercantil en la Castilla bajomedieval', in *Políticas y estrategias socio-económicas en la ciudad medieval atlántica*, J.Á. Solórzano Telechea, D. Ditchburn y M. Álvarez Fernández, eds., Nájera, Instituto de Estudios Riojanos, 2023 pp. 83–133; F. Guidi Bruscoli, 'London and its Merchants in the Italian Archives, 1380–1530', in *Medieval Merchants and Money. Essays in Honour of James L. Bolton*, eds. M. Allen, M. Davies, University of London-Institute of Historical Research, London 2016, pp. 113–135; F. Guidi Bruscoli, 'Los mercaderes italianos en Lisboa y los portugueses, siglos XV-XVI', in *Mercaderes y redes mercantiles en la península ibérica, siglos XV-XVIII*, eds. M.F. Fernández Cháves, R.M. Pérez García, B. Perez, Editorial Universidad de Sevilla, Cátedra de Estudos Sefarditas Alberto Benveniste, Éditions Hispaniques Paris-Seville-Lisbon 2019, pp. 69–85; F. Guidi Bruscoli, 'Perception, Identity and Culture: The Italian Communities in Fifteenth-Century London and Southampton Revisited', in *Resident Aliens in Later Medieval England*, eds. M. Ormrod, N. McDonald, C. Taylor, Brepols, Turnhout 2017, pp. 89–104; A. Orlandi, *Le Grand Parti. Fiorentini a Lione e il debito pubblico francese nel XVI secolo*, Olschki, Florence 2002; A. Orlandi, 'Oro e monete', pp. 981–1004; A. Orlandi, 'Tuscan Merchants in Andalusia: A Historiographical Debate, *European Review of History. Revue Européenne d'Histoire*, 23, 3, 2016, pp. 347–366; P. Pinelli, 'Le relazioni commerciali tra Firenze e Dubrovnik (XV-XVI secolo)', in *Firenze e Dubrovnik all'epoca di Marino Darsa (1508–1567)*. Atti della Giornata di Studi Firenze, 31 gennaio 2009, ed. P. Pinelli, FUP, Florence 2010, pp. 43–50; A. Poloni, 'Banchieri del re. La monarchia angioina e le compagnie toscane da Carlo I a Roberto I', in *Périphéries financières angevines-Periferie finanziarie angioine*, ed. S. Morelli, Publications de l'École Française de Rome, Rome 2018, pp. 1–36, https://books.openedition.or/efr/3568 acccessed 10 August 2018; G. Spallacci, *I rapporti commerciali tra le città delle due sponde adriatiche nella documentazione dell'archivio di Ancona tra 1345 e 1514*, Dottorato di Ricerca in Storia, Ciclo XXVIII, Alma Mater Studiorum-Università di Bologna, Bologna 2017, p. 71, available at http://amsdottorato.unibo.it/7989/1/spallacci_giulia_tesi.pdf accessed on 16 November 2018; S. Tognetti, 'Cenni sulla presenza dei mercanti-banchieri fiorentini a Famagosta di Cipro nei primi anni del Trecento', *Archivio Storico Italiano*, CLXVI, 2008, pp. 53–68; K. Weissen, 'I mercanti italiani e le fiere in Europa centrale alla fine del Medioevo e agli inizi dell'Età Moderna', in *La pratica dello scambio. Sistemi di fiere, mercanti e città in Europa (1400–1700)*, ed. P. Lanaro, Marsiglio, Venice 2003, pp. 161–176.

[18] F. Braudel, *L'Italia fuori d'Italia*, pp. 2092–2248.

When they calculated that they did not need to be directly involved in a particular market, they relied on local correspondents or other businesses, largely fellow countrymen, active in that location. They therefore belonged to one or more networks, through which information essential for making good economic decisions was passed.[19]

They handled problems with notable mental elasticity, sometimes sending associates to places where specific types of presence were needed, further defining their ties. Other times, they turned to locals, because they were better connected or accepted by the population.[20] In some areas, they adopted work agreements similar to those of today. One example is that of Tuccio di Gennaio, from Prato, who had a travelling salesman contract for buying wool from Maestrazgo. Later, and especially during the sixteenth century, we have evidence of agreements with internal and external associates, who, for example, moved between Tuscany and Constantinople as business agents.[21]

In short, Florentine businessmen in the late Middle Ages and early modern period had considerable economic power and, as we will see shortly, a series of particular qualifications.

How was it possible to achieve all this?

2.1.2 Entrepreneurship, Innovation and Risk Culture

The picture outlined above implies possession of a broad range of entrepreneurial skills. Federigo Melis was the first to propose a new way of studying these skills. In his view, the economic historian needs to try to put himself at the table with the merchant from those centuries, 'to experience the way his business was organised,

[19] One exemplary case is that of Francesco Datini, which is reconstructed in A. Orlandi, 'Networks and Models', pp. 81–106. On the circulation of information in particular, see A. Orlandi, *Mercanzie e denaro*, and the more recent *Cultural Exchange in Early Modern Europe, III, Correspondence and Cultural Exchange in Europe, 1400–1700*, eds. F. Bethencourt, F. Egmond, Cambridge 2007, pp. 80–103 and F. Guidi Bruscoli, 'Circolazione di notizie e andamento dei mercati nel basso Medioevo', in *Fama e publica vox nel Medioevo*, eds. I. Lori Sanfilippo, A. Rigono, Istituto Storico Italiano per il Medioevo, Rome 2011, pp. 119–146.

[20] A. Orlandi, 'A Man from Prato in the Maestrazgo. Tuccio di Gennaio, Wool Merchant', in *Francesco di Marco Datini. The Man the Merchant*, ed. G. Nigro, Fondazione Istituto Internazionale di Storia Economica "F. Datini" Prato, FUP, Florence 2010, pp. 377–383; A. Orlandi, 'Ibiza entre el Mediterráneo, el Atlantico y el Mar del Norte (siglos XIV y XV)', *eHumanista*, 38, 2018, pp. 48–64.

[21] A. Orlandi, 'Les précurseurs des voyageurs et représentants de commerce parmi les hommes d'affaires toscans de la Renaissance (fin XIVe-début XVIe siècle)', *Entreprises et Histoire*, no. 66, 2012, pp. 22–36.

the people behind it, the varied goods he dealt with and guided from afar and all the tools created as needed to better serve the main activity'.[22]

The research that has been carried out on governance since then has naturally expanded the initial picture, turning attention to additional aspects of management. A number of interesting points emerge from it. First, Florentine entrepreneurs placed great importance on merit, choosing partners and associates based on their skills and training, without necessarily taking into account families ties. They also got them involved and invested them with responsibilities. They used different methods and tools. Most importantly, the power of money, which sometimes translated into a more advantageous division of profits in favour of the partner-director, providing him with further motivation to keep things running smoothly.[23] Of equal importance was the partners' conduct and especially that of the majority partner, who, with a hint of paternalism, spurred the group to stay unified and identify with the company they worked for.[24]

Of course, this is not to say that the panorama of companies and behaviours was unequivocal. What we wish to point out is that the above noted openness to foreigners and modern governance was already widespread and common to late-fourteenth-century Tuscan merchants.

In addition to their managerial skills, the Florentines also had a talent for innovation. Out of the many examples we could offer, we will limit ourselves to innovations in the credit sector, with the emergence of the modern bank, so dear to Federigo Melis, rooted in the introduction of the written order, the cheque and the correspondence account. To which we will add those in the area of transport, in which the differentiation of maritime freight opened trade routes to less expensive goods.[25]

---

[22] F. Melis, 'Sulle fonti tipiche della storia economica; per una particolare tecnica di lavoro dello storico (relativamente ai secoli XII-XVII)', *Rassegna Economica*, XXXIX, 2, 1975, pp. 307–332, p. 332.

[23] An early example is offered by the companies owned by Datini in which increased profit distribution was frequent. Another interesting case is that of the company founded by Giovanni Bicci dei Medici, Benedetto dei Bardi and Francesco da Gagliano in Venice in 1406. Although Da Gagliano, a partner with operational functions, had contributed only one-eighth of the capital, he received 25% of the profits. F. Melis, *Documenti per la storia economica dei secoli XIII-XVI, con una nota di Paleografia Commerciale a cura di Elena Cecchi*, Olschki, Florence 1973, pp. 336–339.

[24] A. Orlandi, 'Le prestazioni di una holding tardo medievale rilette attraverso alcune teorie di management e la Social Network Analysis', in *Innovare nella Storia Economica: Temi, Metodi, Fonti, Roma 10–11 ottobre 2014*, Fondazione Istituto Internazionale di Storia Economica "F. Datini" Prato, Prato 2016, pp. 117–148, p. 119–123.

[25] On these topics, see the contributions in F. Melis, *I trasporti e le comunicazioni nel Medioevo*, ed. L. Frangioni, Istituto Internazionale di Storia Economica "F. Datini" Prato, Le Monnier, Florence 1984, F. Melis, *L'azienda nel Medioevo*, ed. M. Spallanzani, Istituto Internazionale di Storia Economica "F. Datini" Prato, Le Monnier Florence 1991; F. Melis, *La banca pisana e le origini della banca moderna*, ed. M. Spallanzani, Istituto Internazionale di Storia Economica "F. Datini" Prato, Le Monnier, Florence 1984 and F. Melis, *Documenti per la storia economica*. These subjects, above all linked to the financial sphere and the bank, have been explored in numerous studies. We will limit ourselves here to listing research concentrated on Tuscany that introduces new aspects to the field: R. De Roover, *Il Banco Medici. Dalle origini al declino*

We will conclude with a brief discussion of risk culture understood as appetite for productive investments. The data from the 1427 cadastre reveals that capitalisation of earnings was quite frequent. Instead of redistributing profits for private needs or consumption, they were reinvested in the company.[26] There were many reasons for this phenomenon, but it is reasonable to think that the influence of the mendicant orders had some weight. While the accumulation of personal wealth beyond an individual's need was classified as the sin of greed, many believed that, as confirmed by the religious world, sums invested in trade were helpful to the society of believers, and increasing those sums could therefore be considered legitimate.[27]

2.1.3 Education and Unlocking the Potential of Human Capital

An unknown fourteenth-century Florentine merchant wrote that people need to do business based on 'reason', not 'opinion'. An incisive assertion that underlined awareness of how important it was for businessmen to make decisions based on analysis of the available data. This rationality, the focus of most of the twentieth-century historiography, was a key characteristic of Tuscan entrepreneurs, who were particularly inclined towards gathering information and increasing their knowledge, including in the areas of mathematics and accounting.[28]

Florence, which had a population of around 100,000 in the time of Dante and Petrarch, had a keen interest in the issue of education. In a passage in his famous *Chronicle*, Giovanni Villani provided a statistical summary of the state of education in 1338, calculating 'between 8000 and 10,000 girls and boys learning to read; between 1000 and 1200 boys learning the abacus and algorithm in 6 schools and

(1397–1494), La Nuova Italia, Florence 1970; R.A. Goldthwaite, 'Local banking in Renaissance Florence', *The Journal of European Economic History*, 14 (1997), pp. 5–56; G. Nigro, 'La compagnia del Banco', in *Francesco di Marco Datini. L'uomo il mercante*, ed. G. Nigro, Fondazione Istituto Internazionale di Storia Economica "F. Datini" Prato, FUP, Florence 2010, pp. 525–536. Also see the summary of De Roover's thought in S. Tognetti, 'L'attività di banca locale di una grande compagnia fiorentina del XV secolo', *Archivio Storico Italiano*, CLV, 574, 1997, pp. 595–647.

[26] G. Nigro, 'Il mercante e la sua ricchezza', in *Francesco di Marco Datini. L'uomo il mercante*, ed. G. Nigro, Fondazione Istituto Internazionale di Storia Economica "F. Datini" Prato, FUP, Florence 2010, pp. 81–104.

[27] G. Todeschini, *I mercanti e il tempio. La società cristiana e il circolo virtuoso della ricchezza fra Medioevo ed Età Moderna*, Il Mulino, Bologna 2002, p. 61. Also see R. Greci, G. Pinto, G. Todeschini, 'La riflessione etica sulle attività economiche', in *Economie urbane ed etica economica nell'Italia medievale*, eds. R. Greci, G. Pinto, G. Todeschini, Laterza, Bari, 2005, pp. 151–228.

[28] A. Orlandi, *Mercanzie e denaro*, p. 11.

between 550 and 600 boys learning grammar and logic in four big schools'.[29] Knowing how to read and do calculations were the main educational goals, but importance was also placed on studying foreign languages, especially the langue d'oïl, which made it possible to do without an interpreter at the fairs in Champagne, Bruges and London.[30]

Drawing on the data provided by Villani, Carlo Cipolla determined that 40% of young Florentines attended the different types of school that existed at the time.[31] In 1480, according to Paul Grendler, the level was still high and exceeded 30%.[32] Although to a lesser degree, there was also a broad focus on writing in the other Tuscan cities, making it 'a region with a pen in its hand'.[33]

A Recipe for Ink

Ink was indispensable as much for school as for writing the countless letters sent between the merchants and their correspondents in every corner of Europe. In April 1559, Simone Botti also found the time to reply to a request from his brother Giovanbattista, who wanted some ink for himself in Lyon and specifically, of course, the kind that was made in Florence.[34]

Here is the recipe:

'To make six pounds of ink, which will be one flask.

Six pounds of white vinegar or rainwater. Take 1/2 pound of crushed, not ground, gall and put it to soak in the white vinegar and leave it for 15 days. And then let it boil for 1/8 of

---

[29] '[F]anciulli e fanciulle che stanno a leggere da otto a diecimila; i fanciulli che stanno a imparare l'abbaco e algoritmo in sei scuole, da mille a milledugento e quelli che stanno ad apprendere la grammatica e la loica in quattro grandi scuole, da cinquecentocinquanta in seicento'. G. Villani, *Cronica...a miglior lezione ridotta coll'aiuto de' testi a penna*, Sansone Coen, Florence 1845, t. III, p. 324. On the education of young Florentines in the Middle Ages and Renaissance, see R. Black, *Humanism and Education in Medieval and Renaissance Italy*, Cambridge University Press, Cambridge 2011; R.A. Goldthwaite, 'Schools and Teachers of Commercial Arithmetic in Renaissance Florence', *Journal of European Economic History*, I, 1972, pp. 418–433. A more recent study, focused on teaching grammar, is R. Black, 'Maestri e insegnamento di grammatica allo Studio fiorentino nel XIV e XV secolo', in *Studium florentinum: l'istruzione superiore a Firenze fra XIV e XVI secolo*, ed. L. Fabbri, Edizioni di Storia e Letteratura, Rome 2021, pp. 177–195. For the development of Florentine 'abacus mathematics', see R. Danna, 'Una scienza per la rinascita. Note su Paolo dell'Abaco e la matematica abacista fiorentina', *Rinascimento*, 59, 2019, pp. 245–269.

[30] J. Favier, *L'oro e le spezie. L'uomo di affari dal Medioevo al Rinascimento*, Garzanti, Milan 1990, pp. 64–65. On using foreign languages, see F. Guidi Bruscoli, 'I mercanti italiani e le lingue straniere', in *Comunicare nel medioevo. La conoscenza e l'uso delle lingue nei secoli XII-XV*, Atti del convegno Internazionale (Ascoli Piceno, 28–20 November 2013), eds. I. Lori Sanfilippo, G. Pinto, Istituto Storico Italiano per il Medioevo, Rome 2015, pp. 103–131.

[31] C.M. Cipolla, *Istruzione e sviluppo. Il declino dell'analfabetismo nel mondo occidentale*, Il Mulino, Bologna 2002, p. 53. Cipolla observed that the main strength of the most advanced areas of Renaissance Europe was a large literate middle classes. C.M. Cipolla, *Literacy and Development in the West*, Penguin, London 1969, pp. 101–102.

[32] Grendler considered Villani's figures excessive. P.F. Grendler, *La scuola nel Rinascimento italiano*, Rome-Bari, Laterza 1991, p. 87.

[33] A. Orlandi, *Mercanzie e denaro*, pp. 15–16.

[34] ASF, *Libri di commercio*, 742, Florence-Lyon, Simone Botti to Giovanbattista Botti, 17 April 1559, c. 29v.

an hour and after it has boiled add 6 ounces which is 1/2 a pound of good Roman vitriol and boil it together for 1/8 of an hour. Then remove it from the heat and while hot strain it and take IIIJ of gum arabic soaked in vinegar for 8 days and heat it up well. And while hot add it to said ink and mix everything very well in its container for two hours with a stick of elm or pomegranate and add, while still hot, two ounces of rock alum.'[35]

Besides using the right quantity of ingredients and amount of time, the recipe's success also depended on the powers attributed to elm and pomegranate: these were the woods from which the stirring stick needed to be made. Two plants of rare beauty. The elm was the tree of dreams, fraternal and marital love, the one under which justice was administered. The pomegranate was the symbol of fertility and associated with abundance in Greco-Roman mythology.

The above data is substantially confirmed by a volume on 'abacus workshops' in Florence between the late thirteenth century and early sixteenth centuries. According to the author, there were 20 schools in the city alone, where about 70 abacists alternated.[36] What is striking here is the frequency with which 'mercantile mathematics' was taught, finding ever broader application a century after Leonardo Fibonacci's handbook for merchants, the *Liber Abaci*. The high rate of attendance at abacus schools shows that it was entirely normal, if not necessary, for an artisan or a merchant to know how to read, write and do calculations. Two years before Villani's *Chronicle*, a Florentine teacher wrote that his teaching programme contained all that was '... sufficiens ad standum in apotecis artificis'.[37]

[35] 'Per fare libbre 6 di inchiostro che farà uno fiasco. Libre sei di aceto bianco o acqua piovana; et pigliate 1/2 libbra di ghalluza acciachata et non pesta afatto et mettete in molle in deto aceto bianco et lassatela stare per XV giorni. Et di poi fate bollire al fuocho 1/8 di hora et di poi di bollito, aggiugnete once 6, cioè ½ lib bra di vetriolo romano buono et ribollite insieme per 1/8 di hora. Di poi levate dal fuocho et così caldo il fate colare et pigliate once IIIJ di groma arabica stata in molle 8 giorni in l'aceto et scaldatela bene bene et così calda la mettete in deto inchiostro et fate ben me stare tutto lo inchiosto nel vaso che è per dua hore con bastone di olmo o di melagrano et aggiungete, mentre è ancora caldo, once dua d'allume rocco'. AFS, *Libri di commercio*, 742, c. 28r. One Florentine *libbra* = 12 ounces = 0.339 kg. A. MARTINI, *Manuale*, p. 207.

[36] E. ULIVI, 'Abacisti attivi a Firenze al tempo di Dante', *Bollettino di storia delle scienze matematiche*, 41 (2021), pp. 135–162; E. ULIVI, *Gli abacisti fiorentini delle famiglie 'del Maestro Luca', Calandri e Micceri e le loro scuole d'abaco (secc.XIV-XVI)*, Florence, Olschki 2013; E. ULIVI, 'Scuole d'abaco e insegnamento della matematica', in *Il Rinascimento italiano e l'Europa*, eds. A. Clericuzio, G. Ernst, V, Le Scienze, Treviso 2008, pp. 403–420. E. ULIVI, 'Scuole e maestri d'abaco in Italia tra Medioevo e Rinascimento', in *Un ponte sul Mediterraneo. Leonardo Pisano, la scienza araba e la rinascita della matematica in Occidente*, eds. E. Giusti and R. Petti, Polistampa, Florence 2002, pp. 121–155, p. 133, pp. 150–151. On Pisa in particular, T. ANTONI, 'Le scuole di abaco a Pisa nel secolo XIV', in *Studi di ragioneria, organizzazione e tecnica economica. Scritti in memoria del prof. Alberto Riparbelli*, I, Cursi, Pisa 1975, pp. 57–62; on Siena, R. FRANCI, L. TOTI RIGATELLI, 'La trattatistica matematica del Rinascimento senese', in *Atti dell'Accademia delle Scienze di Siena detta de' Fisiocritici*, XIV, 13, 1981, pp. 1–71; S. MOSCADELLI, 'Maestri d'abaco a Siena tra Medioevo e Rinascimento', in *L'Università di Siena: 750 anni di storia*, Monte dei Paschi di Siena, Siena 1991, pp. 207–216.

[37] C.M. CIPOLLA, *Istruzione e sviluppo*, p. 52.

An aspiring businessman's education was completed with direct experience in trade and finance, which he could gain through an apprenticeship[38] or through his first responsibilities working in a shop or abroad.[39] We learn much about the latter from a letter written by Tuccio di Gennaio to his brother Giovanni, who had recently moved to Ibiza. In the letter, he recommended that his brother keep a notebook for writing 'short and substantial' notes, avoid gambling, stay away from female servants and, most importantly, live frugally, keeping in mind that he was 'on a ship'.[40]

This is not the place to discuss the conditions and social and cultural mechanisms that triggered phenomena and awareness of this kind. Here, it is important to note that this was all also the cause and effect of fourteenth-century economic development. The crisis that followed the plague of 1348 was met by a group of managers and a substantial proportion of agents, ready to take on the challenge of a rapid relaunch.[41]

In any case, the theme of education was also considered to be of great importance elsewhere on the peninsula. In Venice, young men prepared themselves for trade by studying under abacus teachers and specialists in methods of mnemonic learning. Education in the lagoon concluded with practical experience in the warehouses

---

[38] On apprenticeships, see G. Casarino, *Maestri e garzoni nella società genovese fra XV e XVI secolo. Profilo e itinerario quantitativo della ricerca,* Prima Cooperativa Grafica Genovese, Genoa 1988. For Tuscany, F. Franceschi, 'I giovani, l'apprendistato, il lavoro', in *I giovani nel Medioevo. Ideali e pratiche di vita. Atti del Convegno di studio (Ascoli Piceno, 29 novembre-1 dicembre 2012)*, eds. I. Lori Sanfilippo, A. Rigon, Istituto Storico Italiano per il Medioevo, Rome 2014, pp. 122–143; F. Franceschi, 'Les enfants au travail dans la manufacture textile florentine des XIVe et XVe siècles', in *Médiévales*, 30, 1996, pp. 69–82. For Bologna, R. Greci, 'Il contratto di apprendistato nelle corporazioni bolognesi (XIII-XIV sec.)', in *Corporazioni e mondo del lavoro nell'Italia padana medievale*, CLUEB, Bologna 1988, pp. 157–223; for Venice, *Garzoni. Apprendistato e formazione tra Venezia e l'Europa in età moderna*, eds. A. Bellavitis, M. Frank, V. Sapienza, Universitas Studiorum S.r.l., Mantua 2017.

[39] As is well known, Tuscan trade papers and Veneto tariffs were mainly used for consultation but also for training young agents. See A. Orlandi, *«Ora diremo di Napoli». I traffici dell'area campana nei manuali di commercio*, Firenze University Press, Florence 2012 for a fairly exhaustive list of surviving papers and tariffs. There is also an interesting anonymous parchment scroll containing information for calculating transaction costs in the case of Venetian trade: B. Figliuolo, A. Bocchi, L. Passera, *Ragioni di mercatura. Un rotolo pergamenaceo fiorentino trecentesco di argomento commerciale*, Forum Edizioni, Udine 2020.

[40] A. Orlandi, 'Ibiza entre el Mediterráneo', cit., p. 54. Research on agents working at companies owned by Francesco Datini has yielded interesting results, including the still relevant volume F. Melis, *Aspetti della vita economica medievale (Studi nell'Archivio Datini di Prato)*, Monte dei Paschi di Siena, Siena 1962. This type of documentation has been used for many other studies as well, including J. Hayez, 'Un facteur siennois de Francesco di Marco Datini. Andrea di Bartolomeo di Ghino et sa correspondance (1383–1389)', *Bollettino dell'Opera del Vocabolario italiano*, 10, 2005, pp. 203–239; M. Tumino, 'Formazione e attività dei giovani mercanti. Fattori, collaboratori e soci nelle aziende di Francesco Datini', *Mélanges de l'École française de Rome*, 131–2, 2019, pp. 229–237.

[41] G. Nigro, 'Alle origini del fattore Italia'; A. Orlandi, 'Tra austerità e lusso. Modelli di consumo dei mercanti fiorentini tra XIV e XVI secolo', in *Faire son marché au Moyen Âge. Méditerranée occidentale, XIIIe-XVIe siècle*, eds. J. Petrowiste, M. Lafuente Gómez, Casa de Velázquez, Madrid 2018, pp. 31–45.

where it was sometimes possible to set aside a bit of money for starting a company of one's own. Overall, the educational outcomes were high, and indeed the Germans came to the city to learn the principles of accounting.[42] As for Milan, a few documents attest that there was an abacus school in that city in the first half of the fifteenth century. People were convinced at the time that anyone who wished to work in trade needed to start their training at the age of 7. After completing the writing and basic grammar course, those wishing to enter the warehouse needed to attend abacus school and study a few aspects of moral philosophy and proper conduct.[43]

In Genoa, parents seemed more interested in 'the process of learning than the things to learn'. They asked instructors to teach reading, writing and counting, but they more often preferred Latin, which the young people needed to know 'bene, et fideliter et sine fraude', because it helped develop a good memory and an aptitude for reasoning. Education in Genoa 'the Proud' was also competed in a shop or on a ship, all experiences that put the apprentice in direct contact with the economic world.[44]

Mutatis mutandis, it almost seems as though traders in the Middle Ages and early modern period received an education similar to that recommended by current principles of company management.[45] A natural aptitude in the case of the most fortunate and theoretical and practical training for the majority made it possible to become a capable merchant. A profession often described by the traders themselves as an art, one that they could enrich adopting a suitable code of conduct. In a letter dated 1526, sent from Florence to Cádiz, our own Matteo Botti wrote the following in reply to his brother Giovanbattista,[46] who, writing from Andalusia, had asked him to send some costly samite for a garment: 'while the others may dress with much pomp and use lots of silks, I would ask you to choose a middle way that upholds and does not lessen you. For a merchant it is advisable to behave in accordance with the ways of the art of the merchant and not like a gentleman who has an opposite way'.[47]

---

[42] F.C. LANE, *I mercanti di Venezia*, Einaudi, Turin 1982, pp. 14–18.

[43] G. DE LUCA, A. NUOVO, F. PISERI, *La formazione del mercante. Scuole libri cultura economica a Milano nel Rinascimento*, Editoriale Delfino, Milan 2021, pp. 26–27.

[44] F. BORLANDI, *Discorso di inaugurazione dell'anno accademico 1962–1963 dell'Università di Genova*. Società Ligure di Storia Patria, Biblioteca digitale, Genoa 2012, pp. 223-230; G. PETTI BALBI, *L'insegnamento nella Liguria Medievale: scuole, maestri, libri*, Tilgher, Genoa 1979. For Piedmont, see A.M.N. PATRONE, *Vivere nella scuola. Insegnare e apprendere nel Piemonte del tardo Medioevo*, Gribaudo, Cavallermaggiore 1996.

[45] A. ORLANDI, 'Essere mercante: «governare lui et le sue mercantie et denari» (secoli XIV-XVI)', in *Idee di lavoro e di ozio per la nostra civiltà*, eds. G. Mari, F. Ammannati, S. Brogi, T. Faitini, A. Fermani, F. Seghezzi, A. Tonarelli, FUP, Florence 2024, pp. 387–396.

[46] In the letter, the name Giovanbattista is alternated with Battista, which was often affectionately used by those close to him.

[47] '[S]e gli altri vestono tanto pomposi e straccono tanti drappi, io conforto te a pigliare un modo medio, da potere mantenersi e non avere a chalare di basso e sempre uno merchante sarà più chonmendabile andare secondo l'arte e non secondo lo gentiluomo che è artte apposita'. A. ORLANDI, 'Affaires et petites vanités. Un marchand florentin à Lyon au XVIe siècle', in *Commerce, voyage et*

Education and conduct were also important for artisans, who trained in workshops under a master, whose activity was also educational. The master was aided by an assistant, a pieceworker and an apprentice. All working together, they learned the trade. Each piece was made partly by the master and partly by the others, making it an organisational system that stimulated personal creativity. Setting value on manpower in this way, the workers were not only fully involved in the production process, their living conditions were also not unpleasant. As we know, before the advent of the factory system, workers in the Middle Ages and early modern period enjoyed a natural work rhythm and were not subject to that of machines. Their days, while heavy-going, were full of human interaction and pauses to meet personal needs.[48]

2.1.4 Fertile Cultural Ground and Context

As we have seen, Florentines were major players in the most important economic markets of the Mediterranean, Atlantic, North Sea and Near East between the fourteenth and sixteenth centuries. In these places, they discovered unusual or highly valuable foreign goods that they immediately tried to sell in other countries, often buying them for themselves as well. Over time, they adapted these goods to their personal taste and that of their clients. We can add that they were also part of an international trade network built on reciprocity.

Among the countless examples of this, the most famous is that of Spanish majolica. During the fourteenth century, this pottery flooded the Mediterranean market and was produced by Arab potters in Paterna, Càrcer and, especially, Manises, all small towns in the Valencia area.[49] Florentine traders began buying it up to sell in Tuscany, where the pieces, brightened with gold and silver embellishment, quickly conquered the market. Pottery of medium quality reflecting the manufacturing and stylistic canons of Arab-Spanish artisans, in Florence it was distributed by the haberdashers. Alongside demand for this type of majolica was a market for another kind, more limited in scope but important to us here. Distinguished, wealthy families began ordering more valuable pieces, asking the artisans to add their family

expérience religieuse, XVIe-XVIIIe siècles, Colloque international, Lyon, 25–26–27 mars 2004, ed. A. Burkardt, Presses Universitaires de Rennes, Rennes 2007, pp. 341–357, p. 349.

48 G. Nigro, 'Alle origini del fattore Italia', p. 43; G. Nigro, 'Tra diuturno affanno e consolazione: il tempo del non lavoro nel Basso Medioevo' in *Idee di lavoro e di ozio per la nostra civiltà*, eds. G. Mari, F. Ammannati, S. Brogi, T. Faitini, A. Fermani, F. Seghezzi, A. Tonarelli, FUP, Florence 2024, pp. 397–405; also see G. Nigro, *Il tempo liberato. Festa e svago nella città di Francesco Datini*, Istituto Internazionale di Storia Economica "F. Datini" Prato, Prato 1994. Also see F. Franceschi, 'La bottega come spazio di sociabilità', in *Arti fiorentine. La grande storia dell'Artigianato*, Vol. II, Il Quattrocento, eds. F. Franceschi and G. Fossi, Giunti, Florence 1999, pp. 64–83.

49 G.J. de Osma, *Los maestros alfareros de Manises, Paterna y Valencia. Contratos y ordenanzas de los siglos XIV, XV y XVI*, Instituto de Valencia de D. Juan, Madrid 1908 (edición facsímil, Valencia, Librerías París-Valencia 1996).

coats of arms and new ornamentation. These demanding clients sent designs and instructions for which colours to use to fellow Italians resident in Valencia, influencing the aesthetic sensibilities of the Muslim artisans.[50] The 'opere di terra' (works in clay), as our merchants called Spanish majolica, became objects used by clients to demonstrate their taste and prestige. Gianfigliazzi, Gondi, Medici and Ridolfi all fell under the spell of this pottery. Even the less prestigious Francesco Datini ordered pieces with his family coat of arms for his home. Asmet Zulima, a 'Moor' from Manises who was his supplier for more than 20 years, prepared him 'several beautiful big bowls, that is a big one and a large one like sauce bowls, that is sauce boats that are wide and low. They need to be two times bigger than the ones that one uses and they are low and wide and have a beautiful shape' with his shield with 'six stripes, three white and three red'.[51] The papers of the merchant from Prato provide us with much material for further reflection. Even his associates purchased pieces embellished with their insignia. Cristofano Carocci put in his order before leaving his post as head of the Valencia branch. In 1407, Agnolo di Iacopo, the last director of the Grao branch, commissioned a set from Mahomet Albane.[52] In short, majolica with the crests of families major and minor, and even members of the middle class sought to imitate the choices of the wealthy.

At the end of the fifteenth century, when majolica had become fashionable, refined pieces from Montelupo Fiorentino had begun to replace those from the Iberian Peninsula. In 1493, this small Tuscan town had more than 50 kilns and produced more than 6300 pieces for Constantinople.[53]

There are numerous other examples of cultural influence. At the end of the fourteenth century, Tuscans were not just sending splendid religious panel paintings to Avignon, but also chests made in the 'Catalan style' and other items that Florentine artisans were producing in imitation of foreign goods, sometimes copying them but more often improving them. Types of goods that quickly became fashionable and better made. Iron gloves in the Parisian style, swords in that of Bordeaux, lances in the Spanish fashion, Hungarian-style bowstrings and sword tips filled the shelves and chests in Francesco Datini's Avignon warehouses. Sometimes, the specific Florentine artisans selected for the job were listed in the orders. In November 1363, an Oltrarno master was asked to produce 12 pairs of medium-size scissors, and an order was placed with Nicolò di Bongani for small steel hammers clearly marked

[50] R.A. Goldthwaite, *La costruzione*, pp. 129–130; R.A. Goldthwaite, *Ricchezza e domanda nel mercato dell'arte in Italia dal Trecento al Seicento. La cultura materiale e le origini del consumismo*, Milan, Unicopli 1995, p. 179; M. Spallanzani, *Maioliche ispano-moresche a Firenze nel Rinascimento*, SPES, Florence 2006, pp. 10–14.

[51] M. Spallanzani, *Maioliche ispano-moresche*, pp. 339–340.

[52] M. Spallanzani, *Maioliche ispano-moresche*, pp. 398–399.

[53] M. Spallanzani, 'Maioliche di Montelupo per Costantinopoli (1493)', *Faenza*, XCIII, 2007, pp. 36–42. Also see M. Spallanzani, 'Maioliche di Valenza e di Montelupo in una casa pisana del 1480', *Faenza*, LXXII, 1986, 3–4, pp. 164–170.

with his signature mark, a cross.[54] The city of the Popes was an important centre for trade in offensive and defensive weaponry and, more generally, metal tools and utensils from all over the world. Numerous Tuscan merchants had seen and purchased them in its warehouses. Once they arrived in Florence and Lucca, they were quickly reworked and improved.

This aptitude for imitation also extended to goods from the Near East, one example being metalwork. Islamic metalwork was highly prized and sought after across the West in the fourteenth century. At the end of the fifteenth century, as had been the case for silk textiles, it was supplanted by goods from Venice and Florence. One hundred years later, Giorgio Vasari reported weapons and armour embellished with gold arabesques produced in various cities in northern Italy. Benvenuto Cellini wrote of the beauty of a few Turkish daggers, making copies that were even better than the originals.[55]

Through this type of intercultural trade and the internal development of taste, Florence benefited from artisans and merchants who were not just economically well prepared but also aesthetically refined and sensitive. The former produced fine goods; the latter distributed them far and wide.

Cross-influence, imitation and technical skill improved the goods and stimulated creativity, which benefited from increasingly distinguished surroundings. Looking at Tuscany's cities, towns and countryside even today, we can still see the unique harmony that resulted from the collective, almost instinctual intelligence of those who lived in those surroundings, created on the basis of a profound aesthetic sensibility.[56]

---

[54] L. Frangioni, *Chiedere e ottenere. L'approvvigionamento di prodotti di successo della bottega Datini di Avignone nel XIV secolo*, Opus Libri, Florence 2002, pp. 41–42, p. 101.

[55] M. Spallanzani, *Metalli islamici a Firenze nel Rinascimento*, SPES, Florence 2010, p. 4. Among the many analyses of this type of activity, we will limit ourselves to citing F. Trivellato, 'Renaissance Italy', pp. 127–155, which includes a critical examination of studies on the relationship between the Italian Renaissance and the Muslim Mediterranean. In particular, the scholar considers the following texts: N. Bisaha, *Creating East and West: Renaissance Humanists and the Ottoman Turks*, University of Pennsylvania Press, Philadelphia 2004; D. Howard, *Venice and the East: The Impact of the Islamic World on Venetian Architecture, 1100–1500*, Yale University Press, New Haven 2000; L. Jardine, J. Brotton, *Global Interests. Renaissance Art between East and West*, Cornell University Press, Ithaca 2000; M. Meserve, *Empires of Islam in Renaissance Historical Thought*, Harvard University Press, Cambridge 2008; G. Ricci, *Ossessione turca. In una retrovia cristiana dell'Europa moderna*, Il Mulino, Bologna 2002; N. Zemon Davis, *Trickster Travels. A Sixteenth-Century Muslim Across Worlds*, Hill & Wang, New York 2006. For an interesting paper that concentrates on Central Europe, see K. Prajda, 'Mercanti come tramite degli scambi culturali nella Firenze del primo Rinascimento: Il caso del Regno d'Ungheria', *I Tatti Studies in the Italian Renaissance*, vol. 25, no. 2, 2022, pp. 279–308.

[56] G. Nigro, 'Alle origini del fattore Italia', p. 51.

Chapter 3
The Botti in Europe: Merchants, Bankers and Patrons

Know that [...] I have married a young woman of twenty-two years old, called Caterina, daughter of Alamanno de' Medici, relative of our Lord Duke [...] and I made this decision due to the insistence of my brothers and my sister-in-law and all my friends and relatives to whom it seems wrong, as it also seems in the city, for our house to die out because none of my married brothers have male children.

(Giovanbattista Botti) ('Avete a sapere come [...] mi maritai con una donzella di 22 anni, detta Caterina, figla di Alamanno de' Medici, parente del nostro Signor Duca [...] et questo passo ho fatto per inportunatione di mia fratelli et di mia cognate e tutti parenti et amici a' quali pareva pur male, come qua pare, la casa nostra si havessi a spengnere del tutto poi nessuno de' mia fratelli maritati hanno figli masti'. ASF, Libri di commercio, 716, Florence-Seville, Giovanbattista Botti to Lorenzo del Rosso, 12 December 1562, cc. 25v.–26r.)

3.1 The Family and Its Connections

3.1.1 The Tuscan Branch

On 4 October 1562, Giovanbattista wrote to Ana Francisca Fonte, widow of his brother Iacopo, who had died in Seville just over 2 months earlier: 'Muy Magnifica señora hermana mia [...] ha de saver como heramos siete hermanos barones, de los quales quedamos çinco y todos heramos juntos y viviamos a comun'.[1] It was a long letter, full of bitterness and disappointment. In it, Botti relived the salient episodes of his family history, to remind his sister-in-law of them. We can imagine him bent over the letter, remembering the past, in his room in the palazzo in via de' Serragli,

[1] 'Magnificent lady and sister-in-law, as you must know, we were seven brothers, of which five survived and, all close siblings, we lived together'. ASF, *Libri di commercio*, 716, Florence-Seville, Giovanbattista Botti to Ana Francisca Fonte, 4 October 1562, cc. 30r.-30v.

A. Orlandi, *Money, Culture, Beauty. The Botti Family*,
https://doi.org/10.1007/978-3-032-00453-6_3

between the Great Hall and the Camera della Gelosia. Elegant spaces that were filled with coffers decorated with the family coat of arms. The walls were hung with the 'provinces, one of Spain and one of Brittany'.[2] The bed near the writing desk was draped with a black and white cover made from Indian cloth, probably from the years spent in Andalusia.

Among the siblings, Iacopo had influenced him most and the two had an often harsh and difficult relationship. Now he was dead, and Giovanbattista was tracing back over 40 years of family life and business activity. Theirs is a story of a family of merchants who rose from humble beginnings to win a noble title. Its success cannot be explained simply by the power of money earned and carefully invested. The family's ascent required a shrewd combination of ability, appetite for risk and luck.

Much has been said about sixteenth-century Florence and the themes and debate relative to the crisis can lead one to forget that, despite its many difficulties, Florence had a population of about 80,000 residents in the first half of the century[3] and its distinctive characteristics were largely intact. The wool and silk textile trade was still crossing over European borders and merchants' activity was still heavily diversified, as were the markets in which they were active and the investments they made. It remained a city of merchants whose background and mentality conditioned the economic world and life in the city, both socially and in terms of political power.[4]

It was a strong, conscious middle class that did not shrink from translating every aspect of life into the materiality of sums and the impalpable uncertainty of the image: not just business and trade, but also politics and family.[5] For that matter, as Leon Battista Alberti observed, 'wealth [...] is very useful [...] for acquiring amity, honour and fame'[6] and, to cite Gregorio Dati, 'a Florentine who is not a merchant, who has not travelled all over the world seeing different countries and people and who did not then return to Florence with a certain degree of wealth is a man who will garner no esteem'.[7]

---

[2] ASF, *Libri di commercio*, 726, Florence, 30 June 1565, c. 3d.

[3] K.J. Beloch, *Storia della popolazione d'Italia*, introduction by Lorenzo del Panta and Eugenio Sonnino, Le Lettere, Florence 1994.

[4] For a complete overview of the socio-economic situation in Florence at the time, see, most importantly, R.A. Goldthwaite, *L'economia della Firenze rinascimentale*. For the updated perspective on wool textile production, see F. Ammannati, *Per filo e per segno. L'arte della lana a Firenze nel Cinquecento*, FUP, Florence 2020, which provides a reconstruction of the historiography and an interesting interpretation of the complex fortunes of the city's Wool Guild. For a close analysis of the production and distribution of luxury textiles, see F. Franceschi, 'Woollen Luxury Cloth in Late Medieval Italy', in *Europe's Rich Fabric. The Consumption, Commercialisation, and Production of Luxury Textiles in Italy, the Low Countries and Neighbouring Territories (Fourteenth-Sixteenth Centuries)*, Ashgate, Farnham-Burlington 2016, pp. 181–204. On the production of luxury silks, see S. Tognetti, *Un'industria di lusso al servizio del grande commercio. Il mercato dei drappi serici e della seta nella Firenze del Quattrocento*, Olschki, Florence 2002.

[5] J. Lucas-Dubreton, *La vita quotidiana a Firenze ai tempi dei Medici*, Rizzoli, Milan 1985, p. 70.

[6] https://www.liberliber.eu/mediateca/libri/a/alberti/i_libri_della_famiglia/pdf/i_libr_p.pdf, p. 62.

[7] C. Hibbert, *Ascesa e caduta di Casa Medici*, Mondadori, Milan 1990, p. 15.

On the basis of these convictions, Giovanbattista, by now advanced in years and left alone to handle the family's trading, was attempting to find a solution to complicated hereditary issues and matters of family strategy. He was trying to convince his sister-in-law to preserve the continuity of the economic venture launched by his father, Simone, 80 years before (Figs. 3.1 and 3.2).

Simone, the founder of the family, had married Maddalena Riccardi[8] and nine children were born of their union: Matteo, Iacopo, Riccardo, Giovanbattista, Girolamo, Francesco, Simone, Elisabetta and Maria. They were born in the house on the corner of via dell'Ardiglione, in the parish of San Frediano in Cestello, in the Santo Spirito quarter. Their church was Santa Maria del Carmine, where they obtained, through the granting of a privilege, the chapel of the Crocifisso, which became their 'burial place'.[9] In it, they displayed their family coat of arms: 'From

[8] The documentation for Maddalena is scant: we know that she was originally from Pisa, she had a sister, Lady Bartolomea, and she died in Florence on 23 June 1534. In the letters written by her children, we read about her in San Romolo busy caring for Elisabetta and Simone, who were sick, in Careggi with Maria, Elisabetta and Ginevra del Marchi to escape the plague, and at Girone for a pleasant stay in the countryside with her 'brigade' of children and grandchildren. The most beautiful image might be that provided by Matteo, who describes her astonished and absorbed in thought, convinced that she had lost Iacopo, who had been in Spain for many years, but still keeping her son's things, waiting for the day he would come back to get them. The Botti siblings' ties with their maternal relatives were quite strong. As we will see below, Francesco spent part of his time in Pisa at the home of the heirs of Ridolfo Riccardi, described as 'our cousins'. Francesca, the daughter of Gabriello Riccardi, shared a home with Elisabetta Botti and Matteo was the one who saw to her marriage. With a dowry of 2600 ducats, she married Carlo di Niccolò Paganelli. ASF, *Libri di commercio*, 711, Florence-Cádiz, Matteo Botti to Iacopo Botti, c. 158r.; *Libri di commercio*, 711, Florence-Cádiz, Matteo Botti to Iacopo Botti, 10 December 1527, c. 176v.; *Libri di commercio*, 712, Florence-Cádiz, Matteo Botti to the Botti company, 30 November 1530, c. 42r.; *Libri di commercio*, 721, Pisa-Cádiz, Francesco Botti to the Botti company, 28 March 1531, c. 8v.; *Libri di commercio*, 721, Pisa-Cádiz, Francesco Botti to the Botti company, 18 July 1534, c. 216r.; *Miscellanea*, 107, fascicolo 4, Florence-Valladolid, Matteo Botti to Giovanbattista and Francesco Botti, 12 November 1544, c. 47v.; *Miscellanea*, 107, fascicolo 4, Florence-Seville, Matteo Botti to Iacopo Botti, 10 January 1545, c. 62r.

[9] In the Libro dei Padronati of 1689, we read: 'The first Chapel that was made in this form and decoration in pietra serena and officiation began on the day of Pentecost in May 1561, and in the month of December 1563 the Altar Panel was installed with a depiction of the Redeemer dead on the Cross'. As we will see below the table was 'six and a half braccia tall and four and a half wide' and had a predella with the 'Nativity of Christ and a dossal: all of which together were worth 70 scudi'. The panel was painted by Giorgio Vasari, who described it in his *Lives* as a 'Crucified Christ, Our Lady, St John and the Magdalene, all crying'. In the *Sepultuario* of 1657, Rosselli also wrote about the 'Botti family altar with their arms on the right and another on the left and tomb at the foot with arms, and letters of the family'. Vasari also designed the chapel of the Crocifisso. When Iacopo died, Giovanbattista had a Mass officiated in the chapel for the repose of his brother's soul. Matteo also remembered the brothers of the Carmine in his will, providing for the payment of five florins a year to the sacristy for the storage and repair of the albs. He also allotted 140 liras per year and six pounds of worked yellow wax to honour the feast of St Matthew. The religious were obliged to celebrate a low Mass at the altar in the chapel daily and an 'office of the dead' on the anniversary of his death, with ten low Masses and a sung Mass. ASF, *Libri di commercio*, 716, Florence-Seville, Giovanbattista Botti to Ana Francisca Fonte, 30 September 1562, c. 28r.; ASF, *Libri di commercio*, 726, Florence, 30 June 1565, c. 9d.; G. Fossi, *Grandi casati, uomini illustri e committenti*, in *La Chiesa di Santa Maria del Carmine a Firenze*, ed. L. Berti, Cassa di Risparmio di Firenze, Florence 1992, pp. 313–342, p. 334.

Fig. 3.1 Botti Coat of Arms. ASF, *Raccolta Ceramelli Papiani*, 930. On loan from the Ministero della cultura/Archivio di Stato di Firenze

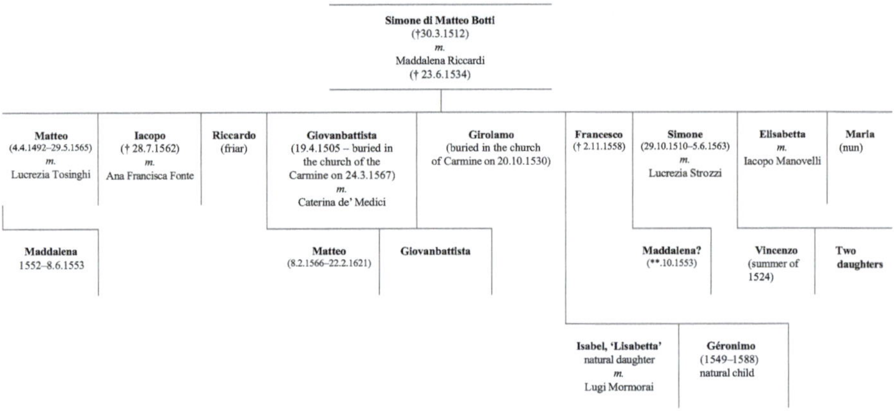

Fig. 3.2 Family tree: The Florentine branch

the blue background, to the mountain of six golden peaks, and to the crossing red band with three eight-pointed golden stars'.[10]

Led by their father until 1512[11] and through the joint effort of all the brothers, a prosperous business group was formed, the flagship of which was the Spanish venture. Matteo,[12] the firstborn, remained in Florence to coordinate the activity; Iacopo, Giovanbattista and Francesco moved to Andalusia, spending most of their lives abroad.

'El señor Jacome Botti mi hermano, que en groria sea, fue a Calis el año de 1519',[13] he wrote in his letter to his sister-in-law. Iacopo, to the disapproval of his family, never saw his hometown again. Andalusia had become his home and he only left it for brief periods since, as he explained, commitments and obligations of various kind prevented him from leaving. Difficulties that Battista saw as poorly concealed excuses: his marriage, daughters and loved ones in general were what kept him indissolubly tied to Spain.

Battista recalled when, in 1527, in Seville, Iacopo confided in him that he planned to marry.[14] And on 31 July, he married Ana Francisca Fonte, daughter of a deceased Catalan merchant by the name of Rafael.[15] She lived in the city with her mother and siblings.[16] Her father had built a considerable fortune in a short period of time, exploiting intense trade between Cádiz and the Canaries. When he died, he left his wife, Paula, an income of 4000 scudi per year. The social status he had acquired in the area of Cádiz and Jerez de la Frontera was equally impressive. He had been

[10] https://archiviodistatofirenze.cultura.gov.it/ceramellipapiani/index.php?page=Famiglia&id=1480 accessed on 4 June 2024.

[11] Simone Botti died on 30 March 1512 and was buried in the church of the Carmine on 30 March 1512. He had drawn up his will 2 years earlier on 30 January, leaving everything to his children, while his wife was named usufructuary and proxy for the entire estate. In addition to being highly regarded, Simone was a Florentine faithful to his duties. This is clear from the measures with which he called for adherence to the requirements of the city statutes when deciding spending for the Opera di Santa Maria del Fiore, the Sacrestia Nuova and work on the city walls. ASF, *Notarile antecosimiano*, 13,918, c. 343; *Arte dei Medici e Speziali*, Libri dei morti, 248, c. 56v.

[12] We will henceforth also refer to Matteo as the 'Eldest'.

[13] 'Mr Iacopo Botti, my brother, who has died, went to Cádiz in 1519', 'ASF, *Libri di commercio*, 716, Florence-Seville, Giovanbattista to Ana Francisca Fonte, 4 October 1562, c. 30v.

[14] Ibid.

[15] For the occasion, as was customary, Iacopo asked for a chest decorated with the family arms and the name of his bride to be sent from Florence. A few years later, also for Ana, he asked his brother Simone for two *albarelli* decorated with 'our arms and those of my wife which is a white fountain on the red ground like the ones that are in the middle of the piazza and spurt water from above and have a round marble basin that receives it. And have them filled with dried grapes the way our mother used to do it.' ASF, *Miscellanea*, inserto 2, 107, Cádiz-Florence, Iacopo Botti to Matteo Botti, 6 June 1541.

[16] ASF, *Libri di commercio*, 711, Florence-Cádiz, Matteo Botti to Iacopo Botti, 18 July 1527, cc. 158r.–158v.; *Libri di commercio*, 711, Florence-Cádiz, Matteo Botti to Iacopo Botti, 10 December 1527, cc. 174v.-175v.

regidor of Cádiz since at least 1508, of San Cristóbal de La Laguna in 1512 and of Jerez de la Frontera in 1521.[17]

Botti had made a wise choice, from every point of view, emotional and material, and they were a good match. Ana Francisca willingly accepted the strong personality of a husband who was ill equipped to tame the harsh aspects of his character. He gave up his country and Tuscan family ties for her. He could consider himself satisfied. The circle was closed. He had found a patient wife, and he would benefit, as a merchant, from the Fonte family's economic strength. The marriage agreements were signed in Cádiz on 17 May 1527 in the presence of five witnesses, two of which, Iacopo Fantoni and Francesco Lapi, were Florentine friends and merchants. The dowry amounted to 3000 ducats. Of these, 2000 were taxes and revenue from the Isla de León which the father and uncle of the promised bride possessed as security for a loan give in 1521 to the duke of Arcos. Of the remaining 1000 ducats, 500 were paid, 30 days after the wedding, in silver, gold, slaves, small plots of land, family jewels, clothing and other things. The remainder was paid in cash at the end of 1531.[18]

The Botti welcomed the wedding, wishing Iacopo prosperity, peace and happiness.[19] Most importantly, they urged him to maintain open business relationships with his wife's relatives: 'there is nothing in the world worse than war with your relatives'.[20] Words of warning and hesitation, since despite the concerns, he found himself time and again involved in legal and financial trouble due to the 'madness

[17] On the activity of the Fonte brothers (Rafael and Miguel) in Andalusia, see E. Otte, 'Los Botti y los Lugos', in *III Coloquio de Historia Canario-Americana (1978)*, Tomo I, Ediciones del Excelentisimo Cabildo Insular de Gran Canaria, Gran Canaria 1980, pp. 47–86, pp. 61–66; F.J. Fornell Fernández, 'Los Fonte, un ejemplo del comercio gaditano con Canarias durante el siglo XVI', *Trocadero*, 23, 2011 pp. 165–173.

[18] The Fonte brothers had a very particular link to the Isla de León. Miguel and Rafael came into possession of it, the first time, in 1516, for 825,000 maravedís (2200 ducats), agreeing to give it back at any time for the same sum. The duke of Arcos maintained his jurisdiction over the inhabitants and the castle. The duke was able to reclaim the property in full 4 years later, but shortly after, in December 1521, he was forced to cede it again to Rafael Fonte. This time as well, the island was sold with 'la barca que en ella está e con todas las dehesas pastos e pradose abrevaderos e con todo el término de la dicha ysla e con todos los mrs. Que se pagan de tributo por algunas casas e vinnas que en la dicha ysla e en los términos della estan edificados e puestas e plantadas e sobre çiertas tierras de la dicha ysla.' All this guaranteed taxes in the amount of 26,170 maravedís (about 70 ducats) of annual income. Iacopo was informed of the right of redemption, which he was then obligated to respect, with some initial resistance, on 19 February 1533, when he gave it back to Don Luis Cristóbal Ponce de León, duke of Arcos. A. Franco Silva, *La Isla de León en la Baja Edad Media*, Excmo. Ayuntamiento de San Fernando-Fundación Municipal de Cultura, San Fernando 1995, pp. 23–31.

[19] ASF, *Libri di commercio*, 711, Florence-Cádiz, Matteo Botti to Iacopo Botti, 18 July 1527, cc. 158r.–158v.; *Libri di commercio*, 711, Florence-Cádiz, Matteo Botti to Iacopo Botti, 10 December 1527, c. 175r.

[20] ASF, *Libri di commercio*, 711, Florence-Cádiz, Matteo Botti to Iacopo Botti, 10 December 1527, c. 175r.

of his brother-in-law',[21] Lázaro Fonte who, among his untold mishaps, had participated in the ill-fated colonisation attempt in Santa Marta in Colombia. An unfortunate enterprise, even though it was organised with Pedro Fernández de Lugo, member of the famed family of conquistadors, with which the Fonte family had close ties.[22]

As we will see below, Anna and Iacopo had seven children: three boys and four girls (Magdalena, Ana Paula, Ginebra, Isabel). None of the boys survived, to the disappointment of the Florentine uncles, who were primarily interested in the lineage. Moreover, it was noted, Iacopo's sizeable estate, estimated at 200,000 gold ducats,[23] would pass in its entirety to his wife and daughters, creating further trouble.[24] These testamentary decisions, which Giovanbattista did not learn of until it was too late, created immense bitterness. Aware that he had no other choice, his letter to Ana was a final attempt to keep the family assets united. Not being able to control his brother's wealth directly, he tried to do it indirectly, proposing that his sister-in-law move to Tuscany with her youngest daughters. His proposed plan left nothing to chance and covered all the bases. Ginebra would be able to look after her health in the 'excellent, hot' Tuscan spas 'and what's more there are also prefect physicians'[25] and Isabel would be able to contract a good marriage from among the 'most important princes of Florence of a social rank no less than the Anriches and Marigues and Gusman have over there'.[26] Magdalena and Ana Paula, who would

[21] ASF, *Miscellanea*, 107, fascicolo 4, Florence-Valladolid, Matteo Botti to Giovanbattista and Francesco Botti, 24 July 1545, c. 113v.; *Miscellanea*, 107, fascicolo 4, Florence-Valladolid, Matteo Botti to Giovanbattista and Francesco Botti, 18 September 1545, c. 143r.

[22] The ties between the Fonte and Lugo families dated back to the time of Rafael, who met Alonso de Lugo in 1506. From that point forward, the Fonte family gave them frequent loans in exchange for farming and, especially, sugar trade concessions. Iacopo was a part of this and involved in various ways in the ventures of the family of conquistadors. Including the Santa Marta expedition, for which Lázaro Fonte, having purchased a ship, was appointed 'capitano de la armada y conquista'. M. Gambín García, 'Sevillanos y andaluces en la colonización Canaria y en la conquista de América', in *XX Coloquio de Historia Canario-Americana*, ed. E. Acosta Guerrero, Cabildo Insular de Gran Canaria, Las Palma de Gran Canaria 2014, pp. 246–261; E. Martín Acosta, 'Don Alonso Fernández de Lugo, III adelantado de las Islas Canarias, conquistador de Santa Marta y San Borondón', in *XV Coloquio de Historia Canario-Americana*, ed. F. Morales Padrón, Cabildo Insular de Gran Canaria, Las Palma de Gran Canaria 2004, pp. 500–512, p. 500; E. Otte, *Los Botti y los Lugos*, cit., pp. 63–71; E. Otte, 'Los Sopranis y los Lugos', in *II Coloquio de Historia Canario-Americana, Cabildo insular de Gran Canaria*, ed. F. Morales Padrón, Tomo I, Excmo. Cabildo Insular de Gran Canaria, Las Palmas de Gran Canaria 1979, pp. 241–259, p. 255.

[23] We do not know how Iacopo managed the Tuscan properties. It seems, however, that he sold most of them. Archivo General de Simancas, *Contaduría de Mercedes* (henceforth AGS, *CME*), 300.27. ASF, *Libri di commercio*, 716, Florence-Sevill, Giovanbattista Botti to Ana Francisca Fonte, 30 September 1562, c. 28v.

[24] ASF, *Libri di commercio*, 726, Florence, 30 June 1565, c.1s.; AGS, *CME*, 300.27.

[25] ASF, *Libri di commercio*, 716, Florence-Seville, Giovanbattista Botti to Lorenzo del Rosso, 1 February 1563, c. 41r.

[26] ASF, *Libri di commercio*, 716, Florence-Seville, Giovanbattista Botti to Ana Francisca Fonte, 20 February 1563, c. 39v.

remain in Seville, would not be an obstacle. According to Battista, the former would be soon following her husband[27] to Genoa. Whereas the husband of the latter, Juan Pérez de Guzmán, had not been speaking to his mother-in-law for more than 4 months, due to his own ghastly character.

Spanish ties and interests prevailed, however, and Ana Francisca and her daughters remained in Seville. Just as Giovanbattista feared, Iacopo's entire estate was slowly squandered. This is another story, which we will return to below.

Battista's letter left out a few members of the Botti family who had distanced themselves from it in search of their own paths, away from the world of business and trade. One was Riccardo, a restless Franciscan who was unable to repress the adventurous instincts of his homeland and rank, travelling without interruption from Pisa to Vicenza, from Milan to Paris, as a student, from Lyon to Cádiz, where, in 1531, he boarded a ship headed to 'Settuar' (maybe Ceuta), leaving again shortly after for Calicut.[28] Maria, facing the choice of 'convent or husband', opted to become a nun, joining the order of 'San Francesco de' zocholi'[29] in the beautiful convent of Fuligno in Florence, which became a recipient of the whole family's attention and charity. Lastly, Elisabetta, who was married to Iacopo Manovelli, with whom she had two daughters and a son, Vincenzo, who opened a Wool Guild shop in the 1560s with his uncle Giovanbattista.[30] Elisabetta died in May 1539, after 6

[27] Agostino di Marino, a Genoese and Magdalena's second husband (her first was Luís de Medina). Agostino was not thought highly of in the Botti household, because he was a relentless gambler.

[28] When Riccardo decided to go to Paris, he was supported by his family: Matteo arranged for him to be provided with 14 *scudi d'oro di sole* for 3 years. His brothers in Florence also sent him money when he was in Lyon. He is last documented in December 1533, when we learn from Francesco that the friar was well. ASF, *Libri di commercio*, 711, Florence-Lyon, Matteo Botti to the Bini company, 22 August 1526, c. 108v.; Florence-Cádiz, Matteo Botti to Iacopo Botti, 20 May 1525, c. 47r.; *Libri di commercio*, 712, Florence-Cádiz, Matteo Botti to Giovanbattista Botti, 1 March 1529 c. 34v.; *Libri di commercio*, 712, Florence-Cádiz, Matteo Botti to the Botti company, 4 March 1531, c. 74v.; *Libri di commercio*, 721, Pisa-Cádiz, Francesco Botti to the Botti company, 10 July 1531, c. 14v.; *Libri di commercio*, 721, Pisa-Cádiz, Francesco Botti to the Botti company, 30 December 1533, c. 181r.

[29] ASF, *Libri di commercio*, 716, Florence-Seville, Giovanbattista Botti to Loreno del Rosso, 30 September 1562, c. 6v.; ASF, *Libri di commercio*, 711, Florence-Cádiz, Matteo Botti to Iacopo Botti, (personal), 26 February 1525, c. 40r. The documentation reveals that the brothers often helped Maria. Iacopo sent her meat and salted fish, Matteo sent alms and both included their sister in their wills. ASF, *Libri di commercio*, 711, Florence-Cádiz, Matteo Botti to the Botti company, 1 January 1527, c. 129v.; *Libri di commercio*, 712, Florence-Cádiz, Matteo Botti to Iacopo Botti, 14 March 1528, c. 14v.; *Libri di commercio*, 712, Florence-Cádiz, Matteo Botti to the Botti company, 4 March 1531, c. 75r.; *Miscellanea,* 107, fascicolo 4, Florence-Seville, Matteo Botti to the Botti company, 12 November 1544, c. 49v.; *Libri di commercio*, 716, Florence-Seville, Giovanbattista Botti to Lorenzo del Rosso, 30 September 1562, c. 6v.; *Libri di commercio*, 726, Florence, 30 June 1565, c. 9s.

[30] ASF, *Libri di commercio*, 711, Florence-Cádiz, Matteo Botti to Iacopo Botti (personal), 10 October 1527, c. 167r.

months of suffering during which she found comfort in her nun sister and her cousin Apollonia.[31]

The story becomes much more detailed when he turns to matters in Andalusia. He wrote about himself, his brother Francesco and the time he spent in Cádiz and Seville, where he visited Iacopo. Far from Florence, it was a difficult but very important period. They were years of demanding commitments during which he acquired the maturity of a man and the balance of a merchant. He noted that he was in a very different position than the one he had been in before, when he went to Pisa in 1524, where his brothers co-owned a company with the Capponi family. Matteo found him to be quite weak and complained about it: 'he will never do anything good, I've never known a man more afraid of himself than him'.[32] He is insecure, he added, and 'it seems to me that he needs a special teacher for everything, who will explain to him, point by point, every smallest thing'.[33] To see Iacopo in Andalusia, he left from Genoa on 5 April 1525 'with good weather'[34] and, after a stop in Alicante, arrived in Seville in early May.[35] When he wrote to Ana Francisca, it had been 40 years since that trip, but he remembered it all with the freshness of someone who had experienced every part of it with youthful enthusiasm. The details flowed quickly through his mind, following one after the other, connecting like links in a chain. His experience in Spain was not without its difficulties. Understanding and adapting to unfamiliar places and economic processes requires time, perseverance and skill. Moreover, his relationship with Iacopo, an expert in the area, seems to have been difficult and stormy from the beginning. Demanding, not very forthcoming and even less patient, irritated by Giovanbattista's falling ill as soon as he arrived, Iacopo complained about the shyness and insecurity of his brother who instead patiently put up with him and in the meantime learned how to buy and sell, make deals with traders and do business 'without getting into disagreements'.[36] During those years, he travelled across Spain, taken up with activities of every sort.

[31] ASF, *Libri di commercio*, 713, Florence-Cádiz, Matteo Botti to the Botti company, 14 May 1539, c. 3v.; *Libri di commercio*, 713, Florence-Seville, Matteo Botti to the Botti company, 14 May 1539, c. 6v. Elisabetta and Iacopo Manovelli's children were raised by the latter's sister, who moved into her sister-in-law's house.

[32] ASF, *Libri di commercio*, 711, Florence-Cádiz, Matteo Botti to Iacopo Botti (personal), 23 June 1524, c. 7r.

[33] ASF, *Libri di commercio*, 711, Florence-Cádiz, Matteo Botti to Iacopo Botti (personal), 11 August 1524, c. 12v.

[34] ASF, *Libri di commercio*, 711, Florence-Cádiz, Matteo Botti to Iacopo Botti (personal), 24 April 1525, c. 45r.

[35] ASF, *Libri di commercio*, 711, Florence-Cádiz, Matteo Botti to Giovanbattista Botti, 14 July 1525, c. 54v.

[36] ASF, *Libri di commercio*, 711, Florence-Cádiz, Matteo Botti to Giovanbattista Botti, 28 May 1526, c. 100v.

As time passed, the lack of understanding between the two of them showed no sign of abating. Working and living together got harder and their fights more frequent, until Battista decided to leave. A few years later, when he was living in Valladolid, where he had moved to found a company with the Bellotti family, he was called back to Seville by Iacopo to resolve the matter of internal relations, which required immediate attention. He stayed in his brother's home for 3 months, 'like a guest in an inn', without anyone deciding what to do. In the end, in the autumn of 1547, he left Andalusia, this time for good.[37] But he was not finished travelling. In 1555, he left Florence for Lyon, to recover a bad debt. He stayed far longer than planned, remaining until 1562, when the Lutheran unrest spreading through the city convinced him to return to Tuscany.[38] After all, his currency trading could be supported by correspondents like the Bini, Del Bene and Panciatichi families.[39]

Francesco, the other brother, worked for the group in Pisa and Spain.[40] He started out in the Tuscan port city, at the company co-owned with the Capponi family, and at the end of 1530 founded a company that he continued to run until 1535,[41] the year in which it seems he realised his long-standing dream of moving to Cádiz.[42] In 1541, he left Andalusia and his brothers to return to Florence.[43] Two years later, although suffering from long-standing kidney pain,[44] he left for Genoa, where he boarded the galleys of Don Bernardo to go to Castille, in Valladolid, and help Battista with the

---

[37] ASF, *Miscellanea*, 107, fascicolo 5, Florence-Seville, Matteo Botti to the Botti company, 31 October 1547, c. 122r.

[38] If it had not been for the Wars of Religion, Giovanbattista would not have left Lyon so hastily and he would have moved to Paris and headed to Antwerp to clinch a deal and, finally, London where the Cavalcanti family was happy to host him. ASF, *Libri di commercio*, 715, Lyon-Venice, Giovanbattista Botti to the D'Adda and Rezzonico company, 4 August 1561, cc. 101v.-102r.; *Libri di commercio*, 715, Lyon-Antwerp, Giovanbattista Botti to the Giacomini and Gondi company, 4 November 1561, cc. 107v.-109r.; *Libri di commercio,* 715, Lyon-Antwerp, Giovanbattista Botti to the Giacomini and Gondi company, 6 January 1562, c. 135r.

[39] On his time in Lyon, see A. Orlandi, 'Affaires et petites vanitas', pp. 341–357, A. Orlandi, *Le Grand Parti*.

[40] For a short time, it was thought that Francesco could be sent to London where 'it seems there is some business being done and more solid'. ASF, Libri di commercio, 711, Florence-Cádiz, Matteo Botti to Iacopo Botti, 14 July 1526, c. 111v.

[41] Francesco lived with the Capponi family until 1531. That autumn, he decided to go live with his cousins, the children of his mother's brother Ridolfo Riccardi. ASF, *Libri di commercio*, 721, Pisa-Cádiz, Francesco Botti to the Botti company, 25 November 1531, c. 27r.

[42] Lack of documentation for the second half of the 1530s makes it impossible to precisely establish the year that Francesco moved to Andalusia. In a letter that he sent to Cádiz on 24 April 1535, he wrote that he intended to join his brothers in Spain in September. According to Enrique Otte, he first arrived in Seville in 1537. ASF, *Libri di commercio*, 721, Pisa-Cádiz, Francesco Botti to the Botti company, 24 April 1535, c. 228v. E. Otte, 'Los Botti y los Lugos', pp. 47–86, p. 66.

[43] He began the return trip on 15 March 1541, stopping in Valladolid, Toulouse and Lyon. ASF, *Miscellanea*, 107, fascicolo 3, Florence-Seville, Matteo Botti to the Botti company, 31 May 1541, c. 89v.

[44] ASF, *Miscellanea*, 107, fascicolo 3, Florence-Valladolid, Matteo Botti to Giovanbattista Botti, 25 May 1542, c. 185v.

company he had just founded. He stayed until 1547, when, after the All-Saint's fair, he went back to Seville to finish some negotiations and organise the move of Isabel, his illegitimate daughter with a local woman, to Italy. He stayed in Spain until the summer of 1554, when he left the country 'to go to Flanders and England'.[45] He stopped in Antwerp, but he did not stay long. He had the time to do business with the Affaitadi family, important Italian merchants who the Botti family had had ties with since 1548.[46] In 1555, Giovancarlo Affaitadi asked him to be a witness for the drafting of his will. The next year, during the Easter fair, he joined a consortium of financiers led by the Affaitadi family, with 6000 ducats for a loan of 50,000 to Philip II.[47] Shortly after, he moved back to Florence permanently, where he died of kidney disease on 2 November 1558.[48] He left two illegitimate children, the above-mentioned Isabel[49] and Géronimo,[50] who was born 9 years earlier in Valladolid.

---

[45] During that trip, Francesco had a terrible experience at the border between Spain and France, where he was captured by the French and they tore up his safe conduct. The Florentines in Lyon lost no time in coming to his aid. The powerful Guadagni family acted immediately and obtained his release. ASF, *Libri di commercio*, 723, Florence-Seville, Giovanbattista to Iacopo Botti, 11 August 1554, c. 58v.; *Libri di commercio*, 723, Florence-Valladolid, Giovanbattista Botti to the Affaitadi and Giraldi company, 14 August 1554, c. 59v.; *Libri di commercio*, 723, Florence-Ancona, Giovanbattista Botti to Niccolò da Barberino, 7 September 1554, c. 62v.

[46] In the 1550s, Francesco was in Medina del Campo, where he got involved in a company with Affaitadi and Bardi. F. Point-Waquet, 'Les Botti. Fortunes et culture d'une famille florentine (1550–1621),' Mélanges de l'École Française de Rome. *Moyen Age Temps Modernes*, 90, 2, 1978, pp. 689–712, pp. 693.

[47] *Inventaire des Affaitadi banquiers italiens à Anvers de l'année 1568*, ed. J. Denucé, Éditions de «Sikkel», Antwerp 1934, pp. 49, 223.

[48] He was buried in the church of the Carmine on 30 November. In his will, he named his heirs as his brothers Giovanbattista and Simone, leaving each 50%. His heirs were to take care of his two children. ASF, *Libri di commercio*, 726, Florence, 30 June 1565, c.1s. ASF, *Arte dei Medici e Speziali*, Libri dei morti, 251, c. 68.

[49] As noted above, Isabel had moved to Italy in the spring of 1548. The journey had gone well and a few days after leaving Andalusia she arrived in Portovenere, where a boy sent by her uncle Matteo was waiting for her with a mule. She was brought to the countryside and provided with a personal servant. Matteo was thinking of having her enter a convent and believed he would be able to convince her, but he had calculated wrong. 'Lisabetta', who threatened suicide, won and was married to Luigi Mormorai with a dowry of 3500 scudi. She died on 28 November 1580 and was buried in the church of San Lorenzo. ASF, *Miscellanea*, 107, fascicolo 5, Florence-Seville, Matteo Botti to Francesco Botti, 8 May 1548, c. 187v.; *Libri di commercio*, 715, Florence-Valladolid, Giovanbattista Botti to the Affaitadi and Giraldi company, 8 November 1559, cc. 35v.–36r.; *Libri di commercio*, 715, Florence-Valladolid, Giovanbattista Botti to Carlo Martelli (personal), 23 January 1562, c. 135v.; ASF, *Libri di commercio*, 716, Florence-Salamanca, Giovanbattista Botti to Géronimo Botti, 16 July 1563, c. 75t.; ASF, *Ufficiali poi Magistrato della Grascia*, 192, c. 239.

[50] When Francesco died, his son Géronimo was in Salamanca, entrusted to Giovan Francesco Tedaldi who was expected to see to his education. Giovanbattista, named ward by his brother, made sure to regularly send the money needed for his care. The life of the young Géronimo Botti reads like a short novel. When Tedaldi needed to move to Rome in 1560, he left him in the care of the *Bacelier* Sales of Salamanca along with the son of Giovancarlo Affaitadi. A bookseller visiting Florence informed Giovanbattista that the two youths were not being sufficiently supervised: they were neglecting their studies and spending all their time hunting and on entertainment. Tedaldi's

In Giovanbattista's account, his brothers come to life one after the other, acquiring identities and precise features. All of them had gradually found a satisfactory place within the family, now that the youngest were ready to come out of their shells and participate in everyday life.

Quick, fragmentary images surfaced in Battista's mind. He even reflected on the introverted Girolamo, who had a short, anonymous life, entirely devoted to manufacturing woollen cloths[51] and abruptly cut short by the plague in 1530.[52]

Simone, the youngest of the brothers,[53] was the opposite: autonomous and independent, he was the family rebel. His life had been eventful and fun, as Giovanbattista remembered it, perhaps with a bit of envy: 'he is not cut out for business and spends his time with as little irritation as possible and it seems to me he is quite good at that'.[54] He does not seem to have dedicated himself much to the Silk Guild.[55] The shop he had been entrusted with was of little interest to him. He preferred to spend most of his time at the country house, where he saw to the management of the landed estates and farm activity. These were not his true interests, however. In April 1542 he left for Loreto to 'walk about a bit'[56] and then to Venice where he stayed a few months 'given over to amusements and [...] governed in everything'.[57] In 1544, he was in Rome to monitor a dispute with the Bagattino, which required the

return was not enough to convince Battista, who decided to bring Géronimo to Tuscany, where he arrived in November 1564. The scion's care had been expensive, amounting to 66,000 maravedís a year, which corresponded to 24 months' salary for a member of the Sei di Mercanzia (Florence's trade tribunal). Géronimo did not stay in Florence long, returning to Andalusia in 1566 to see his aunts and cousins. ASF, *Libri di commercio*, 715, Lyon-Salamanca, Giovanbattista Botti to Leonardo Nicolozzi, 23 January 1562, cc. 135v.–136r.; *Libri di commercio*, 715, Lyon-Valladolid, Giovanbattista Botti a Carlo Martelli, 23 January 1562, c. 119r.–119v.; *Libri di commercio*, 716, Florence-Salamanca, Giovanbattista Botti to Géronimo Botti, 16 July 1563, cc. 75r.–77v.; *Libri di commercio*, 716, Florence-Lyon, Giovanbattista Botti to the Pandolfi company, 16 November 1564, cc. 119r.–119v.; ASF, *Libri di commercio*, 716, Florence-Valladolid, Giovanbattista Botti to the Martelli company, 4 April 1565, c. 145r.; *Libri di commercio*, 727, Florence-Valladolid, Giovanbattista Botti to the Martelli company, 23 September 1566, cc. 46r.–46v. A member of the Sei di Mercanzia received a monthly salary of nine ducats and ten soldi. Biblioteca Nazionale Centrale di Firenze (henceforth Bncf), *Capponi*, 9, c. 98.

[51] As we will see below, a Wool Guild shop was opened expressly for him.

[52] He was buried in the church of the Carmine on 20 October 1530. ASF, *Ufficiali poi Magistrato della Grascia*, 191, c. 445r.

[53] Simone was born on 29 October 1510. ASF, *Tratte*, Libri dell'età, 81, c. 64v.

[54] ASF, *Miscellanea*, 107, fascicolo 3, Matteo Botti to Iacopo and Giovanbattista Botti, 14 June 1541, c. 97v.

[55] Simone was trained for work in the Silk Guild by Bernardo Pandolfini, who was a good teacher according to Matteo. ASF, *Libri di commercio*, 712, Florence-Cádiz, Matteo Botti to Iacopo and Giovanbattista Botti, 15 July 1531, c. 129v.

[56] ASF, *Miscellanea*, 107, fascicolo 3, Florence-Valladolid, Matteo Botti to Giovanbattista Botti, 5 April 1542, c. 171v.

[57] ASF, *Miscellanea*, 107, fascicolo 3, Florence-Valladolid, Matteo Botti to Giovanbattista (personal), 25 May 1542, c. 185v.

constant presence of a representative of the family. Simone did not let the opportunity slip away and stayed in the Eternal City for 4 years. The suit dragged on for years and their opponents repeatedly appealed. According to Battista these delays were due to the fact that 'Rome ... wants to get fat, and its officials willingly draw out disputes as long as possible and especially when they see they are dealing with wealthy people'.[58] On the other hand, we can be certain that the young Botti did nothing to speed things up, 'since he is enjoying the pleasures of Rome, music, song, wine and other delightful things. You will find him where there is money to spend.'[59] Even after he married Lucrezia, the daughter of Strozzo Strozzi, he still preferred the 'villa to the city',[60] houses and farms to 'shops', the pleasures of life to responsibilities of any kind, relationships with artists to those with merchants.[61]

Each sibling was a main character in their own way, but all were sensitive to the authority of Matteo, the firstborn: 'the Eldest' as he was called. Born on 4 April 1492,[62] he gave the Florentine company its business name, maintained relations with correspondents and organised trade and customers. He was the chief executive, while also devoted to 'study',[63] and saw to managing the company and the strategies of the whole group. These commitments did not prevent him, however, from being an active participant in the city's political life. He was a Member of the Consiglio dei Duecento, Officer of the Monte, Magistrate of the Otto and 'one of the forty-five':[64] all prestigious posts and held with dignity and a sense of duty. In keeping with his strong, decisive character, he never neglected the obligations and responsibilities of his role. Skill and prudence guided his behaviour and economic decisions. Not even the wars and outbreaks of the plague could keep him away from Florence for long.[65] When necessary, however, he did not hesitate to travel and go wherever the importance and weight of business required it. This was the case between June

---

[58] ASF, *Miscellanea*, 107, fascicolo 4, Florence-Seville, Matteo Botti to the Botti company, 5 January 1546, c. 178v.

[59] ASF, *Miscellanea*, 107, fascicolo 4, Florence-Valladolid, Matteo Botti to Giovanbattista and Francesco Botti, 17 October 1545, c. 149v.

[60] ASF, *Libri di commercio*, 723, Florence-Seville, Matteo Botti to Iacopo Botti, 11 August 1553, c. 59r.

[61] Simone died on 5 June 1563. He was buried the same day in the chapel of the Carmine. He left a nine-and-a-half-year-old son. In 1561, he had drawn up his will, naming Matteo and Giovanbattista his heirs. They accepted with reservations. His lifestyle had not brought him much wealth and his brothers wanted to assess how much it would cost them to fulfil all his bequests. They were, however, willing to contribute up to 1000 scudi. ASF, *Libri di commercio*, 716, Florence-Seville, Giovanbattista Botti to Lorenzo del Rosso, 20 July 1563, c. 77r.

[62] ASF, *Tratte*, Libri dell'età, 81, c. 50v.

[63] F. Melis, 'Il mercante', in F. Melis, *L'economia fiorentina del Rinascimento*, ed. B. Dini, Istituto Internazionale di Storia Economica "F. Datini" Prato, Le Monnier, Florence 1984, pp. 187–202, pp. 190–194.

[64] ASF, *Libri di commercio*, 712, Florence-Cádiz, Matteo Botti to Iacopo Botti, 23 June 1528, c. 20v.

[65] ASF, *Libri di commercio*, 711, Florence-Cádiz, Matteo Botti to Iacopo Botti (personal), 18 July 1527, c. 158r.

1533 and April 1536, when, as we will see, he was forced to stay in Venice to sell a sizeable consignment of Madeira sugar.[66]

It was not until 1550 that Matteo, by then advanced in years, married. His bride was Lucrezia di Luigi di Tommaso Tosinghi[67] 'a highly distinguished and respected woman, so much so that I do not think there is another in Florence who can hold a candle to her'.[68] He had done as many Florentines at the time, delaying family responsibilities as long as possible, often seeing them as trouble, expense and an imposition.[69] In the 1560s, after having devoted his entire life to goods, tired, ill and 'irritated by business transactions, he expressed and fulfilled his desire to disengage'.[70] Perhaps he felt near death, and indeed he died soon after.

His marriage did not yield the yearned-for progeny. Lucrezia gave birth to a girl, Maddalena, who lived just 1 year, and lost a boy when she was 7 months pregnant.[71] With no heirs, the family put heavy pressure on the writer of our account, vigorously pushing him to marry.[72] This is partly why Giovanbattista decided to do so and his choice fell to Caterina dei Medici, daughter of Alamanno, who was a relative of the duke and granddaughter, on her mother's side, of Raffaello Girolami, from another of the oldest Florentine houses.[73]

---

[66] ASF, *Libri di commercio*, 721, Pisa-Seville, Francesco Botti to the Ricasoli and Ridolfi company, 17July 1533, c. 131v.; *Libri di commercio*, 721, Pisa-Cádiz, Francesco Botti to the Botti company, 17 July 1533, c. 140r. Matteo returned to Venice in June 1559. We do not know how long he stayed, but in November 1560 he was back in Florence. ASF, *Libri di commercio*, 715, Lyon-Venice, Giovanbattista Botti to Matteo Botti, 7 June 1559, c. 16r.; *Libri di commercio*, 715, Lyon-Florence, Giovanbattista Botti to Matteo Botti, 21 November 1560, c. 79r.

[67] ASF, *Manoscritti, Carte dell'Ancisa DD*, 351, c. 141v.

[68] ASF, *Libri di commercio*, 716, Florence-Seville, Giovanbattista Botti to Ana Francisca Fonte, 20 July 1563, c. 80v.

[69] C. De La Roncière, 'La vita privata dei notabili toscani alle soglie del Rinascimento', in P. Ariès, G. Duby, *La vita privata dal Feudalesimo al Rinascimento*, Laterza, Bari 1987, pp. 137–138.

[70] ASF, *Libri di commercio*, 716, Florence-Venice, Matteo Botti to Pandolfo Attavanti, 10 February 1565, cc. 135v.-136r.

[71] Little Maddalena died on 8 June 1553 and was buried in the Carmine. ASF, *Arte dei Medici e speziali*, Libri dei morti, 251, c. 118v.; ASF, *Libri di commercio*, 723, Florence-Seville, Giovanbattista Botti to Iacopo Botti, 24 August 1553, c. 19v.; *Libri di famiglia*, 723, Florence-Seville, Giovanbattista Botti-Iacopo Botti, 11 August 1554, c. 59r.

[72] ASF, *Libri di commercio*, 716, Florence-Seville, Giovanbattista to Lorenzo del Rosso, 12 December 1562, c. 25v.

[73] Giovanbattista wrote about it to Carlo Martelli: 'As I told you in my last letter, on the feast of St Catherine I married a woman of 22 years of age, called Caterina, daughter of Alamanno de' Medici and her mother is the daughter of Raffaello Girolami. I am very happy about this and thank God. In 4 days, I will host a banquet to which I will invite Lady Lucretia and Lady Camilla daughters of your wife Lady Maria. It seemed important to me to involve you as one of my closest friends and I am certain you will be happy about it. I needed to get married because none of my three brothers have male children. We shall see if God by his grace wants to give one to me so that our house does not entirely die out.' ('Come vi dissi per l'ultima mia el dì di Santa Caterina mi maritai con una figla di 22 anni chiamata Caterina, figla di Alamanno de' Medici e la madre d'essa è figla del codan Rafel Girolami della quale cosa ne sono molto contento e ne dò gratia a Dio. E fra 4 giorni farò il

While Battista was writing to his sister-in-law, lamenting Iacopo's will, he did not know that a few years later Matteo would cause similar upset, leaving the house in via de' Serragli to his wife and thereby forcing him to move. When he was dying, on 29 May 1565, 'at 11 o' clock', tormented by the same painful 'bladder trouble' as Francesco,[74] he named Giovanbattista his general heir, but added two codicils to his will, limiting his rights: his widow would not only keep their home with all the furnishings, but also the Monteturli property (the villa, two farms and livestock). Lucrezia had the right to the return of her dowry, worth 2000 scudi, and an annuity of 10 scudi per month. It would go to Battista when his sister-in-law died.[75] Once again, the unity and continuity of the family fortune seemed to be in question, albeit temporarily, specifically in an especially sensitive area: the 'main' house. The residence was a metaphor rich in meaning,[76] representing unity, honour and familial harmony.[77] The public image of the family's power, prestige and wealth, it was part of the impressive building that Matteo had bought from the Del Pugliese family in

convito dove chiamerà dona Lucretia e donna Camilla figle di donna Maria vostra consorte, emi parso farvene parte come uno de' mia principali amici e son certo ve ne ralegrerete insieme con meco et questo passo non ho potuto scusarlo, poi di 3 mia fratelli nessuno di essi ha havuto figli masti; vedreno se Dio per sua gratia ne vorrà dare a me a cciò la casa nostra non spenga del tutto'). ASF, *Libri di commercio*, 716, Florence-Valladolid, Giovanbattista Botti to Martelli company, 12 December 1562, c. 24v.

[74] Since no doctor had identified his brother's illness, Battista had an autopsy done on his body. The autopsy revealed that Matteo 'had 28 stones in his liver and a big stone in his bladder that weighed 5 ounces. It tormented him so much that one could say death freed him, because he suffered every time he urinated. This shows you what we really are in this world.' (aveva nel fiele 28 pietre e nella vescicha una preta grossa quale à pesato presso a once 5 quale era quella li dava tanto gran tormento et si può dire la morte li sia stata vita a secondo penava ogni volta che egli orinava sì che vedete quello siano in questo mondo'). ASF, *Libri di commercio*, 716, Florence-Venice, Giovanbattista Botti to Pandolfo Attavanti (personal), 2 June 1565, c. 154v. The Eldest was also buried in the Carmine. ASF, *Ufficiali poi Magistrato della Grascia*, 192, c. 250.

[75] The will was dated 17 September 1563 and the codicils added by Matteo on 4 February 1564 and 12 April 1565 specified the instructions for his wife's inheritance. If Giovanbattista were to die without any male children, the estate would go to his nephew Vincenzo Manovelli, and should he die without any male children, it would go to the Ospedale degli Innocenti. If it failed to fulfil Botti's wishes, it would lose the assets in favour of the Ospedale di Santa Maria Nuova and this one, in turn, to the benefit of the Ospedale di San Matteo, called Sant'Elmo, in Piazza San Marco. The Eldest also left Vincenzo Manovelli 4000 scudi in cash, Matteo Pasquini 600 and 1200 to various charitable institutions. He left Lorenza, the daughter of his wet nurse, Caterina, 12 bushels of grain a year and left bequests to everyone who lived and worked in his house. All of which shows the painstaking attention that Matteo, like the members of all great Florentine families, paid to specifying how he wished his wealth to be distributed even in the long term. ASF, *Libri di commercio*, 726, Florence, 30 June 1565, cc. 2s.-9s. *Libri di commercio*, 716, Florence-Venice, Giovanbattista Botti to Pandolfo Attavanti (personal), 2 June 1565, cc. 154v.–155v. The Florentine staio was equivalent to 24.36 litres. A. Martini, *Manuale*, p. 207.

[76] G. Duby, 'La vita privata nelle famiglie aristocratiche della Francia feudale', in P. Ariès, G. Duby, *La vita privata dal Rinascimento all'Illuminismo,* Laterza, Bari 1987, pp. 37–71, p. 70.

[77] C. De La Roncière, 'La vita privata dei notabili', p. 141.

1550, paying them 3100 florins.[78] In a letter written in 1552, Vasari congratulated his friend for the 'beautiful and comfortable house that you have acquired. It is worthy not only of Mr Matteo Botti but of any great prince'.[79]

All of Florence talked about this unusual will, especially since Giovanbattista and Caterina had been living with Matteo and Lucrezia in via de' Serragli up until then: 'But this thing of having to leave the Botti home seems very strange to me and all of Florence, and has been heavily criticised, not for the value but for the way of doing it. Everyone endeavours to raise and increase their family stock, but Matteo did the opposite'.[80] Battista's only choice was to return to the family home on the corner of via dell'Ardiglione.[81] And so a vision for the family that he thought Matteo had shared came crashing to an end. He had thought Matteo was not like the other brothers, who were more detached, possibly because they had spent so much time away from Florence. Until then, he had imagined that the importance attributed by the Eldest to the idea of family unity, a dominant concept in the Florentine 'establishment', was linked to a desire to give importance to the family and the unity of the fortune that had been the fruit of all their combined efforts and included their official residence. And so, his brother's decision was a source of bitterness. His sole consolation might have been being appointed soon after to the Duecento by the 'Prince of Florence and Siena'.[82]

Indeed, Matteo's behaviour, which gave more autonomy to his wife, contradicted the idea that family tradition needed to always be the priority, to the point of

---

[78] ASF, *Decima repubblicana*, 1842, arroti, n. 37. Matteo bought the part of the building towards Borgo Stella, while the part that was closer to the Arno remained the property of the Del Pugliese family. See M. Bucci, R. Bencini, *Palazzi di Firenze*, IV, Quartiere di Santo Spirito, Florence 1973, p. 117; G. Fossi, 'Grandi casati, uomini illustri e committenti', in *La Chiesa di Santa Maria del Carmine a Firenze*, ed. L. Berti, Cassa di Risparmio di Firenze, Florence 1992, pp. 313–342, p. 332; L. Ginori Lisci, *I palazzi di Firenze nella storia e nell'arte*, Giunti, Florence 1985, p. 773. The building was purchased on 11 February 1622 by Claudia d'Albon, wife of Camillo Coppoli, who paid the Medici, who had inherited it from Giovanbattista's son Matteo, 5300 scudi. G.V. Parigino, 'Il patrimonio di Ferdinando II de' Medici. Una prima ricognizione', *Mediterranea ricerche storiche*, VI, 17, 2009, pp. 479–516, p. 515.

[79] ASF, *Diplomatico*, Rome-Florence, Giorgio Vasari to Matteo Botti, 25 February 1551.

[80] '[M]a questa cosa d'avere a uscire della casa de' Botti e a me e a tutta Firenze pare molto strano e ne à ricevuto gran biasimo non per il valore, ma per il modo del fare e ognuno procura di inalzare e aumentare e' ceppi delle case loro e Matteo à fatto il contrario'. Giovanbattista did everything he could to avoid leaving the house in via de' Serragli. He consulted with his lawyer, considered taking legal action to stay in the home and tried offering his sister-in-law the value of the property plus 700 scudi. In the end, he was forced to yield. ASF, *Libri di commercio*, 716, Florence-Venice, Giovanbattista Botti to Pandolfo Attavanti (personal), 16 July 1565, c. 158v.; *Libri di commercio*, 716, Florence-Venice, Giovanbattista Botti to Pandolfo Attavanti (personal), 22 June 1565, c. 159v. *Libri di commercio*, 716, Florence-Venice, Giovanbattista Botti to Pandolfo Attavanti, 7 July 1565, c. 162r.

[81] Which was made possible by the death of the actuary Lorenzo Gianfigliazzi. ASF, *Libri di commercio*, 716, Florence-Venice, Giovanbattista to Pandolfo Attavanti, 28 November 1565, c. 181v.

[82] This appointment was made in January 1567. ASF, *Libri di commercio*, 726, Florence, 5 January 1567, 24d.; *Libri di commercio*, 726, Florence, 5 January 1567, c. 25s.

influencing the societal structures created and almost always influenced by the desire to be self-sufficient, rejecting the contribution of outsiders. This was not a attitude unique to Giovanbattista. As we will see below, when Iacopo, in Cádiz and Seville, founded a company with Zanobi Guidacci and Giovanni Morelli, the Eldest, working from Florence, opposed it and convinced his brother to break up the company taking advantage of Battista's arrival in Spain.

It is difficult to say whether this approach precluded the further expansion of the family and its wealth. Nor can we exclude the possibility that its decline was partly caused by the withering of almost all the branches of the family tree. What is certain is that the Botti did not pass unscathed from the 'generation of merchants' to that of marchesi. The coat of arms and elevation to knight of St Stephen bestowed upon Giovanbattista's son date to the last decade of the sixteenth century. At the very end of the period covered by our documentation, we learn that the family got its long yearned-for progeny. On 8 February 1566, in the house in via dell'Ardiglione,[83] Caterina gavc birth to a boy. Battista had managed to ensure the continuation of the line.[84] The next day, the baby was baptised with the names Matteo, Zanobi and Romolo.[85] Lucky names: Matteo was the head of the family; Zanobi (Zenobius) was the first bishop of Florence; Romolo (Romulus) was the founder of the Eternal City. That said, his family tie to the Medici family and its wealth held greater weight in his life, considering that he began a diplomatic career in 1587 during which he was a part of numerous missions across Europe (Savoy, Transylvania, Lorraine, Low Countries, Spain, France). He became a knight of the Order of St Stephen (25 May 1591),[86] was an associate of the Accademia degli Alterati, a member of the Accademia fiorentina (1583) and that of the Arti del disegno (1594).[87] In 1608, he was made First Majordomo.[88] He gave generous alms to the church and monastery

[83] ASF, *Libri di commercio*, 726, Florence, 8 February 1566, c. 17d.

[84] Giovanbattista was born on 19 April 1505 and, like his brothers, he was buried in the chapel of the Carmine, on 24 March 1567. ASF, *Tratte*, Libri dell'età, 81, c. 40v.; *Ufficiali poi Magistrato della Grascia*, 192, c. 159v. Caterina became guardian of their children. She joined her husband in May 1592. ASF, *Ufficiali poi Magistrato della Grascia*, 193, c. 120.

[85] Giovanbattista himself described the event: 'I remember that on this day the 9th of February, a Saturday, at 11 o'clock PM I had my little boy baptised in San Giovanni and I named him Matteo, Zanobi and Romolo. My godfather Alamanno di Tomaso da Filicaya was there and so was Monna * Giacomini, wife of Bindaccio de' Ricasoli and they made an offering of seven gold scudi'. ('Ricordo come questo dì 9 di febbraio in sabato a hore 23 feci battezzare a San Giovanni el mio figliuolo e li posi nome Matteo, Zanobi e Romolo. Fu mio compare Alamanno di Tomaso da Filicaya et Monna * Giacomini, moglie di Bindaccio de' Ricasoli e messono nelle pere in tutto scudi 7 d'oro'). ASF, *Libri di commercio*, 726, Florence, 9 February 1566, c. 17s. At that time, 11 o'clock PM was what 5 o'clock PM is today.

[86] F. Point-Waquet, 'Les Botti', p. 697. On 28 February 1568, Francesco's illegitimate son, Géronimo, was also made a knight of St Stephen. He died in 1588. ASF, *Manoscritti*, 594, Carte Pucci, inserto 26. F. Angiolini, *I cavalieri e il principe. L'Ordine di Santo Stefano e la società toscana in età moderna*, EDIFIR, Florence 1996, pp. 81–82.

[87] https://www.aadfi.it/accademico/botti-matteo-di-giovanbattista/ accessed on 4 June 2024.

[88] F. Point-Waquet, 'Les Botti', p. 697.

of San Michele e San Gaetano in Florence's Piazza Antinori, where his brother Giovanbattista had taken holy orders in 1592. Giovanbattista was the second born of Caterina, who contributed to the construction of the monastery with 13,000 piastres. He was a courtier of Grand Duchess Christina of Lorraine, who regularly attended that church.[89]

On 28 June 1609, Matteo became marchese of Campiglia. He was enormously cultured and not only an expert in art and music but also a sophisticated linguist. He associated with Galileo Galilei, Torquato Tasso and many other personalities of his time.[90]

In conclusion, this account confirms the feeling that the Botti family was also representative of a process that involved many of the major Florentine houses. They were able to maintain wealth, affluence and a propensity for investment until the end of the sixteenth century. Then, the unmistakable signs of decline began to emerge, characterised by disengagement from manufacturing and trade investments in favour of unearned income. As noted above, the marchese of Campiglia neglected commodities to carry out numerous diplomatic missions for Ferdinand I.[91] The years of greatest prosperity and a high standard of living fell between 1591 and 1596, when he was receiving income equal to 250,000 scudi. But a few unsuccessful diplomatic missions and the abandonment of all economic activity marked his end and that of the family. In 1615, a few years before his death, in exchange for all his assets, valued at 200,000 scudi, Grand Duke Cosimo II settled his unpaid debts in the amount of 150,000 and used the remainder to provide him with a life annuity.[92] And that is how the Florentine branch of the Botti family died out.

[89] E. Chini, *La chiesa dei Santi Michele e Gaetano a Firenze*, Edizioni Cassa di Risparmio di Firenze, Florence 1984, p. 15, p. 335, p. 338; *La chiesa dei Santi Michele e Gaetano*, ed. G. Piccirillo, Becocci Editore, Florence 2006. Giovanbattista wrote in his will that if Matteo, his sole heir, died childless, the church would receive 1000 scudi a year for 16 years.

[90] For a detailed picture of Matteo di Giovanbattista Botti, see F. Point-Waquet, 'Les Botti'.

[91] On the diplomatic missions, see F. Martelli, C. Galasso, *Istruzioni agli ambasciatori e inviati medicei in Spagna e nell'"Italia spagnola" (1536–1648) II 1587–1648*, Ministero per i beni e le attività culturali, Direzione Generale per gli Archivi, Rome 2007, pp. 223–230; F. Point-Waquet, 'Les Botti', pp. 698–702; R. Cantagalli, 'Matteo Botti', in *Dizionario Biografico degli Italiani*, vol. 13, 1971. Available online at https://www.treccani.it/enciclopedia/matteo-botti_(Dizionario-Biografico)/ accessed 19 February 2024. There are some inaccuracies in the entry, such as the Botti family's origins in Cremona. G.V. Parigino, 'Alcune riflessioni sulla politica patrimoniale di Ferdinando II de' Medici', *Mediterranea-ricerche storiche*, VII, 19, 2010, pp. 279–294, p. 290.

[92] Matteo di Giovanbattista died on 22 February 1621 and was buried in the chapel of the Carmine. G. Fossi, 'Grandi casati', pp. 332–334. The inventories of the estate of Marchese Botti are kept in the Guardaroba Medicea in the Archivio di Stato, Florence, at no. 398. The properties included the buildings in Fiesole and Petrognano and the Petrognano, Camugliano and Mandri farms with all their contents. When Botti died, the contents of the house in via de' Serragli were also distributed to different Medici residences. See P. Barocchi, 'Sulla collezione Botti', *Prospettiva*, 93/94, II, 1999, pp. 126–130; G. Gaeta Bertelà, *La Tribuna di Ferdinando I de' Medici. Inventari 1589–1631*, Panini Editore, Modena 1997. For an in-depth, complete analysis of the Medici's entire inheritance, see G. V. Parigino, 'Il patrimonio', pp. 488, 497, 512.

3.1.2 The Andalusian Branch

As was the case for the Tuscan line, the Andalusian branch produced families of great import in the Spanish nobility.[93] Iacopo died in Seville the night of 28 July 1562. The following day, a Wednesday, his will was opened in his house in the *colación* of Santa María Magdalena.[94] His widow, Ana Francisca Fonte, presented those in attendance with a signed and sealed letter. The group gathered in her home including the *alcalde ordinario* of Seville, Cristóbal de Montiel, the notary for the testamentary procedure, Pedro Gutiérrez de Padilla, and the witnesses: the *licenciado* Martin Alonso and the notaries Joan de Salvatierra, Alonso Palaçio and Gonçalo de Mazuecos. After they swore to tell the truth, to have verified the death of the merchant and declared that they were present when the will was drawn up, De Padilla was able to begin the process of opening and publishing the document. He cut the threads used to sew shut the document, opened it and read it out loud. Its content reflected the events of a life lived to the full, not without numerous challenges, in a country far from home and a social context undergoing profound change following the discovery of the New World.

Iacopo's wishes revealed his strength and fragility to all the world. Like all men of his time, his first thought was for the salvation of his soul. A salvation that rich merchants in particular believed could be earned through bequests to religious institutions or the needy. Iacopo was no different. He began with an appeal to God, begging his forgiveness, ordered Masses for the repose of his soul and made bequests for confraternities in Seville and the poor. A few examples include a bequest of ten ducats each to the confraternities of 'Obispo de Escalas e de las Donzellas', of which he was a member, a contribution to the monasteries of Santísima Trinidad and Nuestra Señora de las Mercedes to be used for the redemption of Christian prisoners, a contribution to the house and hospital of San Lázaro, 20 ducats to the homeless and 6 to convalescents.

He also left precise instructions for his funeral. He wished to be buried in Seville in the church of the monastery of San Pablo.[95] The tomb was to be chosen by the executors of his will, who would also decide the number and quality of the candles needed to honour the cross during the funeral. In the interest of sobriety, he asked that everything be as simple as possible.

We cannot escape the fact that the will was written on 25 July, just 3 days before he died. Iacopo was undoubtedly already very sick, and we do not know that he was still fully lucid. We might make a conjecture and wonder whether his wife exploited her husband's weakness, making him draft a document that, voiding any previous

---

[93] F. Fernández de Béthencourt, *Nobiliario y blasón de canarias: diccionario histórico, biográfico, genealógico y hèraldico*, Imprenta isleña, Santa Cruz de Tenerife 1878–1879, Tomo I. Available online at https://bibliotecadigital.jcyl.es/es/catalogo_imagenes/grupo.do?path=10130529 (accessed 24 June 2024).

[94] AGS, *CME*, 300.27.

[95] A chantry was founded in this monastery in 1591 by his daughters. AGS, *CME*, 79, 36.

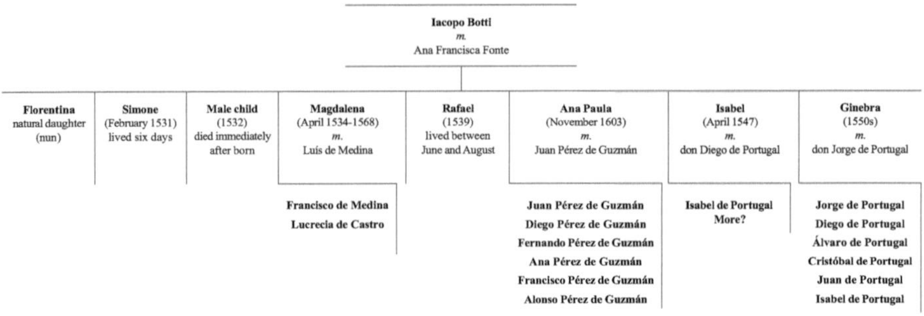

Fig. 3.3 Family tree: the Andalusian branch

ones, was to the sole advantage of herself and their daughters. We will never know if Botti truly wanted to exclude his brothers, or if he was influenced by the fact that in Spain his patronymic would not be lost, since all mothers gave their children, then and now, their own surname as well. Perhaps Ana took the opportunity to safeguard herself and their daughters even more.

Among the various bequests, there was 1 for 15 ducats for Florentina Botti, a nun in the convent of Santa Clara in Seville. We have no further information about her, but she was undoubtedly Iacopo's illegitimate daughter, since Giovanbattista referred to her as a niece in one of his letters (Fig. 3.3).[96]

Children were a source of endless worry for Iacopo and Ana Francisca. Their first child was Simone, who was born in 1531 and lived for just 6 days. The following year, Ana gave birth to another boy, but he also died soon after. Anxiety about having a male child drove them to procreate, but Ana continued 'to be thin', to the point that Iacopo decided to ask for 'detailed information about how to make babies' from Florence. The brothers took care that this information was prepared by 'a competent man' but warned Iacopo 'that it will not be of much use to you since it's all down to practice and learning from that when it's good to do it or not, since one learns by doing'. Finally, Magdalena was born in April 1534. Five years later, another boy, Rafael, who lived just over a month, and then just girls: Ana Paula in November 1541, Isabel in April 1547 and, last, Ginebra in the 1550s.[97] In short, Iacopo's marriage was a fruitful one, albeit all girls.

These children, even if all female, guaranteed the Botti family nobility in Spain. The wealth of the shrewd Tuscan, accumulated through his various economic ventures, was undoubtedly the most effective motivation, and his daughters all made

[96] AGS, *CME*, 300.27, c. 17.

[97] ASF, *Libri di commercio*, 721, Pisa-Cádiz, Francesco Botti to the Botti company, 25 November 1531, c. 28r.; *Libri di commercio*, 721, Pisa-Cádiz, Francesco Botti to the Botti company, 22 April 1534, c. 204v.; *Libri di commercio*, 721, Pisa-Cádiz, Francesco Botti to the Botti company, 11 May 1534, c. 208r.; *Libri di commercio,* 713, Florence-Cádiz, Matteo Botti to the Botti company, 21 June 1539, c. 31r.; *Libri di commercio*, 713, Florence-Cádiz, Matteo Botti to the Botti company, 6 August 1539, c. 59r.

prestigious matches. Magdalena's first husband was Luis de Medina and her second a Genoese. Ana Paula married Juan Pérez de Guzmán, Isabel wed Don Diego de Portugal, and Ginebra married Don Jorge de Portugal, Don Diego's brother. Through these unions, the merchant's daughters married into the Braganza house and after two generations their descendants became nobles. Specifically, in 1626 when Don Luis de Medina y Carillo de Mendoza Botti became a knight of the Order of Calatrava. Medina Botti was the son of Francisco de Medina and Lady Beatriz Carillo de Mendoza. His grandmother was Magdalena Botti and his great-grandfather Iacopo.[98]

The Seville house, in the *collación* de la Magdalena, where Iacopo had lived most of his life, also remained in the family. In 1614, the portion inherited by Ginebra was sold for 6000 ducats by her brother Diego de Portugal to their uncle and aunt Diego de Portugal and Isabel Botti.[99] The symbol of family unity was saved.

The Will of Ginebra, Iacopo's Youngest Daughter

On 7 June del 1581, in Gelves, Don Jorge de Portugal appeared before Antonio de Cuenca, the city *alcalde*, and the notary Alonso de Herrera, to report the death of his wife Ginebra and publish her will.

Ginebra, of fragile health, died young, just over 30 years old, leaving six children. Her last will and testament reflected the customs of the time. She indicated that her tomb was in the family church, Nuestra Señora de Santa María in Gelves. The building was commissioned by her father-in-law, Don Jorge Alberto del Portugal, first duke of Gelves, who, complying with the wishes of his wife, Isabel Colón, granddaughter of the Genoese admiral,[100] had left a bequest of 2000 gold ducats.

After indicating her tomb, she provided for 330 Masses for the repose of her soul to be given in different shrines in Seville, including the monastery of San Pablo where her father was buried and the church of the Magdalena in the quarter where she had spent much of her life. She left numerous bequests for relatives, friends and household staff. She freed a few young people from servitude, gave money to those who had helped her when she was ill and contributed to the dowries of her granddaughters. She left her sister Isabel a diamond rosary and Ana Paula a string of pearls set in gold.

She named her children her sole heirs (Don Jorge, Don Diego, Don Álvaro, Don Cristóbal, Don Juan and Donna Isabel) as well as her husband, Don Jorge, who she designated their warden. She asked him to raise them in 'buena doctrina y virtud' (good doctrine and virtue), but most importantly making sure that they all studied and guaranteeing that those among them who wished to could continue their studies to the highest level. We do

[98] M.V. Vera Morín, 'El acceso a la nobleza como estrategia social en el ámbito mercantil. Los Botti y los Fonte entre Sevilla y Canarias en el siglo XVI', in *Nuevas perspectivas de investigación en Historia Moderna: Economía, Sociedad, Política y Cultura en el Mundo Hispánico*, eds. M.Á. Pérez Samper, J.L. Betrán Moya, Fundación Española de Historia Moderna, Madrid 2018, pp. 150–158, p. 158. Also see F. Fernández de Béthencourt, *Nobiliario y blason*, p. 133 (https://bibliotecadigital.jcyl.es/es/catalogo_imagenes/grupo.do?path=10130529 accessed 24 June 2024). The Fantoni family from Florence also joined the local nobility. See J.J. Iglesias Rodríguez, 'Los Fantoni. Fuentes y metodología para el estudio de la familia y el patrimonio en Toscana y en la Andalucía moderna', *e-Spania*, 43, 11, 2022, pp. 1–21 (https://idus.us.es/bitstream/handle/11441/139834/Iglesias%20Rodriguez%20JJ%20-%20Los_Fantoni_PDF.pdf?sequence=1&isAllowed=y accessed 24 June 2024).

[99] E. Otte, 'Los Botti y los Lugos', pp. 47–87, p. 82.

[100] https://dbe.rah.es/biografias/jorge-de-portugal-y-melo

not know if this was a customary request, but we cannot exclude the possibility that Ginebra had learned from her father the importance of a good education for success in life and business.

Her main concerns were for Isabel, who was still very young and who she entrusted to the care of her sister, who had married her husband's brother. Aunt Isabel was to take her niece into her home and raise her like a daughter. The young child, the only girl, received 6000 ducats and all her mother's gold, jewellery and objects in precious, including a lavish diamond pin that was in the shop of the silversmith Cristóbal López.[101]

3.2 Wealth and Patronage

The cityscape of Renaissance Florence was, as we know, the result of the work of a great number of wealthy merchants who, working with the leading artists of the time, shaped the image of their city. Patronage was the fruit of economic prosperity and a high level of knowledge that, as we have seen, were together among the main reasons for their financial success. One need only think of the forms of education and cultural activities that benefited from broad circulation in the population. These phenomena had no equivalent in other cities governed by the oldest courts, which tended to centralise politics and artistic investments, putting the brakes on private initiative and stimulation of natural competition. Whereas in Florence, the grounds for debate and imitation were particularly significant. A contributing factor in all this was the city's large middle class made up of merchants, bankers and artisans. Men who, as Leonardo Bruni observed, used the arts to document their prestige and demonstrate their virtues.[102]

The effects of this phenomenon still symbolically mark the city today. Every street was characterised by splendid architecture, not least the countless proud palazzos expressing their patron's power: Medici, Rucellai, Strozzi, Pitti, Antinori,

[101] AGS, *CME*, 300.27.

[102] On Florentine patronage, see, among the more relevant publications, C. Acidini Luchinat, 'Il mecenatismo familiare', in *'Per bellezza, per studio, per piacere'. Lorenzo il Magnifico e gli spazi dell'arte*, ed. F. Borsi, Giunti, Florence 1991, pp. 101–124; E. Capretti, *I Medici mecenati a Firenze: da mercanti a signori*, Polistampa, Florence 2004; M. DePrano, *Art Patronage, Family and Gender in Renaissance Florence*, Cambridge University Press, Cambridge 2018; P. Findlen, 'Ereditare un museo. Collezionismo, strategie familiari e pratiche culturali nell'Italia del XVI secolo', Quaderni storici, 39, 115, 2004, pp. 45–81; P.D. McLean, *The Art Network. Strategic Interaction and Patronage in Renaissance Florence*, Duke University Press, Durham 2007; L. Tanzini, *Cosimo de' Medici. Il banchiere statista padre del Quattrocento fiorentino*, Salerno Editrice, Rome 2022; S. Tognetti, 'Gli affari di messer Palla Strozzi (e di suo padre Nofri). Imprenditoria e mecenatismo nella Firenze del primo Rinascimento', *Annali di Storia di Firenze*, IV, 2009, pp. 7–88; M. Wyatt, *The Cambridge Companion to the Italian Renaissance*, Cambridge University Press, Cambridge 2014. For a complete account of religious patronage, see F. Salvestrini, *Il carisma della magnificenza. L'abate vallombrosano Biagio Milanesi e la tradizione benedettina nell'Italia del Rinascimento con l'edizione critica del* Memoriale *dell'abate Biagio Milanesi*, Viella, Rome 2017.

Pazzi, Gondi. Buildings designed by great architects, like Leon Battista Alberti, Michelozzo, Giuliano da Sangallo, Filippo Brunelleschi, Luca Fancelli and Giuliano da Maiano. The merchants had magnificently decorated chapels built in these residences and in the churches they attended. A complete list would be very long, and we will limit ourselves here to the Chapel of the Magi by Benozzo Gozzoli in Palazzo Medici, the Brancacci Chapel by Masaccio and Masolino in Santa Maria del Carmine, the Tornabuoni Chapel by Ghirlandaio in Santa Maria Novella, the Sagrestia Vecchia, Brunelleschi's masterpiece in the basilica of San Lorenzo, the Pazzi Chapel in Santa Croce also by Filippo Brunelleschi and the Strozzi Chapel in Santa Maria Novella, frescoed by Filippino Lippi. The inventory of furnishings, paintings and sculptures that decorated those spaces would be nearly infinite. As observed by Richard Goldthwaite, these works contributed to the emergence of true art collecting.[103] We could say that these riches expressed choices that linked aesthetic sense to luxury for display. We can only imagine the reaction of visitors to the costly intarsia, the elegant curtains' play of colours and forms, the valuable drapery, lavish decorations and omnipresent frescoes. Their recurrence in the account books of businessmen attests to the ubiquity of these kinds of objects. To give an example, in the last decade and a half of the fifteenth century, the Serristori family was hiring embroiderers and painters, including Lorenzo di Credi, a student of Verrocchio, who painted a cornice and the decoration of some drapery in their home. And Averardo had his study decorated with works by the painter Niccolò di Bartolomeo and spent more than 30 florins to furnish the room of his son, Antonio, with wardrobes, chests and cornices.[104] In short, fine pieces that stood as expressions of economic, financial and political power.

The members of the Botti family neatly represent these merchant-patrons. The property and most of the works of art that Matteo di Giovanbattista left to the Medici were the fruit of the economic initiative and artistic sensibility of his father and uncles. Men who grew up breathing in Renaissance taste who could also recognise the quality of works of art and were most importantly quick to help the artists who were invigorating Florentine cultural life. In his *Life* of Raphael, Giorgio Vasari described Matteo di Simone Botti as 'an intimate friend of every able person, and particularly of painters'[105] A little further down, he continued, 'And no less esteem is shown to the works of our arts and to the craftsmen by his brother, Simon Botti, who, besides being held by us all to be one of the most loving spirits that show favour to the men of our professions, is held in estimation by me in particular as the best and greatest friend that ever man loved after a long experience; not to mention the good judgment that he has and shows in matters of art'.[106] To give just one

[103] See R.A. Goldthwaite, *Ricchezza e domanda.*

[104] A. Orlandi, 'Tra austerità e lusso', p. 37.

[105] G. Vasari, *Lives of the Most Eminent Painters, Sculptors and Architects*, trans. Gaston du C. De Vere, London 1913, vol. IV.

[106] '[N]é meno di lui stima l'opere dell'arte nostra e gli artefici il fratello suo Simon Botti, che oltra lo esser tenuto da tutti noi per uno de' più amorevoli che facciano beneficio agli uomini di queste professioni, è da me particolare tenuto e stimato per il migliore e maggiore amico si possa per lunga esperienza aver caro oltra al giudicio buono che egli ha e mostra nelle cose dell'arte'. Ibid.

example among many, the sculptor Daniello Ricciarelli was hosted in a house owned by Simone, thanks to Vasari, while he was making plaster copies of the marble statues sculpted by Michelangelo in the Sacrestia Nuova.[107]

So, the link between the Botti family and the maestro from Arezzo was profound. Indeed, Vasari described Matteo and Simone often in the *Lives* as his 'very dear friends'. The paintings he created for them included the panel of 'Christ Crucified, with Our Lady, S. John and the Magdalene weeping' in the family chapel in the Carmine[108] and the 'Our Lady with her Son in her arms, and Joseph' that Francesco brought with him to Andalusia.[109] Vasari was closest to Simone. In his *Ricordanze*, the youngest Botti figures as an important liaison for business and commissions. In 1545, he gave him an advance of 50 scudi on behalf of Raffaello Acciaiuoli, who had ordered two large pictures that he intended to bring to Spain and six works on canvas 'full of landscapes and other small figures in oil'.[110] Three years later, the painting with portraits of Dante, Petrarch, Guido Cavalcanti, Cino da Pistoia, Boccaccio and Guittone di Arezzo that had been commissioned by the bishop of Nocera, Monsignor Iovio, was sent to none other than Simone, who was in Rome at the time, so that he could take care of the delivery.[111] In 1555, the Florentine merchant obtained a commission for his friend, on behalf of Mariotto Alberighi, for a painting of the crucified Christ, the Virgin Mary, St John and the Magdalene for the nuns of Luco di Mugello; he was paid 50 scudi for it (Fig. 3.4).[112]

Brushes for Giorgio Vasari

On 24 October 1556, Simone Botti wrote a letter, probably from his country house, to the company of the Attavanti family, eminently trusted friends in Venice:

'Please send me 100 painter's brushes as soon as possible. They need to be 100 bristle brushes, a mix of big and small, for oil painting and another 100 vair brushes, a mix of big and small. Since I think you will not be able to send them here, please send them to Rome with instructions to then send them here. And there is a master in San Lio who makes good ones and so inform me of what you will do. For the cost, don't make me the debtor because I don't want to keep track of it. Make Mr. Giorgio Vasari the debtor on my behalf.'[113]

---

107 G. Vasari, *Lives*, vol. VIII.

108 G. Vasari, *Lives*, vol. X.

109 Ibid.

110 G. Vasari, *Ricordanze,* 1527–1573, c. 15v. (https://www.memofonte.it/home/files/pdf/vasari_ricordanze.pdf, accessed 24 June 2024).

111 G. Vasari, *Ricordanze*, c. 17v. (https://books.google.it/books?id=dnGxfe4YCwcC&printsec=frontcover&hl=it&source=gbs_ge_summary_r&cad=0#v=onepage&q&f=false, accessed 24 June 2024).

112 G. Vasari, *Ricordanze*, c. 23r. (https://books.google.it/books?id=dnGxfe4YCwcC&printsec=frontcover&hl=it&source=gbs_ge_summary_r&cad=0#v=onepage&q&f=false, accessed 24 June 2024).

113 'Vorrej che quanto prima mj mandassj ciento pennelli da pittori. Hanno a essere ciento di setole fra grossi e sottili da lavorare a olio, et altri ciento in fra grossj e sottilj di ogni sorte dj vaio, e sia più presto si pò. Ma perché penso che qua non possiate mandare niente, vi prego li mandiate a Roma con ordinare siano poi mandati qui. Et a San Lio è un mastro che li sole fare bonj, in però di grazia avvisatemj il seguito. E del costo non ne fate debitore me che non voglio tenerne conto, ma faretene debitore messer Giorgio Aretino sopra di me e qui sianno pagatj e i danari a lui ordinerete'. ASF, *Libri di commercio*, 742, Florence-Venice, Simone Botti to the Attavanti company, 24 October 1556, c. 12r.

Fig. 3.4 Botti Chapel with Vasari's *Crucifixion* today. Giorgio Vasari, *The Crucifixion* (1562–1563), Florence, Basilica di Santa Maria del Carmine. (Photo by Carlo Gianni)

This is the umpteenth attestation confirming the link between Simone and the multifaceted artist from Arezzo. It is notable that Simone did not turn to the Florentine market. The order for 200 brushes of varying size was sent to Venice, where it was thought it would be possible to find better ones. Botti's familiarity with both the products and the Venetian market emerges clearly from the letter. He was the one to suggest that Pandolfo Attavanti go to the talented brushmaker with a shop in San Lio, in the Castello quarter near the church with the painting of St James completed by Titian a few years before.

The Botti family expressed and refined their taste associating with artists and acquiring artworks, furniture and other furnishings. The first acquisitions were made for the old family home on the corner of via dell'Ardiglione. Later, they were brought to the part of the building in via de' Serragli that Matteo had bought the year he got married (Fig. 3.5).

The property was not chosen by chance. Firstly, it was very close to their longtime residence and some of their other properties. They had two other houses in Borgo Stella, one of which on the corner of via de' Serragli. And, in Fondaccio Soderini, near the Arno, the brothers owned a cobbler's shop and a bakery at the end of the street. Secondly, the building belonged to the descendants of Piero del Pugliese, a politician and important merchant who had it built in the mid fifteenth century, filling it with masterpieces. It would seem that the new owners 'inherited' a fine painting by Fra' Bartolomeo of San Marco depicting St George wearing

Fig. 3.5 Palazzo Botti-Del Pugliese today. (Photo by Carlo Gianni)

armour and killing a dragon while jousting, 'in an antechamber at the head of a staircase'.[114]

An inventory drawn up in 1565 provides us with a valuable list of the rooms in the home: cellar, male servants' room, courtyard and loggia, ground floor room of the salon, salon, ground floor room to the left of the stair, stove, well room, great hall, Giovanbattista's room and its antechamber, the 'camera della gelosia', room of the sitting room antechamber, sitting room, attic, second attic, female servants' room, bread-making room, dining room, room of the great hall, antechamber of the upper salon, room of the salon, great hall of the terrace, room facing the bridge or chimney room, ground-floor room and salon.[115] The document only provides information about the furniture and other furnishings that were left to Matteo's widow in

[114] G. Vasari, *Lives*, vol. IV.

[115] The order of the rooms follows that of the inventory. ASF, *Libri di commercio*, 726, Florence, 30 June 1565, cc. 2d.-8d.

usufruct. It does not include the belongings that Battista took with him when he moved back to the old family home. Even so, it is not hard to imagine the sumptuousness of the salons decorated with red and light blue leather and golden ornament, benches lining the walls, panels with oak frames and trestles and intarsia wardrobes. Other, equally rich rooms were decorated with gold and silver hangings, beds embellished with lion's paws and complete with 'a stool and canopy', coffers painted with the Botti and Tosinghi coats of arms, painted canopies and much more. And then there was the lavish study that the Eldest had decorated by Alessandro del Barbiere. Raffaello Borghini described it as follows:

> For Matteo Botti, a most courteous young man who takes much pleasure in virtues, he painted a private study in which he created the seven liberal arts in oil the octagonal panels in the ceiling and other virtues associated with those arts in a ring around them with grotesques, with little birds and with other fair things, that are playing. Under the ceiling in a frieze amidst very beautiful decoration there are prints by Alberto Duro [Albrecht Dürer]. These are arranged in the middle of some shelves, on top of which there are worthy men setting down little wax models. Below there is another frieze with heads of emperors and balls of different stones set upon a carved and gilded cornice beneath which there are 11 oil paintings of ancient games, hunts, fishing and other country pleasures and between the pictures there are paintings on pillars of the 12 months of the years and the four elements.[116]

The private study was accessed from the bedroom, probably the one called the 'camera della gelosia', going through a door with a 'Christ in relief' above it.[117]

The walls of the home were hung with the family's painting collection. In 1591, Francesco Bocchi wrote in the volume *Bellezze della città di Firenze* that the collection included works by Andrea del Sarto, Raphael and Leonardo.[118] The first had made 'a panel painting of a Charity' and the Virgin 'with Our Lord sitting on a small

---

[116] 'A Matteo Botti, giovane gentilissimo e che molto si diletta delle virtù, ha dipinto uno scrittoio dove negli ottangoli del sopracielo ha fatto le sette arti liberali a olio et altre virtù conformi a dette arti fanno a quelle corona intorno con grottesche, con uccelletti e con altre vaghe cose, che scherzano. Sotto il sopracielo in un fregio fra bellissimi adornamenti sono accomodate stampe d'Alberto Duro (Albrecht Dürer) messe in mezo da certe mensole, sopra cui più valentuomini posano modellini di cera e sotto segue un altro fregio con teste d'imperadori e palle di pietre mistie fini di più sorte, posanti sopra una cornice intagliata, e messa d'oro, sotto cui fanno spalliera intorno undici quadri a olio rappresentanti giuochi antichi, cacce, pescagioni et altri piaceri villeschi e fra quadro in certi pilastri sono dipinti con bell'ordine i dodici mesi dell'anno et i quattro elementi'. R. Borghini, *Del riposo in cui della pittura e della scultura si favella, de' più illustri pittori e scultori e delle più famose opere loro si fa menzione; e le cose principali appartenenti a dette arti s'insegnano*, libro IV, Giorgio Marescotti, Florence 1584, pp. 635–636 (https://www.memofonte.it/home/files/pdf/guide_borghini_4.pdf accessed 24 June 2024).

[117] ASF, *Libri di commercio*, 726, Florence, 30 June 1565, c. 4d.

[118] P. Barocchi, 'Sulla collezione Botti', *Prospettiva*, 1992, 93–94, pp. 126–130; F. Bocchi, *Le bellezze della città di Fiorenza dove a pieno di pittura, di scultura, di sacri tempii, di palazzi i più notabili artifizii et più preziosi si contengono*, Sermartelli, Florence 1591, pp. 83–84 (https://www.memofonte.it/files/2019/12/Bocchi_LE_BELLEZZE_DELLA_CITTA_DI-FIORENZA_1591.pdf accessed 24 June 2024).

Fig. 3.6 Andrea del Sarto, *The Botti Madonna* (1528–1530), United States, private collection

pillow' for the family.[119] It is likely that 'the painting of Our Lady with the gilt frame' that the inventory of the furnishings drawn up in 1565 reports in the Camera della Gelosia was the famous painting by Andrea del Sarto. We know that Matteo di Giovanbattista, the last of the Botti line, left the painting to Cosimo II. The painting is not found in the Medici inventory of 1637, since during those years it had been given to Charles I of England. When the king was executed in 1649, the Madonna was purchased by the artist and art dealer Remigius Van Leempunt. After various other episodes, it found its way into the collection of Laurence W. Boothe.[120] The Botti Madonna has remained in the United States ever since and now belongs to anonymous private collector (Fig. 3.6).

[119] This is how it was described in 1621 in an inventory of Matteo Botti's collection drawn up specifically for the Medici, c. 16 and c. 37. P. Barocchi, 'Sulla collezione Botti', pp. 126–130.

[120] A. Turpin, 'The Frame of the Botti Madonna', in *Andrea del Sarto. The Botti Madonna*, catalogue and appendix prepared in connection with the display of the painting at the Galleria Doria Pamphilj, Courtauld Institute of Art, London 2001, pp. 56–69; A. MacGregor, 'The Collection-History of the Botti Madonna', in *Andrea del Sarto. The Botti Madonna*, catalogue and appendix prepared in connection with the display of the painting at the Galleria Doria Pamphilj, Courtauld Institute of Art, London 200, pp. 43–53. In general, see the catalogue and appendix prepared in for the display of the painting at the Galleria Doria Pamphilj, *Andrea del Sarto. The Botti Madonna*, Courtauld Institute of Art, London 2001–2001. We can therefore answer the author's question about who the second name written on the slip of paper attached to the painting referred to.

Fig. 3.7 Raphael, *La Velata*, (1512–circa 1515), Florence, Palazzo Pitti

The *Velata* that Matteo kept in his home like a relic was instead by Raphael.[121] Our documents mention a Lady by Raphael that Simone sent to his brother Francesco in Spain between February and April 1554, which was probably this painting (Fig. 3.7).

Lastly, again according to Bocchi, there was a Leonardo:

> A small panel painted in oils … of immense beauty, in which the Virgin is painted with supreme mastery and extreme diligence: the figure of Christ, as a child, is beautiful and wondrous; the rendering of his raised face is singular and admirable.[122]

Raphael's *Velata* and a St Jerome in Valladolid

In February 1554, Simone Botti sent his brother Francesco two paintings on wood. All we know about one was that it was a St Jerome, while the other was probably Raphael's *La Velata*, now in the Palazzo Pitti, Florence. The veil covering the sitter's hair tells us that she was a married woman, but her identity is uncertain. According to Giorgio Vasari, who saw the painting in Matteo's house, it is Raphael's beloved Margherita Luti, called La Fornarina.

---

[121] G. Vasari, *Lives*, vol. IV.

[122] 'Una tavoletta colorita a olio […] di eccessiva bellezza, dove è dipinta una Madonna con sommo artifizio et con estrema diligenza: la figura di Cristo, che è bam bino, è bella a maraviglia; si vede in quello uno alzar del volto singolare et mirabile'. F. Bocchi, *Le bellezze della città di Fiorenza*, pp. 83–84 (https://www.memofonte.it/files/2019/12/Bocchi_LE_BELLEZZE_DELLA_CITTA_DI-FIORENZA_1591 accessed 24 June 2024).

According to others, it was, judging by the sitter's clothing and jewellery, a noblewoman painted on commission.

Simone informed his brother in a letter[123] and sent him a statement of the costs for packing the paintings and shipping them to Pisa. The two crates were loaded onto the Santa Maria Togignia, a Portuguese ship headed to Cádiz, from where they would continue their journey to Valladolid. That is where Francesco received them.

We do not know why Botti had the two paintings sent. Perhaps, like his fellow merchants, he was thinking of selling them or filling an order he had received. We like to think that he wanted to keep them and enjoy them during his time in Spain; it is no accident that the sublime painting returned to Italy.

Studying the costs involved is interesting and reveals the care with which they were packed.

+1554

+Copy of a bill for II paintings sent to Cádiz on instructions from Francesco Botti to whom this bill is being sent and firstly:

The following is the bill for the expenses incurred for sending two paintings to Cádiz to the Botti and Peri on the Portuguese ship called Santa Maria Togignia, captained by Manuello Alvaro, Portuguese resident of Vila do Conde.

For one large crate *a lanciaio* for the St Jerome,	lb.	8	
Per 13 *braccia* of wide cloth at 8 s. per *braccio* for said crate,	lb.	5	4
Per 20 *braccia* of waxed fabric at 9 s. per *braccio* for said crate,	lb.	9	
For the binder for the binding of said crate,	lb.	1	15
For nails to nail it,	lb.	–	1
For transport to customs house,	lb.	–	8
For *fogli reali* and *pasta* for arranging it in the crate,	lb.	1	8
Total expenses incurred for said crate,	lb.	25	16

+ The following is the bill for expenses incurred for the small crate

For a smaller crate for Raphael's lady,	lb.	3	–
Per 4 *braccia* of wide cloth at 8 s. per *braccio* for said,	lb.	1	12
Per 8 *braccia* of waxed fabric at 9 s. per *braccio* for said,	lb.	3	12
For the binders for the binding,	lb.	1	5
For nails to nail it,	lb.	–	1
For transport to customs house,	lb.	–	2
Total for twine, sheets of paper and *pasta* for arranging it,	lb.	–	12
	lb.	10	4

[123] ASF, *Libri di commercio*, 743, Florence-Cádiz, Simone Botti to the Botti and Peri company, 22 February 1554, c. 9v.

And paid for transport from here to Pisa lb. 14 *piccioli*, lb. 10 of which for the large crate and lb. 4 for the small crate,	lb.	14		
+The cost breakdown follows, and the expenses add up as shown	lb.	50		
And so, tax paid for both crates lb. 12.4.4 of which one could say 2/3 for the large crate,	lb.	12	4	4
In total, the expenses incurred were lb. 62.4.4 *piccioli*, for which I will be debtor on your behalf, enter them in your books and if there are any mistakes, say so and they will be corrected,	lb.	62	4	4
Simone Botti in Florence				
+9 April 1554				
And for the Livorno expenditures, I credited Bertini of Livorno	lb.	4	–	–
	lb.	66	4	4[124]

Being a merchant did not only mean commissioning works to decorate one's own country houses and city residences. In Florence, merchants also contributed to spreading the beauty of art for the benefit of everyone. Matteo commissioned Raffaellino del Garbo to create a small shrine depicting the Virgin and Child with St Catherine and St Barbara at the corner of a house he owned between the Ponte alla Carraia and the Canto alla Cuculia.[125] This was another way in which the unique animus loci of Renaissance Florence took shape.

We have only offered a few exemplary cases since it is sufficient to look at the inventory of the Guardaroba Medicea of 1621 to grasp the richness and variety of the art and more or less costly furnishings from the Botti house, like a bookcase valued at more than 10,000 ducats.[126] The already rich original collection built by Simone, the founder of the family, and his children, had been expanded by Matteo di Giovanbattista, who made the bequest to the Grand Dukes, who in turn brought the countless items thereby inherited to their homes in the city and countryside (Fig. 3.8).[127]

Iacopo, the brother who had left Tuscany for Andalusia, also had a fine artistic sensibility. It is again Vasari who provides us with information in this regard. Writing about Pietro Torrigiano, the author of the *Lives* reported that the artist had left England in 1521 and moved to Spain, where he proved his talent in many sculptures, including a 'Crucifix of terra-cotta, which is the most marvellous thing that

[124] ASF, *Libri di commercio*, 743, Florence-Cádiz, Simone Botti to the Botti and Peri company, 9 April 1554, cc. 11r.–12r.

[125] G. VASARI, *Lives*, vol. IV.

[126] F. POINT-WAQUET, 'Les Botti', pp. 689–712, pp. 701.

[127] P. BAROCCHI, 'Sulla collezione Botti', pp. 126–130; G. GAETA BERTELÀ, *La Tribuna di Ferdinando I de' Medici*.

Fig. 3.8 A surveyor's compass that belonged to Matteo and Giovanbattista Botti, Museo Galileo, Florence. (Photo by Franca Principe)

there is in all Spain'.[128] For the monastery of the friars of San Jerónimo Buenavista, just outside Seville, he sculpted another Crucifix and a St Jerome in penitence. He gave the saint the likeness of an old steward who worked in Botti's home. The choice of model tells us that the sculptor had visited the home of the Florentine merchant, who, like his brothers, was devoted to supporting artists (Fig. 3.9).

Considering the relationships that Iacopo was forming with the Andalusian aristocracy, he was undoubtedly the one who introduced Torrigiano to the Duke of Arcos, who fell in love with 'a Madonna and Child' that was so beautiful that he wanted a similar one for himself. The nobleman made so many promises to the sculptor that the latter thought he would become rich. This is how Giorgio Vasari described the moment of payment and the way the episode ended:

> The work being finished, the Duke gave him so many of those coins that are called "maravedis," which are worth little or nothing, that Torrigiano, to whose house there came two persons laden with them, became even more confirmed in his belief that he was to be a very rich man. But afterwards, having shown this money to a Florentine friend of his, and having asked him to count it and reckon its value in Italian coin, he saw that all that vast sum did not amount to 30 ducats; at which, holding himself to have been fooled, he went in a violent

[128] 'There is no tradition in Spain that the Crucifix in clay and the Virgin and Child, mentioned by Vasari above, ever existed. But the St Jerome in penitence, a statue in terracotta, larger than life size, is a work that has few rivals in Spain.' Fr. Quilliet, *Les arts italiens en Espagne ou Histoire des artistes italiens qui contribuerent a embellir les Castilles*, Ange Ajani, Rome 1825 p. 7 (https://books.google.it/books?id=ZrL9n3dhQ5oC&printsec=frontcover&hl=it&source=gbs_ge_summary_r&cad=0#v=onepage&q&f=false accessed 21 February 2024). On the works of Pietro Torrigiani, see M. Riddick, *Pietro Torrigiani. Discovery of a St. Anthony in Wood* (https://renbronze.files.wordpress.com/2020/05/pietro-torrigiani-_-a-saint-anthony-in-wood-1.pdf accessed 21 February 2024).

rage to where the figure was that he had made for the Duke, and wholly destroyed it. Whereupon that Spaniard, considering himself affronted, denounced Torrigiano as a heretic; on which account he was thrown into prison, and after being examined every day, and sent from one inquisitor to the other, he was finally judged to deserve the severest penalty. But this was never put into execution, because Torrigiano himself was plunged thereby into such melancholy, that, remaining many days without eating, and thus becoming very weak, little by little he put an end to his own life; and in this way, by denying himself his food, he avoided the shame into which he would perchance have fallen, for it was believed that he had been condemned to death.[129]

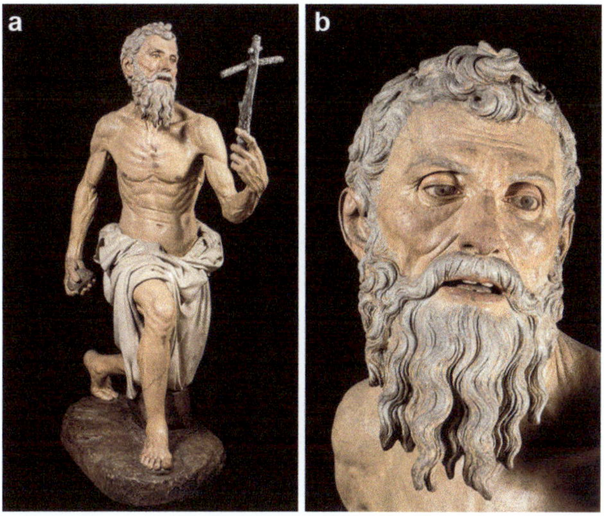

Fig. 3.9 (**a**, **b**) Pietro Torrigiano, *Penitent St Jerome*, (c. 1525), Seville, Museo de Bellas Artes

[129] 'La quale opera finita, gli donò quel duca tante di quelle monete che chiamano maravedís, che vagliono poco o nulla, che il Torrigiano, al quale ne andarono due persone a casa cariche, si confermò maggiormente nella sua opinione d'avere a essere ricchissimo. Ma avendo poi fatta contare e vedere a un suo amico fiorentino quella moneta e ridurla in modo italiano, vide che tanta somma non arrivava pure a trenta ducati; perché tenendosi beffato, con grandissima collera andò dove era la figura che aveva fatto per quel duca, e tutto guastolla. Onde quello Spagnolo tenendosi vituperato, accusò il Torrigiano per eretico; onde essendo messo in prigione ed. ogni dì esaminato e mandato da uno inquisitore all'altro, fu giudicato f inalmente degno di gravissima punizione; perché esso Torrigiano per ciò venne in tanta malinconia, che stato molti giorni senza mangiare, e perciò debolissimo divenuto, a poco poco, finì la vita: e così col. torsi il cibo, si liberò della vergogna in che sarebbe forse caduto, essendo come si credette, stato condannato a morte'. G. VASARI, *Lives*, vol. IV.

Chapter 4
Being Merchants

This profession is also a crafty, shrewd, subtle, ingenious, arduous one, and requires great memory, intellect and knowledge [...] of all the types of currency [...]; knowledge of and familiarity with the trading done between one place and another; and, similarly, knowledge of which goods do well in this place and which in the other.

(Tomaso Garzoni) ('Questa professione poi è una professione ac corta, scaltrita, sottile, ingegnevole, laboriosa, e cui bisogna grandissima memoria, intelletto e cognizione [...] di tutte le sorti di monete [...]; la cognizione e prattica de' cambi che si fanno da un luogo all'altro; e similmente il co noscere che mercanzie hanno buon recapito in questo, e quali in quell'altro luogo'. The merchant's profession as defined by Canon Tomaso Garzoni at the end of the sixteenth century. T. Garzoni, La piazza universale di tutte le professioni del mondo, eds. P. Chierchi, B. Collina, Einaudi, Turin 1996, pp. 874–886.)

4.1 Companies and Business Culture

4.1.1 Company Types Between Modernity and Tradition

In the first half of the sixteenth century, the Botti family's trade activity was a combination of different national and international interests that corresponded to a changeable corporate structure.

As noted above, study of the inner workings of the business is limited by the lack of complete and continuous account books. We cannot reconstruct, except fragmentarily, the individual brothers' contributed capital, that of possible other partners and overall turnover.

In any case, at the apex of the group, we find the family company 'Matteo Botti and partners', a corporation in which each of the male siblings had an equal share,

A. Orlandi, *Money, Culture, Beauty. The Botti Family*,
https://doi.org/10.1007/978-3-032-00453-6_4

the amount of which is unknown.[1] Firmly situated within the rich context of the time, running the company forced Matteo to devote more attention to strategy and management. He carried out his role as manager (which fell to him as the eldest brother and due to his personal, recognised skills) with profound commitment. His moral authority was also keenly felt later when the time came to formally divide up the family's businesses, skills and assets.

Other businesses grew out of the Florentine parent company, with headquarters in Tuscany (Pisa and Florence) and, in Spain, Andalusia and Castile (Cádiz, Seville and Valladolid). The family's activity was supported by the individual brothers' prolonged working sojourns in some of the most important economic centres of the time. Venice, Lyon and Antwerp were the choice markets where the family personally carried out activities of various kind, generating substantial earnings.

It is likely that its first business venture in Spain (1519) was a simple limited partnership in which the Botti brothers all had equal share. Our merchants worked together with the Capponi family, or so it seems, deploying Iacopo as its representative in the region.

The limited partnership and its laws in Florence

The needs of merchants, who had to adapt themselves to the changing economic landscape they worked in, resulted in the rise, especially in inland cities, of the limited partnership (*accomandita*) derived from the maritime *commenda*. In November 1408, the City of Florence, upon request from the Mercantile Court (*Tribunale della Mercanzia*), approved the so-called law on limited partnership. The law was restricted to affirming the principle of limited responsibility, already in use even if not yet regulated, for silent partners who participated in this simple joint venture, which did not yet have a true corporate structure. The law did not provide for a time limit within which it was obligatory to join, and so many avoided doing so until the moment in which it was necessary to object to the limits on their responsibility.

In 1455, a further regulation established a strict time limit beyond which failure to register caused the limit of liability to lapse. These provisions, uncertain and partial, remained in force throughout the 15th century until they were updated by the law enacted on 21 March 1495. In practice, a phase opened up in which forms of companies (*società per via di accomandita*) began to be experimented with by way of limited partnership and thus ways of gradually introducing the concept of a real company.

The indication of the name of the company and the share paid by the partners, which up to that point had not been expressed very explicitly, proved with reasonable certainty that the relationship between the associating and managing partners would no longer be based on the old principles. This formally happened with the Statute of Mercanzia of 1577–1585.

Recent studies and research still in progress reflect on how much space was, in effect, given to the use of the limited partnership, understood as an innovative moderniser of the capitalistic organisation of trade. The initial results seem to reveal scant use, which might dull the idea that it was more effective than the company.[2] All this clearly emerges from Matteo Botti's uncertainty when faced with the possibility of using these corporation types.

---

[1] ASF, *Libri di commercio*, 716, Florence-Seville, Giovanbattista Botti to Ana Francisca Fonte, 4 October 1562, c. 30v.

[2] R. Cessi, 'Note per la storia delle Società di commercio nel Medioevo in Italia', *Rivista italiana di Scienze Giuridiche*, 59 (1917), fasc. I, pp. 1–140; G. Fierli, *Della societa chiamata accomandita e di altre materie mercantili secondo le leggi, e statuti veglianti in Toscana*, Antonio Brazzini, Florence 1803 (https://archive.org/details/bub_gb_uKVuath84WQC/mode/2up accessed 5 June 2024); F. Melis, 'Le società commerciali a Firenze'; G. Mignone, *Le regole dei mercanti. Introduzione al diritto commerciale*. Università degli Studi di Torino, Turin 2022; A. Sapori,

We know little about the structure of the family's activity in Pisa. The Eldest was thinking about investing a few thousand ducats and expanding the company to include an outside partner, but we have no confirmation for the latter. That said, the organisational structure chosen by our merchants was a system of partnerships: a group of legally distinct companies linked by elements of a real and personal nature.[3] And so, Pisa was a company separate from Florence and both were autonomous in relation to those of Cádiz and Seville.

The need to reassert belonging to the same group is reasonable proof of an organisational decision in line with the divided company. In this regard, it is telling that Matteo wrote, in May 1531, to the Beni family in Lyon: 'In Pisa, we have our brother Francesco and we are a single entity'[4] and that Francesco wrote to Lorenzo Grazia of Cádiz: 'work with him as you would over there with our company, which you can freely do since we are a single unit'.[5]

As noted above, the corporate structure corresponded to the type most common at the time, the system of partnerships, even though it seemed, on the surface, simpler and less complex than the norm. It was not akin to a holding company because it did not own the majority of shares. Its egalitarian configuration seems to evoke the medieval *fraterna.*

This link to blood ties was emphasised on multiple occasions. In 1521, when Iacopo 'formed a company' in Andalusia with Zanobi Guidacci and Giovanni Morelli, Matteo did not hold back in showing his perplexity. He did not want his brother to acquire, with Botti money, too much autonomy, weakening his dependence on Florence. He had no intention of losing control over the family's activity in Spain, especially in Seville where Iacopo was a minority partner, and convinced him not to renew his contract with Guidacci and Morelli. Taking advantage of the arrival of Giovanbattista and Francesco in Spain, he persuaded Iacopo to continue his trade activity working exclusively with his brothers. And so, unlike many other

'Dalla «compagnia» alla «holding»', *Rivista delle società*, 1, 1956, pp. 72–84; F. Trivellato, 'Renaissance Florence and the Origins of Capitalism: A Business History Perspective', *Business History Review*, 94, 2020, pp. 229–251.

[3] After the well-known failures of Tuscan companies in the first half of the fourteenth century, company structures underwent numerous changes. Generally speaking, these financial difficulties began in a peripheral branch and then extended to the entire corporate structure. To avoid this, the sole juridical entity of the undivided fourteenth-century company was replaced by the divided one, in which all the businesses were independent from the parent company and legally and administratively independent. This way, the failure of a single branch would not lead to the ruin of the whole organisation. This structure has been described as a 'system of partnerships', since its individual parts could be traced back to a single body. F. Melis, *Aspetti della vita economica medievale*, F. Melis, 'Le società commerciali a Firenze'. Also see F. Melis, *Tracce di una storia economica di Firenze e della Toscana in generale dal 1252 al 1550*, ed. B. Dini, Università degli Studi di Florence, Facoltà di Economia e Commercio, Istituto di Storia Economica, a.a. 1965–1966, pp. 27–30.

[4] ASF, *Libri di commercio*, 712, Florence-Lyon, Matteo Botti to the Beni company, 15 May 1531, c. 111r.

[5] ASF, *Libri di commercio*, 721, Pisa-Cádiz, Matteo Botti to the Botti company, 28 March 1531, c. 10r.

Florentine companies, our merchants' decisions limited access to further financial funds to the family. The system seemed to work smoothly despite this.

Iacopo's wedding was the first development to create problems, with the event raising the issue of descendants and therefore potential for hereditary conflict.

This first family crisis transformed into a company crisis, the solution to which required rational revision of the company structure in the form of even clearer distinction of activities, roles and areas of competence.

1527, the year Iacopo married Ana Francisca Fonte, was the year when the Botti family first started thinking about dividing businesses, capital and responsibilities: 'I would like you to think carefully about the fact that we were forced to change because you changed your situation, and so ask you to gather the fruit from the tree as it comes',[6] Matteo wrote to his brother.

The change in the partnership came in 1540, after a laborious, conflictual process during which attempts were made to balance the different positions using numerous expedients and temporary solutions. The Eldest believed that a complete company overhaul was needed, abandoning the original legal structure in favour of the *società per via di accomandita*, which differed from the limited partnership in that it made it possible to keep family capital clearly separate from capital invested in economic activities.[7] However, they did not adopt that path and chose instead to separate the Andalusian companies from the Italian ones, liquidating Iacopo's interests in the Tuscan company and Matteo, Giovanbattista, Francesco and Simone leaving the others.

Free to decide the future of the Spanish businesses, Iacopo founded new ones, partnering with Andrea and Pierozzo Peri. In Florence, Matteo, Giovanbattista, Francesco and Simone used the *società per via d'accomandita* with increasing frequency for their manufacturing activity. More generally, the five brothers, in remarkable solidarity, continued to help each other, ensuring themselves reciprocal services free of charge.[8] It is, however, clear that the division of assets did not have a particularly negative influence on their economic activity. While on the one hand the division did not entirely do away with the shared intent and collaboration

[6] '[I]o voglio che ben tu consideri da che noi fumo mossi che avendo tu mutato stato, quale ongni gorno può poco govarci, a mnoi hè [...] guoco forza mutare conditioni, sì che io ti pregho che vogli piglare le pome come dallo arbore le venghono'. ASF, *Libri di commercio*, 712, Florence-Cádiz, Matteo Botti to Iacopo Botti (personal), 9 February 1529, c. 27v.

[7] In application of the provision of 1495. See the box on the limited partnership and its laws in Florence.

[8] This was Matteo's thinking on the matter: 'what we can do to your benefit, we will do because we are obligated by love. We will think about what one can do there for here and we will take care to keep you fully informed. You do the same, since we will do all we can, since this is one of our obligations.' ('quello che noj senpre potremo fare in vostro benefitio, non si mancherà di niente con ongni amore come siamo obrighati. Andremo pensando quello si potrà fare di costà per qua e non manchere mo senpre con avisarvi di tutto e voi se di qua per costà vi accadrà cosa alchuna l'a viserete e non vi mancherà di quanto fare potremo e in quello potremo avertire non mancheremo come è nostro debito.') ASF, *Miscellanea*, 107, fascicolo 3, Florence-Seville, Matteo Botti to Iacopo and Giovanbattista Botti, 8 April 1541, c. 76r.

between Spain and Italy, it is also true that Matteo, first, and then Giovanbattista, Francesco and Simone were able to autonomously increase their fortunes.

In conclusion, the structure and operation of the group was never fully outside the logic of the family, almost as if the strength of family ties, even more so than sentimental ones, was a greater guarantee for contractual arrangements.

Perhaps it was precisely the influence of family that precluded the possibility of building an even bigger and more rational group. It might have also been the mentality of Matteo, who, cautious in his assessment of risks and opportunities, seemed to prefer forms of controlled expansion.

Comparing the Botti family with the other big groups of the time, we can say that theirs was quite unlike those of the Medici or the Capponi. The Medici family's business system was similar to a modern holding company[9] in which the Bank, the parent company, controlled the others with majority shares.[10] The structure created by the Capponi family at the end of the fifteenth century included further modernisations. The Florentine parent company directly controlled two companies in Florence and Lyon, sub-holdings, which ran the group's activities in the banking, trade and manufacturing sectors. Here, the novelty lay in the insertion of these two companies between that of the family and the others.[11]

Compared to these complex structures, the Botti group was simple. It was successful regardless, and the family was considered very rich, forcing Matteo to complain about the high taxes they had to pay, more, he said, than those paid by the Capponi, which was a more famous and wealthier family.[12]

And so, we have seen that the coexistence of family and business was a constant in every decision made by the brothers. What emerges is continuous, often unresolved, confrontation between old and new and between strength and weakness. If it is true that, when the time came for internal restructuring, the Eldest proposed a *società per via d'accomandita*, it is also true that he recommended against it shortly after for the company in Valladolid that was about to be formed.

---

[9] These structures were still combinations of general partnerships, which is to say with unlimited and joint responsibilities, and not anonymous groups with limited responsibilities.

[10] R. De Roover, *Il Banco Medici*. The business organisation conceived by Francesco Datini in the middle of the fourteenth century, in particular that of the Compagnia di Catalogna, was one of the first examples of the holding company. F. Melis, 'Le società commerciali', pp. 165–167.

[11] G. Conte, *La holding della famiglia Capponi, 1485–1516. (Con trascrizione del libro segreto paghonazzo segnato *, 1485–1516)*, Università degli Studi di Firenze, Facoltà di Economia e Commercio, Istituto di Storia Economica, a.a. 1988–1989, pp. 157–167.

[12] In March 1527, the Capponi were subject to 440 ducats, while the Botti had to pay 600. ASF, *Libri di commercio*, 711, Florence-Cádiz, Matteo Botti to the Botti company, 18 March 1527, c. 137v.

4.1.2 *Pisa, the Beginning*

Almost nothing is known of the Botti's activity before 1523. In 1492, Simone, their father, was part of a company founded in Pisa with the Capponi and Francesco da Empoli, and he might have had a business in Florence dedicated to trade. Here, we are obviously in the realm of pure conjecture, since Simone's roots in Pescia and his wife's in Pisa prevent us from ruling out the possibility that his activity actually began in the city on the Tuscan coast.

Between 1492 and 1516, the Pisan company was renewed five times, although its structure changed slightly. Simone died in 1512 and Matteo succeeded him in the company.

The brothers' activity continued in both Florence and Pisa and in Spain. In 1531, the Eldest decided to send the young Francesco to Pisa where he could 'live without a boss'[13] and 'do business'.[14] He arrived on 3 January and was hosted by the Capponi family. His job was to take care of the tuna shipment that had just been unloaded.[15] He was of course eager to find different accommodation, and so in the spring went to live with his cousins Iacopo and Alessandro Riccardi,[16] who were moving for health reasons to the country house at Calci. To keep the cost of rent down, they shared the house with a certain Martino Orbina, a Spaniard who was working in the city on behalf of Gian de Salamanca and other merchants from Burgos.[17]

Initially, the family's activity in Pisa was concentrated on a warehouse that needed to be continuously replenished so that they could 'comfort the shopkeepers'.[18] And then came the more difficult phase: conquering the market. For months, Matteo carried out an intense campaign to promote the new company: 'I've given up sleeping here, to further Francesco's cause'.[19] And so he instructed Spain to send only quality goods,[20] sometimes sending lists of products considered suited to the Tuscan market.

---

[13] ASF, *Libri di commercio*, 712, Florence-Seville, Matteo Botti to Iacopo Fantoni, 29 November 1530, c. 43v.

[14] ASF, *Libri di commercio*, 712, Florence-Cádiz, Matteo Botti to the Botti company, 30 November 1530, c. 40r.

[15] ASF, *Libri di commercio*, 721, Pisa-Cádiz, Francesco Botti to the Botti company, 30 January 1531, cc. 1r.-5v.

[16] ASF, *Libri di commercio*, 721, Pisa-Cádiz, Francesco Botti to the Botti company, 28 March 1531, c. 8r.

[17] ASF, *Libri di commercio*, 721, Pisa-Cádiz, Francesco Botti to the Botti company, 25 November 1531, c. 27r.

[18] ASF, *Libri di commercio*, 712, Florence-Cádiz, Matteo Botti to the Botti company, 4 March 1531, c. 73v.

[19] ASF, *Libri di commercio*, 712, Florence-Cádiz, Matteo Botti to the Botti company, 12 August 1531, c. 144v.

[20] ASF, *Libri di commercio*, 721, Pisa-Cádiz, Francesco Botti to the Botti company, 30 January 1531, c. 4r.

In the meantime, the Florentine companies in Lyon, Bini and Del Bene, the ones in Rome, Montaguti and Palloni, the one in Naples, Giovanni and Bartolomeo Dini, and also the individual operators, like Agnolo Bolgherini from Siena and Zaccaria Alidoni from Bologna, were kept informed about the activity in Pisa. Relations were so close and the trading so complex that the Eldest even kept the Guicciardini of Antwerp up to date, in the interest of setting up a possible partnership.[21]

The group's activity in Pisa and later Livorno had precise economic motivations. During the late Middle Ages, northern Italy had been led by the 'Pisan centre',[22] which made it possible for its varied, notably extensive hinterland to trade in any port in the Mediterranean.[23] It is therefore clear why numerous Florentine companies had launched trade, financial and manufacturing businesses there.

The silting up of Porto Pisano and, then, the Medici's favourable customs policy had launched the growth of the Livorno coast, which became the preferred landing. Livorno was becoming cosmopolitan, an international port of call where ships from every country docked, a vast trading centre and lively market filled with goods of every kind.[24] Pisa, by this point on the decline, saw its activity closely tied to that of

---

[21] ASF, *Libri di commercio*, 712, Florence-Antwerp, Matteo Botti to the Guicciardini and Vernacci company, 22 July 1531, cc. 137v–138r.

[22] In addition to the classic studies by Federigo Melis (F. Melis, *La banca pisana*; F. Melis, *L'economia fiorentina del Rinascimento*, ed. B. Dini, Istituto Internazionale di Storia Economica "F. Datini" Prato, Le Monnier, Florence 1984), Marcello Berti (M. Berti, *Nel Mediterraneo ed oltre. Temi di storia e storiografia marittima toscana (secoli XIII-XVIII)*, ETS, Pisa 2000) and Marco Tangheroni (M. Tangheroni, *Politica, commercio, agricoltura a Pisa nel Trecento*, Pacini, Pisa 1973 and *Medioevo Tirrenico*, Pacini, Pisa 1992), see *A Companion to Medieval Pisa,* eds. K.R. Mathews, S. Orvietani Busch, S. Bruni, Bril,l Leiden 2022, in particular the essay O. Vaccari, 'The Mediterranean Port System of Pisa: Role, Management, and Evolution', pp. 337–358; *Firenze e Pisa dopo il 1406. La creazione di un nuovo spazio regionale, Atti del convegno di studi (Firenze, 27–28 settembre 2008)*, ed. S. Tognetti, Olschki, Florence 2010; A. Poloni, 'Un lungo Trecento: economia e mobilità sociale a Pisa nel XIV secolo', in *La mobilità sociale nel Medioevo italiano. 4: Cambiamento economico e dinamiche sociali (secoli XI-XV)*, eds. S. Collavini and G. Petralia, Viella, Rome 2019, pp. 163–205; O. Vaccari, 'Il porto di Pisa, un osservatorio mediterraneo nel tardo Medioevo', in *Quel mar che la terra inghirlanda: in ricordo di Marco Tangheroni*, eds. F. Cardini, M.L. Ceccarelli Lemut, Pacini, Pisa 2007, pp. 781–796; O. Vaccari, 'Il sistema integrato Arno-Tirreno: vie d'acqua e infrastrutture a Pisa e a Livorno tra medioevo ed. età moderna', in *Vallis Arni - Arno Valley. La Toscana dal fiume al mare: tra eredità storica e prospettive future*, eds. M.L. Ceccarelli Lemut, F. Franceschini, G. Garzella, O. Vaccari, Pacini, Pisa 2019, pp. 83–93. On the relationship between Pisa and Piombino, see P. Meli, S. Tognetti, *Il principe e il mercante nella toscana del Quattrocento. Il Magnifico Signore di Piombino Jacopo III Appiani e le aziende Maschiani di Pisa*, Olschki, Florence 2006.

[23] F. Melis, 'Uno sguardo al mercato die panni di lana a Pisa nella seconda metà del Trecento', in *Industria e commercio nella Toscana Medievale*, ed. B. Dini, Istituto Internazionale di Storia Economica "F. Datini" Prato, Le Monnier, Florence 1989, p. 108–156; F. Melis, *Tracce*, pp. 264–265.

[24] 'Da Porto Pisano a Livorno: i 'tempi della modificazione' del sistema portuale pisano', in *"Un filo rosso" studi antichi e nuove ricerche sulle orme di Gabriella Rossetti in occasione dei suoi settanta anni*, eds. G. Garzella, E. Salvatori, ETS, Pisa 2007, pp. 127–144. For an updated, detailed overview of research on sixteenth-century Livorno, see L. Frattarelli Fischer, *L'Arcano del mare. Un porto nella prima età globale: Livorno*, Pacini, Pisa 2018. The classic studies on the

Livorno.[25] After the plague in the 1510s, various trading companies were still active, and thanks to Francesco we have a clear picture of them.[26] Among the most important Florentine groups, he noted the Salviati, Capponi, Quaratesi, Bartolini (with Bernardo Strozzi acting on their behalf) and Michele Bonaccorsi (on behalf of Luca di Bono, from Ragusa [Dubrovnik]). Curiously, and in some ways worryingly, there was also a 'Burgos colony': a large group of operators from Castile that sometimes upset trade by selling Iberian products at much lower prices than the Tuscans, including the Botti.

In any case, the companies that operated in Livorno set up branches in the city so they could oversee their individual dealings more closely.[27] This organisational model was also used by the Botti, whose company in Pisa was headed by Francesco, while their agent in Livorno was Salvatore Quaratesi, who was in charge of loading and unloading goods. In the Livorno port, the goods were unloaded from ships and galleons onto the smaller vessels of boatsmen called *scafaioli*, which could quickly reach the mouth of the Arno. The journey was not, however, always easy. In winter, the river became choppy near the sea and bad weather often made it difficult to navigate.

On the other hand, the vitality of the market was closely linked to the regular landing of boats and a host of port workers who moved the goods from the barges to the warehouses, which were not always close to the Arno.[28] In short, Pisa and Livorno were, for the Botti, a junction, or crossroads between Italy and Spain.

Francesco was unable to handle the workload in Pisa on his own, and so the youngest brother, Simone, joined him there in 1532, to help. Just then, a ship loaded

topic include M. Berti, 'Aspetti dell'attività commerciale di Livorno all'inizio del regime di porto franco colti da un osservatorio significativo: la società di Giulio del Beccuto', in *Atti del Convegno "Livorno e il Mediterraneo nell'età medicea" 23–25 Settembre 1977*, U. Bastogi Editore, Livorno 1978, pp. 278–291 and G. Nuti, 'Livorno, il porto e la città nell'età medicea', in *Atti del Convegno "Livorno e il Mediterraneo nell'età medicea*", Livorno 23–25 September 1977, U. Bastogi, Livorno 1978, pp. 330–345.

[25] R. Mazzei, *Pisa Medicea. L'economia cittadina da Ferdinando I a Cosimo III*, Olschki, Florence 1991; F. Melis, 'Industria, commercio e credito (secoli XIV-XVI)', in *L'economia fiorentina nel Rinascimento*, ed. B. Dini, Le Monnier, Florence 1984, pp. 31–185, pp. 136–137. On the projection of Pisa in the Iberian Peninsula, see R. Mazzei, 'In margine all'attività di un mercante pisano a Siviglia nella seconda metà del Cinquecento: curiosità del Nuovo Mondo inviate a Ferdinando I dei Medici', in *Toscana e Spagna nel secolo XVI. Miscellanea di studi storici*, ETS, Pisa 1996, pp. 309–321.

[26] ASF, *Libri di commercio*, 721, Pisa-Cádiz, Francesco Botti to the Botti company, 28 March 1531, cc. 8v.–9r.

[27] F. Melis, *Industria*, p. 137.

[28] ASF, *Libri di commercio*, 721, Pisa-Cádiz, Francesco Botti to the Botti company, 25 November 1531, cc. 27v.–28r.

with grain, 'which was a huge hassle',[29] arrived in the port. The warehouses needed to be prepared in advance.[30]

Matteo left for Venice the following year. This increased Francesco's burden and, after an illness that wore on for 5 months, he convinced the family to close up shop. His idea was to move to Andalusia, and he wrote as much in a letter in 1535: 'Our company is done and since I, Francesco, do not want to stay in Pisa any longer, we will not continue with it'[31] 'and I think my base will be Spain'.[32]

When the Botti left Pisa in 1535, they decided to keep a key contact on the coast: the company of the Piombini family, which received the goods sent to Tuscany from the companies in Cádiz and Seville.

4.1.3 Florence, Achieving Stability

Simone, their father, had probably set up the Florence company in the 1480s. The company, at least at the beginning, was run from the house where the brothers were born, at the intersection of via dell'Ardiglione and Borgo Stella. When his sons succeeded him, they added working in the wool, silk and gold beaters' guilds to the family's trade activity. Among their manufacturing activities, it would seem that wool production was the main vocation, since a wool mill was always part of their portfolio, even amidst interruptions and changing fortunes; in 1546, there is still mention of a company with Niccolò Castrati.[33] The oldest was 'Matteo e conpagni lanaioli' (Matteo and fellow wool merchants),[34] set up out of love for Girolamo[35] and in keeping with a well-defined policy that, in a certain sense, obligated every

---

[29] ASF, *Libri di commercio*, 721, Pisa-Cádiz, Francesco Botti to the Botti company, 20 February 1532, c. 40v.

[30] ASF, *Libri di commercio*, 712, Florence-Naples, Matteo Botti to Tommaso Busini, 3 October 1531, c. 166v.

[31] ASF, *Libri di commercio*, 721, Pisa-Lyon, Francesco Botti to the Dei company, 2 July 1535, c. 230v.

[32] ASF, *Libri di commercio*, 721, Florence-Savona, Francesco Botti to Bartolomeo Ferrero, 20 July 1535, c. 231r.

[33] We know that when the contract ended, the partner, unhappy with the profit he obtained (8%), had no intention of renewing it. The Eldest was instead thinking of continuing, reinvesting that profit in the shop's capital stock. In September, the shop was reopened, although high prices and difficulty acquiring raw material meant lower earnings. The material must have been of good quality, since the fibre often came from England. ASF, *Miscellanea*, 107, fascicolo 4, Florence-Castile, Matteo Botti to Giovanbattista and Francesco Botti, 28 April 1546, c. 114v.; *Miscellanea*, 107, fascicolo 5, Florence-Valladolid, Matteo Botti to Iacopo Botti, 4 June 1547, c. 74r.; *Miscellanea*, 107, fascicolo 5, Florence-Seville, Matteo Botti to Francesco Botti, 24 February 1548, c. 172v.

[34] ASF, *Libri di commercio*, 711, Florence-Cádiz, Matteo Botti to Iacopo Botti (personal) 14 August 1525, c. 60v.

[35] ASF, *Libri di commercio*, 711, Florence-Cádiz, Matteo Botti to Iacopo Botti, 11 August 1524, c. 12r.

family member to find their own place within the group. The company was formed in February 1524, and soon after the Eldest began sending cloth to Andalusia and the Levant.[36] It was running at full capacity from the start, and by early May the fibre that had been imported from Spain was already gone.[37] In autumn, the first, partial audit of the results forecast modest earnings, but it would have mattered little since Girolamo was happy with the job.[38]. Over time, the shop began trading regularly in the Levant. The fabric was sent by their associate Iacopo Miniati from Ancona to Constantinople and Pera. Some of the goods came to Antonio del Corazza in Adrianople, through the intermediation of Gerini. It would seem that an impressive seven *mandate di balle* were sent to the East between 1524 and 1527.[39] In May 1527, the Signoria closed the shop, probably due to failure to pay 'loans, duty and tithes'.[40] When the liquidation was complete, it was reopened and remained active until Girolamo died in 1530. The final closure took longer than expected, and there were still some outstanding accounts in March 1531. Matteo considered passing the company to Simone, who was undecided between 'wool and silk'. In the end he chose the Silk Guild[41] and the Botti had a silk mill from July of that year until at least 22 April 1534. During his long apprenticeship, Simone was supervised by a skilled master, Bernardo Pandolfini, who taught him all the secrets of the trade. The total lack of documentation after 1535 deprives us of all further information.

In the meantime, the family's manufacturing activity was expanded to include Vincenzo Manovelli, who had a plan to open a woollen cloth factory of his own in early 1559. He asked his maternal aunts for help, and they gave him their support: the result was 'Vincenzo Manovelli e compagni lanaioli' (Vincenzo Manovelli and fellow wool merchants).[42] The limited partnership was worth 1800 ducats and was to have a duration of 4 years.[43] Giovanbattista, in Lyon at the time, contributed 500 *scudi d'oro in oro*. Matteo probably gave the same amount, while the amount contributed by Simone is unknown. Their assistance did not stop there, and Vincenzo's

---

[36] ASF, *Libri di commercio*, 711, Florence-Cádiz, Matteo Botti to Iacopo Botti (personal), 18 February 1524, c.1r.

[37] ASF, *Libri di commercio*, 711, Florence-Cádiz, Matteo Botti to Iacopo Botti (personal), 11 August 1524, cc.11v.–12v.

[38] ASF, *Libri di commercio*, 711, Florence-Cádiz, Matteo Botti to Iacopo Botti (personal), 7 May 1524, c. 4r.

[39] B. Dini, 'Aspetti del commercio di esportazione dei panni di lana e dei drappi di seta fiorentini in Costantinopoli, negli anni 1522–1531', in *Studi in memoria di Federigo Melis*, Giannini, Pisa 1978, 5 vols., IV, pp. 1–54. p. 46. 'Mandate di balle' were documents drawn up to accompany shipments of goods. F. Melis, *Documenti*, pp. 32–37.

[40] ASF, *Libri di commercio*, 711, Florence-Cádiz, Matteo Botti to the Botti company, 18 March 1527, c. 137v.; *Libri di commercio*, 711, Florence-Cádiz, Matteo Botti to the Botti company, 15 February 1527, c. 132v.

[41] ASF, *Libri di commercio*, 712, Florence-Cádiz, Matteo Botti to Iacopo and Giovanbattista Botti, 15 July 1531, c. 129v.

[42] ASF, *Libri di commercio*, 715, Lyon-Valladolid, Giovanbattista Botti to the Martelli company, 29 May 1561, c. 95v.

[43] ASF, *Mercanzia*, Libri delle accomandite, 10832, c. 123v.

relatives made sizeable purchases, including Uncle Battista, who bought eight lengths of frieze (seven black and one white) finished with silk tassels.[44] The latter, in collaboration with the Martelli in Valladolid, was able to quickly ensure considerable turnover and sizeable earnings for his nephew. When the contract expired in May 1564, the shop was closed and then reopened the following year, with only Giovanbattista contributing, 3/4, since Matteo and Simone had in the meantime both died.[45]

In addition to wool, gold: in November 1561, Battista, Simone and Matteo opened a gold beating shop. This probably meant that they were limited partners in the workshop of Luigi Mormorai, husband of their niece Isabel, Francesco's illegitimate daughter.[46] The capital amounted to 2500 ducats, 1500 of which were contributed by Matteo and Simone.[47] Giovanbattista's involvement is documented until December 1564. The following year, he decided to cut back on his investments to devote himself to the Silk Guild 'in other people's names'.[48] And so 'Berto da Filicaia e conpagni setaioli' (Berto da Filicai and fellow silk merchants), another *società per via d'accomandita*,[49] was set up in March 1565.[50] But its required registration in the Libro dei Giuramenti dell'Arte di Por Santa Maria was not formalised until June 1566.[51] Besides Botti, whose contribution was 3000 florins, the company's other partners were Alamanno and Giovanbattista da Filicaia.[52] We do not know why the business ended just a few months later.[53] There was, however, talk about opening a second fabric mill, as we learn from a letter addressed to Francesco Soldani and Rinieri del Forese in Messina, asking for information about the Sicilian market and its silks.[54]

[44] ASF, *Libri di commercio*, 715, Lyon-Florence, Giovanbattista Botti to Vincenzo Manovelli, 6 November 1559, cc. 34r.–34v.

[45] ASF, *Libri di commercio*, 727, Florence-Seville, Giovanbattista Botti to Lorenzo del Rosso, 7 December 1565, c. 8v.; *Libri di commercio*, 716, Florence-Valladolid, Giovanbattista Botti to the Martelli company, 4 April 1565, c. 144v.; *Libri di commercio*, 726, Florence, 11 September 1566, c. 21s.; *Mercanzie, Libri delle accomandite*, 10832, c. 189r.

[46] ASF, *Libri di commercio*, 716, Florence-Valladolid, Giovanbattista Botti to the Martelli company, 23 December 1564, c. 133r.

[47] ASF, *Mercanzie*, Libri delle accomandite, 10832, c. 147v.

[48] ASF, *Libri di commercio*, 716, Florence-Messina, Giovanbattista Botti to Francesco Soldani and Rinieri del Forese and partners, 9 June 1565, c. 156r.

[49] ASF, *Mercanzie, Libri delle accomandite*, 10832, c. 103v.

[50] ASF, *Libri di commercio*, 726, Florence, 25 October 1566, c. 22s.

[51] ASF, *Libri di commercio*, 726, Florence, 22 June 1566, c. 18d.

[52] ASF, *Mercanzie, Libri delle accomandite*, 10832, c. 185r.

[53] ASF, *Libri di commercio*, 726, Florence, 17 October 1566, cc. 22 sd.

[54] 'Since things have not been going well in exchange for a while, I opened that Silk Guild shop and I am thinking of starting to trade in silk from the Kingdom of Messina as well as from here. Even though one does not earn much from it, I think it would be better than exchange.' ASF, *Libri di commercio*, 716, Florence-Venice, Giovanbattista Botti to Pandolfo Attavanti, 19 May 1565, c. 152v.; *Libri di commercio*, 716, Florence-Messina, Giovanbattista Botti to Francesco Soldani and Rinieri del Forese, 9 June, 1565, c. 156r.

Concluding this section on Florence, we will limit ourselves to briefly mentioning the outcome of the division of property after Iacopo left the parent company. Although interest had been expressed in dividing up the property many times, it was continuously postponed until early 1554. In January of that year, the brothers held a meeting to agree on the composition of five equal parcels.[55] On 9 April, they drew lots. Each was entitled to a value of about 2000 ducats.[56]

---

[55] ASF, *Libri di commercio*, 723, Florence-Valladolid, Giovanbattista to Francesco Botti, 6 January 1554, c. 39r.

[56] 'In the name of God and good luck, we divided things up and then we drew lots. The first went to Matteo, and he gets Pretognano and 36 *staiora* of Cecco Cappelli's land in Pontormo. You (Francesco) got the second, which was the Fibbiana farm, a few plots of land in the Scarsa holding, a house in Pontormo and 100 florins from the trees on that land. I got the third, which is the Scarsi holding with a few other pieces of land, rent for the holding set at 10 f. per year. The fourth went to Simone, with the Legnaia farm and, over there, the Arno farm with the rent from the priests of San Michele. The fifth went to Iacopo, and this was the Padule land plus 18 *staiora* of land worked by Cecco Cappelli and a house in Pontormo with two fields and these are the five divisions that were made. The one in Pretognano is the worst and Matteo is very unhappy about it. Then there are the trees that were estimated at 512 ducats to be divided between all of us. Then there is the house, which will not be divided for now. It is valued at 750 ducats and we would get more than 150 each. All of this was done on 9 April. The taxes still need to be divided, we thought about dividing them one-fifth each, but we cannot do this since each property will pay its share. In this division, they say that your part and mine are the best, the worst is Pretognano and Matteo does not want it. God bless those who enjoy their share in holy peace.' ('Col nome di Dio e di buona ventura faciemo le parte fra noi e buttamo sorte: la pri ma tochò a Matteo, Pretognano e più 36 staiora di Ciecho Cappelli di quele terre di Puntormo; a voi (Francesco) tochò numero 2 e fu el podere di Fibiana, que' di Betto di Nardo, manco cierte staiora entrorno in e podere avemo dallo Scarsa che hè un'altra parte come si dirà e più una casa in Puntormo co [...] e più vi tocha ciento fiorini sopra questa parte, quali si ànno a cavare delli abri sono sopra la terra; numero 3 tochò a me che è il podere avemo dalli Scarsi con più cierte terre di quelle fa que di Betto di Nardo, la casa di Borgo e più el podere de livello e 'l podere e ne ò a pagare f. 10 l'anno e più la ciera a Orto San Michele; numero 4 tochò a Simone e fu el podere di Legniana e quello di là d'Arno con e livello de' preti di San Michele e lui ne à a pagare e 'fitto e più ancora f. 100 della stima delli alberi per raguaglio; numero 5 tochò a Iacopo e fu Padule cor un livello che v'è e più 18 staiora di terra deputorno di quello lavora Ciecho Cappelli e più una casa in Puntormo con dua canpi e queste sono le cinque parte fatte. A Pretognano è la pegio di tutte e Matteo ne resta molto discontento come vi dirò un dì a bocha. Sonvi poi li abri quali furno stimati duc. 512 tutti: di questi se n'à a dare a voi e a Simone cien to per raguaglio, el restante che saranno 312 saranno a ripartire per quinto e tocherà f. 62 per uno e quelli alberi àn tocho a me e Simone di modo no' dua aremo a sborsare. Èvi poi la casa quale resta per non divisa e si starà così per ora; esce apreziata in duc. 750 e ne viene a tochare di più 150 ducati per uno e questa è la divisione fatta e se n'è fatto con tutto questo dì 9 d'aprile. Resta ora a dividere le graveze: pensavamo poterle divi dere per quinto e non si può e bisognerà andarle ponendo canpo per canpo e chi n'arà più e chi manco. Èvi poi l'albitro quanto non si potrà dividere e ongniuno arà a pagare la parte sua delle quale parte costoro dicono la vostra e la mia sono delle meglio, ben ché io non me ne intendo e la più trista di tutte è Pretognano e Matteo non l'arè voluta come è detto e Dio dia grazia a ciascuno la godi in santa pacie. / La quale parte vostra si resterà a Simone come l'aveva prima e mi à ancora ricierco li concieda la mia e credo lo conpiacerò') ASF, *Libri di commercio*, 723, Florence-Valladolid, Giovanbattista Botti to Francesco Botti, 16 April 1554, c. 52r. The content of the notarial act of 9 April 1554 with which the properties of the Botti brothers were divided is found in *Libri di commercio*, 714. Details are provided about their com-

4.2 Adventures in Spain

4.2.1 Cádiz and Seville, the Doors to America

Setting up shop in Andalusia and conquering its market were the result of rational decisions and appropriate actions. Sensitive to the economic potential of places like Cádiz and Seville, Matteo and his brothers embarked on their Spanish adventure aware that the best opportunities were concentrated in that area, a crossroads between the Mediterranean and the Atlantic and between the Old World and the New.

'And if in that land there is, as you say, a lot of profit to be made, I affirm it and know it very well. I would like us to consider that place, and it seems like a good idea for you to remain there for a few years and to send Battista and Francesco there, so that we can earn something.'[57]

This was the Eldest, writing to Iacopo, who had already been on the Iberian Peninsula for some time.

As emerges from their letters, the merchants were drawn to Cádiz and Seville for their economic vibrancy and the interactions underpinning it. Keeping businesses in both met a need to ensure a quick response to market trends and maintain close, direct relations with operators active in both cities. Matteo was the only brother who had some doubts about the advisability of being present on the shores of Guadalquivir, considering the uncertainty that, in his view, derived in part from the tensions caused by the sometimes-nerve-racking waits for the precious metal brought on ships from the Americas. Metal that was still primarily stolen, rather than mined. Most importantly, while Cádiz was essentially a port, a vast market that privileged trade and required local presence on the ground, speculation and finance dominated in Seville. As we will see more clearly below, the Seville company's alternating fortunes were due to these and other reasons.

The Botti's first initiative dates to winter 1519, when Iacopo, together with Zanobi Guidacci, received authorisation from Sebastiano Alvarez, representative of the king of Portugal, 'para cobrar todas las ropas y mercaderías que le fueren enviadas de las islas de Lanzarote y Fuerteventura'.[58] He left Florence that same year, bringing along his own and his brothers' money earmarked for doing business.[59] As mentioned, the company probably took the form of a limited partnership with the participation of the Capponi. He was therefore the key contact person for the two

position, especially the ones in the parish of San Giusto and of Pretognano (Montelupo Fiorentino), in *Libri di commercio*, 710.

[57] 'Et se in lo paese sono, chome tu di', da fartti buone incette; io l'affermo e chonoscholo benissimo e quella chosa che io ti dicho che io vorria lo prendessimo cotesto luogho e chi mi pareva da ffermarsi qualche anno e da 'nchaminarvi Battista e Francesco, a cciò che noi avessimo uno traino da ghuadangniare qualchosa.' ASF, *Libri di commercio*, 711, Florence-Cádiz, Matteo Botti to Iacopo Botti (personal), 12 October 1524, cc. 24r.–24v.

[58] E. Otte, 'Los Botti', p. 59.

[59] The brothers who contributed capital to the business in Spain were Matteo, Giovanbattista, Girolamo, Francesco and Simone: they all put in equal shares, the amount of which is unknown.

Tuscan families, and fully responsible for their cash. The first signs of trouble began to emerge three years later. The capital he was sent from Florence seemed insufficient. And so, on 5 December 1521, he started up two companies with Zanobi Guidacci and Giovanni Morelli to increase his liquid assets. The company in Cádiz was called Iacopo Botti and Giovanni Morelli and partners, while the one in Seville took the name Giovanni Morelli and Zanobi Guidacci and partners.[60] Their agreements were put in a *capitulación*, a simple private contract, which was followed by a notarial act to specify the powers that the partners assigned to each other. Zanobi, who was already linked to another Florentine, Iacopo Fantoni, was the head of the Seville branch. Fantoni also played an important role in the group and, after just a few days, was granted *poder general* (power of attorney).[61]

According to Enrique Otte, the Botti-Guidacci-Morelli companies also represented various other Florentine businesses between 1522 and 1523, including those of Bernardo Peri and Iacopo del Vigna, Bernardo Ricasoli and Iacopo Gualterotti.[62]

The Eldest did not approve of this flurry of activity: 'And when our money and that of the Capponi seemed insufficient to you, you could have said so and I would have found someone here to get involved with the company',[63] Matteo complained, noting the perplexity of Giuliano and Niccolò Capponi as well.

It is clear that he was not just critical of the group's presence in Seville, he was also unhappy with Iacopo entering in partnership with outsiders. He proposed a very different programme in alternative. His brother needed to end his partnership with Guidacci and Morelli, reduce activity in Cádiz and liquidate the Seville company in which he had a minority share.[64] What emerges from these early differences is Iacopo's strong character and an independent spirit that led to his permanent but not total detachment from the family when he married Ana Francisca.

In order to convince him to accept his plan, the Eldest offered him more money and promised to limit his interference in the management of the Andalusian companies, leaving him free to organise trade and other merchant activity as he saw fit: 'and then organise all of our stuff in your own way [...] as you know I've always had faith in you, better still, I've had more in you than the Hungarians had in the Hispanic [Pippo Spano]'.[65]

---

[60] The duration of the contract was three and a half years. E. Otte, 'Los Botti', p. 59.

[61] Fantoni in turn granted the three Florentines an equivalent 'holding' that he had also granted to Zanobi Guidacci in 1519. Ibid, p. 60.

[62] Ibid, pp. 59–60.

[63] 'E quando e' nostri danari e de' Chapponi ti paino pochi potevi dirlo e io aria pensato qua e cerchato qualchuno di danaro e averlo invitato a chonpagnia.' ASF, *Libri di commercio*, 711, Florence-Cádiz, Matteo Botti to Iacopo Botti (personal), 12 October 1524, cc. 23v.–24v.

[64] ASF, *Libri di commercio*, 711, Florence-Cádiz, Matteo Botti to Iacopo Botti (personal), 23 June 1524, c. 7r.; *Libri di commercio*, 711, Florence-Seville, Matteo Botti to Morelli and Guidacci and partners, 11 August 1524.

[65] ASF, *Libri di commercio*, 711, Florence-Cádiz, Matteo Botti to Iacopo Botti (personal), 23 June 1524, c. 7r. In this curious comparison, Matteo used the term 'Hispanic' to refer to Filippo Scolari, a late fourteenth-century Florentine merchant in the service of the king of Hungary.

Filippo Scolari, the Hispanic in the service of the king of Hungary

Filippo Scolari, a late-fourteenth-century Florentine merchant, proved himself to be such a trustworthy advisor at the court of Sigismund of Hungary that he made him count of Temesvár. When Sigismund, by this point emperor, asked him to return to Florence as his representative and mediator in the dispute between the pope in Rome, Gregory XII, and the antipope in Avignon, John XXIII, his fellow townsmen saw that he had become rich and famous and, unintimidated, nicknamed him 'Pippo Spano' (in Hungarian, *ispán* meant count).

The prestige he had won is confirmed by Bartolomeo del Corazza, a Florentine 'wine seller', in a diary in which he described Scolari's arrival in the city in minute detail: 'In Anno Domini 1410 one of our townsmen passed through here by the name of Filippo Iscolari. He came on 23 June as ambassador of the king of Hungary. That citizen came as a great lord, and that is what they said he was in Hungary. And he came with perhaps 150 horses, all big Hungarian horses. And truly this Mr. Filippo kept the court open for the whole time he stayed and held many noble banquets for the citizens and women, and drew almost all Florence, day and night. He stayed opposite the Crown's hotel [...] And some citizens held banquets for him, including many young citizens who prepared him a meal at the home of Piero of Luigi Guicciardini, at the Grieve Bridge. They offered him a fine, rich banquet and a hunt on Piero's grounds. And then, after the meal, they held a joust along the Grieve with six or eight young men. More than 4000 thousand Christians went there from Florence. It was one of the most beautiful celebrations I have ever seen.'[66]

Iacopo was not unmoved by his brother's continuous, prolonged urging and, in June 1524, he began making the first arrangements to liquidate Giovanni Morelli.[67] Two months later, with all the accounts settled, the company name was officially changed in Cádiz and in Seville. From then on 'it was known by the name of Iacopo Botti e Zanobi Ghuidacci'[68] (and according to the agreement the latter could be liquidated simply with 6 months' notice).

Iacopo thought that he had thus met the requests of the Eldest: he was wrong. While the latter was pleased with the new business arrangement, the issue of the

[66] 'Negli anni Domini millequattrocentodieci passò di qua un nostro citta dino, il quale ebbe nome messer Filippo Iscolari, il quale venne per imbasciadore del re di Ungheria, addì 23 di giugno; il quale cittadino venne come grande signore, e così si diceva ch'egli era in Ungheria. E venne forse con centocinquanta cavalli, e tutti cavagli grossi un gheri. E veramente questo messere Filippo tenne, il tempo che gli ci stette, corte bandita, e fece di molti e nobili conviti a cittadini e a donne, e quasi tutto Firenze traeva, sera e matti na; stava sua dirimpetto a l'albergo della Corona, per modo che non vi si poteva capere. E alcuno cittadino fece a lui convito; fra' quali furono molti giovani cittadini che gli feciono un desinare al luogo di Piero di messer Luigi Guicciardini, al ponte a Grieve: e feciono un bello e ricco convito e una caccia nel giardino di detto Piero. E poi, doppo il mangiare, feciono in sulla Grieve una bella giostra: furono da sei o otto giovani. Andovvi di Firenze più di IIII mila cristiani. Fu delle belle feste ch'io vedessi mai di simile cose.' B. del Corazza, *Diario Fiorentino (1405–1439),* ed. R. Gentile, De Rubeis, Rome 1991, p. 26; P. Bargellini, *La Splendida Storia di Firenze dal Duca d'Atene a Cosimo I*, Vallecchi Editore, Florence 1964, 4 vols., II, p. 58. Pippo Spano and his doings were used to show how the gifts exchanged during his diplomatic missions between Hungary and Florence were an example of the permeability of cultural barriers. See K. Prajda, 'Mercanti come tramite', p. 288.

[67] ASF, *Libri di commercio*, 711, Florence-Cádiz, Matteo Botti to the Botti and Guidacci company, 23 June 1524, c. 6v.

[68] ASF, *Libri di commercio*, 711, Florence-Seville, Matteo Botti to Morelli and Guidacci and partners, 11 August 1524, c. 9v.

family's presence in Seville remained unresolved. Matteo insisted that they absolutely needed to pull out of that market.[69] Iacopo, rightly, put forward a series of justifications and clarifications. He said it would be impossible for a single person to control two such important and demanding markets and, most importantly, he was convinced that he would not 'be able to do anything good outside Seville'.[70] The Eldest was, however, unyielding, and demanded that his brother's management of wealth, business and trade remained unconditioned by others' will:[71] 'I do not at all want our interests to be handled but anyone but you or Battista. Deal with it.'[72] Scheming, problems and, in case of cessation of activity, the long process of liquidating accounts and loss of hard-won goodwill were the risks of indirect control of business. Matteo worried endlessly. The future and occupation of the younger brothers were a source of further anxiety and concern. And so, he pressed Iacopo to end his partnership with Guidacci as well, while Giovanbattista was on his way from Tuscany.[73] Only a cautious, orderly approach and extra prudence with people from Siena and Lucca could open up more well-grounded opportunities.[74]

These divergent positions were exacerbated by imprudence, the consequences of which threatened to create serious difficulties for the Eldest. According to the investment plan agreed between the two, Iacopo could draw from Florence, with regular bills of exchange, sums no greater than 500/600 ducats per month. These amounts, added to the normal available funds in Andalusia, should have been enough for the buy ups. In early 1525, those limits were exceeded, due to the issue of three payment orders in quick succession totalling almost 1400 ducats. The Eldest was caught unprepared and, without liquidity, risked the group's image. This imprudence was aggravated by the fact that 250 of those ducats were at 12% interest, while the profit on the corresponding parcel of leather would not exceed 16%.

Perhaps it was partly due to this mistake that Iacopo gave into his brother's repeated requests and came to an agreement with Guidacci to wind up the companies.[75] The liquidation of the assets ensured an advance of about 2000 ducats,

[69] ASF, *Libri di commercio*, 711, Firenze-Cádiz, Matteo Botti to Iacopo Botti (personal), 12 October 1524, c. 24r.

[70] ASF, *Libri di commercio*, 711, Florence-Cádiz, Matteo Botti to Iacopo Botti (personal), 14 December 1524, c. 31v.

[71] ASF, *Libri di commercio*, 711, Florence-Cádiz, Matteo Botti to Iacopo Botti (personal), 12 October 1524, c. 23v.

[72] ASF, *Libri di commercio*, 711, Florence-Cádiz, Matteo Botti to Iacopo Botti (personal), 12 October 1524, c. 24v.

[73] ASF, *Libri di commercio*, 711, Florence-Cádiz, Matteo Botti to Iacopo Botti (personal), 12 October 1524, c. 24r.

[74] ASF, *Libri di commercio*, 711, Florence-Cádiz, Matteo Botti to Iacopo Botti (personal), 12 October 1524, c. 23v.

[75] ASF, *Libri di commercio*, 711, Florence-Cádiz, Matteo Botti to Iacopo Botti (personal), 26 February 1525, c. 38r.

which was viewed as a positive[76] and provides us with further confirmation of the immense potential of those markets.

Iacopo found himself without enough business support. He had two choices: leave Spain or think about new partnerships. So, the Eldest agreed for the first time to a collaboration outside the family, in the form of 'partnering with Fantoni'. He accepted Iacopo Fantoni largely because of his close ties to the Capponi who, in turn, promised to support the businesses in Cádiz and Seville by directing trade there.[77] Fantoni's long residence in the City of the Guadalquivir had made him one of the key contacts for Florentine traders, and so if the Botti had tried to compete with him, it would have been met with surprise and damaged their reputation.

When Giovanbattista arrived in Spain,[78] Iacopo bet 'name and brand on Cádiz'.[79] Fantoni was in some way involved in the new company, Iacopo and Giovanbattista Botti and partners, and a meeting was held with him shortly after to define their respective positions and reciprocal roles. The Botti, therefore, relied on him for trade in Seville and he, in turn, referred to Iacopo and Battista for Cádiz.

Matteo learned from Niccolò Capponi, not from Iacopo, that the company had been set up and he was irritated by his brother's excessive independence. Theirs was a complex relationship. They both had strong personalities and little tolerance for criticism and advice.[80]

There was also conflict between Iacopo and Giovanbattista. The latter, tired of the impatience of the former, thought about returning to Italy many times, without doing so. His brother's imminent wedding accentuated uncertainties that would have only increased if he were left alone to run the business.[81]

Even before the wedding, the Eldest had suggested dividing the assets and cash to allow each one to 'know his own'. This type of division was an ideal solution and would also permit more equitable and less burdensome taxation.[82]

It had been months, or perhaps it would be more accurate to say years, that Matteo and the other brothers who had remained in Tuscany did not want to have commitments in Andalusia without clear terms.[83] In this situation, it was decided, on

---

[76] ASF, *Libri di commercio*, 711, Florence-Cádiz, Matteo Botti to Iacopo Botti (personal), 14 November 1525, c. 74r.

[77] ASF, *Libri di commercio*, 711, Florence-Cádiz, Matteo Botti to Iacopo Botti (personal), 24 April 1525, cc. 45r.–45v.

[78] Battista had arrived in Seville in April.

[79] The duration of the contract was three years. ASF, *Libri di commercio*, 711, Florence-Cádiz, Matteo Botti to Iacopo Botti, 28 October 1525, c. 69r.

[80] ASF, *Libri di commercio*, 711, Florence-Cádiz, Matteo Botti to Giovanbattista Botti, 28 October 1525, c. 66r; *Libri di commercio*, 711, Florence-Cádiz, Matteo Botti to Iacopo Botti (personal), 14 November 1525, c. 74r.

[81] ASF, *Libri di commercio*, 711, Florence-Cádiz, Matteo Botti to Iacopo Botti (personal), 10 December 1527, c. 177v.

[82] ASF, *Libri di commercio*, 711, Florence-Cádiz, Matteo Botti to Iacopo Botti (personal), 10 October 1527, c. 168v.

[83] ASF, *Libri di commercio*, 712, Florence-Cádiz, Matteo Botti to Giovanbattista Botti, 1 March 1529, cc. 32v.–34r.

the urging of Francesco and Girolamo most of all, to come up with a plan that would require Iacopo to return to Florence, at least temporarily. A family meeting would take some of the pressure off their differences and clarify positions that had long been murky.[84] The idea was to find a solution that would work for everyone.[85] For the Eldest, it was fundamental to safeguard such geographically distant interests with more rigorous management. The only reasonable option was the limited partnership, which would make it possible to continue 'transacting business together', but 'having done the calculations', which is to say with a quantitatively defined and limited stake that was known to everyone. Matteo was in this way offering his brothers the opportunity to freely decide whether to contribute or not.[86] The need for change was heightened by Iacopo's increasing involvement in the Fonte family's risky initiatives: 'and it also seems to me that Iacopo has found chaotic relatives who cost him a few hundred ducats a day'.[87] That family's trade and conquest ventures, begun by Rafael Fonte and continued by his son Lazaro, seem to have ended in catastrophe in 1529.[88] Their failure forced Botti to step in in the name of his mother-in-law, wife, brother-in-law and Luis Jorva, who was part of the complex network of interests built by Ana Francisca's family.[89]

Iacopo did not go to Florence. He had decided against losing control of the Andalusia business and rejected the idea of a new company structure.[90] All appeals fell on deaf ears, and he made multiple excuses for not leaving Cádiz.

Since there was no way for him to oppose Iacopo's autonomous decisions, Matteo was forced to deal with the problem from a distance, filling every letter with lengthy sections on the subject of internal relations. In a letter dated 10 January 1531, he presented the outline of a plan aimed towards gradually clearing the accounts between the Spanish partnerships and the family company as well as the more rational organisation of trade between Florence and Andalusia.

Two months later, a kind of temporary management plan was launched that made it possible to settle the old, shared account and start new, distinct accounts, 'the

---

[84] ASF, *Libri di commercio*, 711, Florence–Cádiz, Matteo Botti to Iacopo Botti, 10 December 1527, cc. 177v.–178r.

[85] ASF, *Libri di commercio*, 712, Florence-Cádiz, Matteo Botti to Giovanbattista Botti, 1 March 1529, cc. 32v.–34r.

[86] ASF, *Libri di commercio*, 711, Florence-Cádiz, Matteo Botti to Iacopo Botti, 10 December 1527, c. 177v.–178r.

[87] ASF, *Libri di commercio*, 712, Florence-Cádiz, Matteo Botti to Giovanbattista Botti, 1 March 1529, c. 32v.

[88] On the Fonte family's New World expeditions, see: A. Cioranescu, 'La aventura americana de los hermanos Silva', in *Anuario de Estudios Atlánticos*, 18, Patronato de la "Casa de Colón", Madrid-Las Palmas 1972, pp. 277–304; L. ó Olivera, 'Don Pedro Fernández de Lugo prepara la expedición a Santa Marta', in *Anuario de Estudios Atlánticos*, 5, Patronato de la "Casa de Colón", Madrid-Las Palmas 1959, p. 399–433; F.J. Fornell Fernández, 'Los fonte'; E. Otte, 'Los Sopranis y los Lugos'.

[89] E. Otte, 'Los Botti', p. 65.

[90] ASF, *Libri di commercio*, 712, Florence-Cádiz, Matteo Botti to Giovanbattista Botti (personal), 9 February 1529, c. 30r.

bookkeeping for which will keep your account separate from ours, even though it is all one'. One, in the name of Iacopo and Giovanbattista, was the account of the new Andalusian company set up to ensure the separation of Iacopo and Ana Francisca's interests from those of the original Botti family. The other, transacted in the name of Matteo, was for the trade activity carried out in Florence.[91]

We do not know the duration of these transactions, which were slowed down by Matteo's period in Venice between 1533 and 1536. What is certain is that Francesco also found himself on the shores of Guadalquivir in 1537. There, he devoted himself to trade and financial activity alongside Iacopo and Giovanbattista. In April 1538, the company in Seville was called 'Iacopo e Francesco Botti' and the following year the three brothers gave each other reciprocal power of attorney for trade in the two Andalusian markets.[92] The new company broke all formal relationships with Fantoni.

Francesco was director of the company and his permanent residence in Seville was calming to the Eldest. In the meantime, in Cádiz, Iacopo and Giovanbattista threw themselves into their company, which was probably still in the midst of closing accounts. Between late 1539 and early 1540, Francesco and Battista were determined, however, to also put an end to the recent activity in Seville.[93] In November 1540, after more than 20 years of shared business names, the Spanish companies were formally separated from the Italian ones. The results were clearly positive if Iacopo was able to write from Cádiz: 'but in the end take yours from here and thank Christ that it went better for you than for any Tuscan who has come here in the last 80 years, whether from Siena or Lucca or Perugia'.[94]

Sixty four thousand ducats were distributed in the first sharing out of liquid assets. Iacopo, Giovanbattista and Francesco were all present, with the latter representing Matteo and Simone by proxy. Iacopo received 40,000 ducats, and the others 6000 each. In the letter from Battista in which he tried to convince Ana Francisca that her husband's will was unjust, he said that his deceased brother had forced them to accept this arrangement. In truth, it is difficult to believe this. On the one hand, it is rather unlikely that Iacopo could have taken advantage of his brothers' good will. On the other hand, it seems just as strange that Matteo, Giovanbattista, Francesco

[91] ASF, *Libri di commercio*, 712, Florence-Cádiz, Matteo Botti to the Botti company, 4 March 1531, c. 74v.

[92] E. Otte, 'Los Botti', p. 66.

[93] ASF, *Miscellanea*, 107, fascicolo 3, Florence-Seville, Matteo Botti to Giovanbattista Botti, 25 January 1541, c. 53v.

[94] '[M]a infine chavate el vostro di qua e date grazie a Cristo che v'è ita meglio que nissuno toscano que qua sia venuto da 80 anni in qua, chosì sanese chome luchese e perugino.' ASF, *Miscellanea*, 107, fascicolo 2, Cádiz-Florence, Iacopo Botti to Matteo Botti, September 1540. In the same letter, Iacopo expressed 'an extraordinary desire to settle our accounts', certain that he would be able to count on help from his brothers in any case: 'as for helping each other there is no need to repeat ourselves since we are more than certain of it'. ASF, *Miscellanea*, 107, fascicolo 2, Cádiz or Seville-Florence, Iacopo Botti to Matteo Botti, 6 June 1541.

and Simone would have allowed themselves to be swindled. It is more probable that the calculation included buying Iacopo out of the family business.[95]

In the meantime, in Florence, the Eldest managed the land and real estate that had not yet been divided. It was not until the end of 1541 that attention turned to a preliminary definition of the patrimonial situation. When he returned from Spain, Francesco brought a document with him suggesting how to split it up.[96]

Matteo, for his part, sent a summary of current assets to Cádiz and repeated that houses and land were 'a final reef where we can land during a shipwreck'.[97] Safe haven investments that provided image and protection in case of temporary difficulty.[98] And this is how the whole affair ended, at least so it seems. Almost everything was divided up. It was a distribution of assets that, despite a few disagreements, left their solidarity in business intact. Iacopo prepared himself for his new chapter and it was precisely then that the company structure in Andalusia took the form of a small, completely independent business group. Alone, his connections to his birth family slackened and,free from contractual ties to his brothers, Botti could make his decisions with total autonomy and without having to answer to anyone for his conduct. He was on a new path that seemed to him more efficient and modern. In Andalusia, he partnered with outsiders, lightened the management load by hiring more staff and paid more attention to monitoring the actions of associates. And so, he often went to Cádiz from Seville, where he had moved in 1541, to personally check on the activity of the partner-director.

More impulsive than Matteo, after so many years in Andalusia perhaps he was no longer the moderate, restrained Florentine merchant.[99] Perhaps he no longer wore heavy fustian coats 'that cost no more than one ducat each',[100] indulging instead in the silks and velvets, eccentricities and luxuries of Spanish knights. But he certainly knew how to organise and run his business. When he died, a time when one could live well in Florence with 1000 scudi a year and 4000 were needed in rich Seville, as we have noted, he left his wife and daughters an inheritance of more than 200,000 gold ducats.[101]

95 ASF, *Libri di commercio*, 716, Florence-Seville, Giovanbattista Botti to Ana Francisca Fonte, 4 October 1562, c. 31v.

96 ASF, *Miscellanea*, 107, fascicolo 3, Florence-Seville, Matteo Botti to Iacopo Botti, 16 September 1541, cc. 121r.–122r.

97 ASF, *Miscellanea*, 107, fascicolo 3, Florence-Seville, Matteo Botti to Iacopo Botti, 16 September 1541, c. 122r.

98 ASF, *Miscellanea*, 107, fascicolo 3, Florence-Seville, Matteo Botti to Iacopo Botti, 16 September 1541, c. 122r.

99 ASF, *Libri di commercio*, 711, Florence-Cádiz, Matteo Botti to Giovanbattista Botti, 28 May 1526, c. 101r.

100 ASF, *Libri di commercio*, 711, Florence-Cádiz, Matteo Botti to Giovanbattista Botti, 28 May 1526, c. 101r.

101 According to M.V. Vera Morín, Ana became very rich, in part thanks to her inheritance from her husband. In 1568, her liquid assets totalled 120,000 gold ducats, she collected taxes from the duke of Medina Sidonia in the amount of more than 25,000 ducats, she received 18,000 from the residents of Maestrazgo di Santiago, 5000 from Cádiz and 900,000 from Jerez. She also had houses in

The new Cádiz company was set up at the end of March.[102] The company's capital amounted to 1500 ducats, with 1000 from Iacopo and 500 from his partner Andrea Peri.[103] The profits were split equally, since Andrea served as manager, remaining in Cádiz with Giovanbattista Ciachi, called Ciacco.[104] Moreover, the company was not a source of worry and Peri's hard work translated into efficient and high turnover, a large part which from sugar trading with the Canaries. Wanting to strengthen that trade, Iacopo sent Ciacco there in October 1544, although his skills as a bookkeeper were very poor. The young man performed poorly in Tenerife as well and, even worse, he failed to send the kind of detailed information that managers needed from their associates, deficiencies that were even more critical considering that he was working in unfamiliar territory. He had not taken care to describe 'the features of the island, how big it is, what the cities, marinas and ports are like, who lives there, how they do the sugar trade, how many sugar mills there are, how much sugar they produce, how good it is, how they sell good, medium and low quality … and how their price varies'.[105] And so he was forced to return to Cádiz in the summer of 1545.[106]

Things were more complicated in Seville, as we know. The market was demanding and dangerous, and management of the company needed more attention and care. It required a constant presence. And so Iacopo, who had always preferred living in Cádiz, moved. He bought a house with attached storerooms and sent for his wife and daughters, who would lighten his load in that arduous world.[107]

This was the period during which he asked Giovanbattista, who was still in Andalusia, to join his company. When his brother declined, they came to a

Seville worth 20,000 ducats, assets in Cádiz and Tenerife and numerous *juros*. M.V. Vera Morín, 'Patrimono familiar, herencia y ascenso social: el caso de la familia Botti en las *Islas Canarias del Quinientos'*, in *Hacer Historia Moderna. Líneas actuales y futuras de investigación*, eds. J.J. Iglesias Rodríguez, I. Mª. Melero Muñoz, Editorial Universidad de Sevilla, Seville 2019, pp. 416–427, p. 424.

[102] ASF, *Miscellanea*, 107, fascicolo 3, Florence-Seville, Matteo Botti to Giovanbattista Botti, 8 March 1541, c. 71r.

[103] Andrea Peri was in Cádiz by at least July 1533, when he was working with the Ricasoli and Ridolfi who sent him to Chios in January the following year. ASF, *Libri di commercio*, 721, Pisa-Cádiz, Francesco Botti to Andrea Peri, 17 July 1533, c. 133v.; *Libri di commercio*, 721, Pisa-Seville, Francesco Botti to the Ricasoli and Ridolfi company, 21 January 1534, c. 192r.

[104] Giovanbattista Ciachi, called Ciacco, had arrived in Cádiz in the autumn of 1540.

[105] ASF, *Miscellanea*, 107, fascicolo 4, Florence-Tenerife, Matteo Botti to Giovanbattista Ciachi, 25 October 1544, c. 44v.

[106] 'la qualità dell'Isola, come sia grande, come vi sia villa e lle marine e in fra terra che porti, come vi sia vicini, come vanno negotj di zucheri, quanti ingegni, che somma di zuccheri vi fanno, come buoni, come si vendono, li buoni, li mezani e bassi […] e come vanno aumentando e diminuendo.' ASF, *Miscellanea*, 107, fascicolo 4, Florence-Cádiz, Matteo Botti to the Botti and Peri company, 8 June 1545, c. 101r.

[107] ASF, *Miscellanea*, 107, fascicolo 3, Florence-Seville, Matteo Botti to Iacopo and Giovanbattista Botti, 8 March 1541, c. 71r.

compromise. Battista would add his name to the company[108] to 'darles mas favor y credito en lo negotios',[109] without making any kind of financial contribution. In short, he agreed to help him preserve the goodwill built up over the previous 20-odd years and maintain stability, which served as an index of solidity and reliability.[110] Giovanbattista remained in Seville for almost a year, helping Iacopo 'como a criado suyo y syn yntereses mio d'un maravedis',[111] keeping the accounts and working as if the two had a real business partnership. He left the city at the end of 1541, although the company continued to bear his name until 1547.

In the meantime, he found himself in need of a young associate. The choice fell to Vincenzo Ardinghelli, who had arrived in Seville in the summer of 1541.[112] His solid professional training, in Florence at the Banco de' Fazi da Puttino, in Rome with Giovanni Ardinghelli and then with Berardi, suggested that he would be an expert clerk. Botti instead discovered that Vincenzo was unable to 'work as a merchant because he has none of the concepts and entirely lacks the merchant foundation',[113] and so he was moved to the less demanding Cádiz market.[114] At the end of 1542, he made another hire, this time a local, Fernando de Torres[115] who he worked with until 1553 when he decided to leave for the Indies.

---

[108] ASF, *Miscellanea*, 107, fascicolo 3, Florence-Seville, Matteo Botti to Giovanbattista Botti, 9 April 1541, c. 78v.

[109] ASF, *Libri di commercio*, 716, Florence-Seville, Giovanbattista Botti to Ana Francisca Fonte, 4 October 1562, c. 31v.

[110] Matteo was plagued by the same concern and he stepped in from Florence to convince Battista to stay in Andalusia a little longer, even going so far as to propose an limited partnership of 3000 ducats: 'If Giovan Battista becomes content to stay and you agree to give him money for a limited partnership, we would be happy if you would give it for the three of us, Simone, myself and you, up to 1500 ducats, and Iacopo will need to give him the same amount. If you want to do this, you will need to write up a contract, or better I will send you a summary.' ('Quando Giovanbattista si contentassi di fermarsi e che voi vi concordassi dargli danarj per accomandita e nunc noj siamo contentj che tu gli dia per noj tre, Simone, tu e io, sino a millecin quecento ducati, e Iacopo gle ne doverrà dare altantj. Se così volessi fare, aresti a fare una scritta e dire in questo modo, cioè anzi ti mando un poco di minuta') ASF, *Miscellanea*, 107, fascicolo 3, Florence-Seville, Matteo Botti to Francesco Botti (personal), 25 November 1540, c. 36v.

[111] ASF, *Libri di commercio*, 716, Florence-Seville, Giovanbattista Botti to Ana Francisca Fonte, 4 October 1562, c. 31v.

[112] ASF, *Miscellanea*, 107, fascicolo 3, Florence-Lyon, Matteo Botti to Francesco Botti, 8 July 1541, c. 103r.; *Miscellanea*, 107, fascicolo 3, Florence-Seville, Matteo Botti to the Botti company, 14 July 1541, c. 105r.

[113] ASF, *Miscellanea*, 107, fascicolo 4, Florence-Seville, Matteo Botti to the Botti company, 12 December 1545, c. 169r.

[114] He was still in Cádiz in 1551. Archivo Histórico Provincial de Cádiz (henceforth AHPC), *Protocolos notariales de Cádiz*, 4339, cc. 742v.–743v.

[115] ASF, *Miscellanea*, 107, fascicolo 3, Florence-Sibilia, Matteo Botti to the Botti and Peri company, 11 November 1542, c. 205v.

Despite the high costs and chancy trade, Iacopo was satisfied. Things seemed to him to be going in the right direction. Peri was running the Cádiz company well.[116] The Seville company was also running at full capacity and with good results, and in autumn 1542 Botti was again looking for a 20-year-old who could help him with 'things'.[117]

In the meantime, another project was taking shape. Between the end of 1542 and early 1543, Iacopo got involved in an initiative that bordered on the illegal. 'The Granata affair'[118] involved opening a Silk Guild shop that could guarantee excellent results, a potential for success that led him to underestimate the prohibition imposed on Florentines abroad by the law at home. He was dragged into the deal by Luigi Pecori and Francesco Gondi, and this was possible in part because while Matteo had viewed it with a lot of caution, he had not actually opposed it. In his view, they shouldn't call it a 'silks concern', precisely to avoid the intervention of the Florentine Silk Guild, and could instead describe it generically as 'general business'. But he did not leave it at that. The Eldest had little faith in the two partners, who had in the past shown themselves to be dishonest and lacking in professional integrity. For these and other reasons, he advised his brother to participate in the venture in the form of a *società per via d'accomandita*.[119]

Once again, Iacopo did not follow his suggestions and paid for his lack of prudence a few years later: the company failed. The insolvency of some of their clients and his partners' non-payment caused him a substantial loss.

In Cádiz, in August 1545, Andrea Peri fell ill, and the company was neglected, compounding the problems that had already begun to emerge. Many of his correspondents complained about how slowly the orders were being processed, lack of punctuality in sending bills and most importantly 'scant communication'. Even Matteo was unhappy with the service being provided.

These were not the only troubles, however, and, in April 1546, not even the contract with the bishopric of Cádiz[120] for 4500 ducats[121] went through. Moreover,

[116] ASF, *Miscellanea*, 107, fascicolo 3, Florence-Seville, Matteo Botti to the Botti company, 9 January 1542, cc. 147v.–148v.

[117] ASF, *Miscellanea*, 107, fascicolo 3, Florence-Seville, Matteo Botti to the Botti company, 15 September 1542, cc. 197v.–198v.

[118] ASF, *Miscellanea*, 107, fascicolo 3, Florence-Valladolid, Matteo Botti to Giovanbattista Botti, 4 December 1542, c. 211v.

[119] ASF, *Miscellanea*, 107, fascicolo 3, Florence-Valladolid, Matteo Botti to Giovanbattista Botti, 4 December 1542, c. 211v.; *Miscellanea*, 107, fascicolo 3, Florence-Seville, Matteo Botti to the Botti company, 1 January 1543, c. 217r.

[120] ASF, *Miscellanea*, 107, fascicolo 4, Florence-Cádiz, Matteo Botti to Andrea Peri (personal), 26 June 1546, c. 8v.; ASF, *Miscellanea*, 107, fascicolo 4, Florence-Seville, Matteo Botti to the Botti company, 27 April 1546, c. 2r.

[121] ASF, *Miscellanea*, 107, fascicolo 4, Florence-Seville, Matteo Botti to the Botti company, 28 April 1546, c. 111v.; *Miscellanea*, 107, fascicolo 5, Florence-Cádiz, Matteo Botti to Andrea Peri, 26 June 1546, c. 8v.

Ardinghelli wanted to leave the city[122] and Peri was growing increasingly old and sick. And so Iacopo decided to overhaul the management of the company and, between October and December 1547, changed the company name, adding Pierozzo Peri,[123] Andrea's younger brother.

Change was underway in the city of Guadalquivir as well, with Giovanbattista leaving in October 1547.[124] We have no information about the company's new organisation, or whether Iacopo, now alone, transformed it into an individual venture or expanded it to include others. What is certain is that in July 1562, when he died, Lorenzo del Rosso was working with him in Seville.[125] In Cádiz, the Iacopo Botti and Pierozzo Peri company had been active since February 1555. From the will, we learn that in 1562, the partner/director was probably Francesco de' Santis, another Florentine merchant.[126]

Although some problems arose in his dealings with the Canaries in his final years, Iacopo's professional legacy and most importantly his business goodwill passed to Nerozzo del Nero, who opened a company in Cádiz with de' Santis. In December 1562, the two Florentine merchants became partners, giving us important documentation of the still vital presence of Tuscans in that region. In Seville, his activity was continued by Lorenzo del Rosso (Table 4.1).[127]

[122] In October 1546, Vincenzo wanted to leave Cádiz, where he felt 'he did not have good teachers'. And so, he ended his partnership with the Botti shortly after. In February 1554, when he died, he seemed to have links with Niccolò del Setaiolo, another Florentine active on the Cádiz market. ASF, *Miscellanea*, 107, fascicolo 5, Florence-Castile, Matteo Botti to the Botti company, 25 September 1546, c. 26v.; *Libri di commercio*, 743, Florence-Cádiz, Simone Botti to Niccolò del Setaiolo, 24 February 1554, c. 10r.

[123] ASF, *Miscellanea*, 107, fascicolo 5, Florence-Seville, Matteo Botti to the Botti company, 31 October 1547, cc. 122r.-123r.; *Miscellanea*, 107, fascicolo 5, Florence-Seville, Matteo Botti to Francesco Botti, 31 October 1547, cc. 123v.-124v. Pierozzo had been working with the Botti at the Cádiz company for a long time. In April 1541, Iacopo had sent him to 'make sugar' in the Canaries.

[124] ASF, *Miscellanea*, 107, fascicolo 5, Florence-Seville, Matteo Botti to Iacopo Botti (personal), 6 October 1547, cc. 105r.-105v.

[125] E. Otte, 'Los Botti', p. 81. Lorenzo del Rosso had been working with him since 1544. 'Take care of the male and female slaves that my brother left there. Who, being Christians like us, need to live in the Christian way. I would have liked you to free Bonifazio and his brother.' ('Racomandovi li stiavi e le stiave arà lasciato costà la buona memoria di mio fratello, 'sendo cri stiani come noy e fate vivino cristianamente. Arei hauto charo avessi lasciato li bero a Bonifazio e 'l fratello') ASF, *Libri di commercio*, 716, Florence-Seville, Giovanbattista Botti to Agostino Marino, 30 September 1562, c. 5v. AGS, *CME*, legajo 300.27.

[126] ASF, *Libri di commercio*, 716, Florence-Cádiz, Giovanbattista to Francesco de' Santis, 1 February 1563, cc. 46r.-47r.; *Libri di commercio*, 716, Florence-Seville, Giovanbattista Botti to Lorenzo del Rosso, 31 March 1563, cc. 59v.–62r.; AGS, *CME*, legajo 300.27. Also see E. Otte, 'Los Botti', p. 81.

[127] ASF, *Libri di commercio*, 716, Florence- Cádiz, Giovanbattista Botti to Francesco de' Santis, 1 February 1563, cc. 46r.-47r.; *Libri di commercio*, 716, Florence-Seville, Giovanbattista Botti to Lorenzo del Rosso, 31 March 1563, cc. 59v.-62r.

Table 4.1 The Botti Companies in Andalusia (1519–1562)

Date of incorporation	Cádiz	Seville
1519	Botti-Capponi	Botti-Capponi
5 December 1521	Giovanni Morelli and Zanobi Guidacci and partners	Iacopo Botti and Giovanni Morelli and partners
11 August 1524	Iacopo Botti and Zanobi Guidacci	Iacopo Botti and Zanobi Guidacci
October–November 1525	Iacopo and Giovanbattista Botti and partners	Partnership with Fantoni until at least 1531
1531	Iacopo and Giovanbattista Botti	Partnership with Fantoni
1538	Iacopo and Giovanbattista Botti	Iacopo Botti and Francisco Botti
March–April 1541	Iacopo and Andrea Peri	Iacopo and Giovanbattista Botti
October–November 1547	Iacopo Botti and Andrea and Pierozzo Peri	Iacopo and Giovanbattista Botti
February 1555–1560	Iacopo Botti and Pierozzo Peri	?
1560–1562	Iacopo Botti and Francesco de' Santis	Iacopo Botti and Lorenzo del Rosso

4.2.2 Valladolid, 'marcha con tutte le provincie del mondo'

'It is a safe place in terms of both business and trade and exchange. A place where people look well upon foreigners and that does business with all the provinces in the world.'[128] Matteo, drawn to this important economic centre, carefully assessed the

[128] 'Per essere el luogho sichuro e di facciende, tanto di mercanzie quanto di canbi, loco dove è buona giustitia, dove li forestieri sono bone visti, marcha con tutte le provincie del mondo.' ASF, *Miscellanea*, 107, fascicolo 3, Florence-Villalón, Matteo Botti to Giovanbattista Botti, 11 February 1542, c. 164v. For the economic context beyond the classic B. Bennassar, *Valladolid au siècle d'or, une ville de Castille et sa campagne au XVI siècle*, Mouton &Co., paris-La Haye 1967, see D. Carvajal de la Vega, 'Valladolid y el servicio de cortes a inicios del siglo XVI. Evolución y gestión', in Los dineros de la corona. Finanzas y cambio fiscal en la monarquía hispánica (siglos XVI-XVII), ed. R. Lanza García, Comares, Granada 2023, pp. 23–51; H. Casado Alonso, 'Comercio textil, crédito al consumo y ventas al fiado en las ferias de Medina del Campo en la primera mitad del siglo XVI', in *Historia de la propiedad. Crédito y garantía*, V Encuentro Interdisciplinar. Salamanca, 31 de mayo-2 de junio, eds. S. de Dios de Dios, J. Infante Miguel-Motta, R. Robledo Hernández, E. Torijano Pérez, Colegio de Registradores de Madrid, Servicio de Estudios, Madrid 2007, pp. 127–160; H. Casado Alonso, 'Comercio y mercaderes en el valle del Duero (siglos XV y XVI)', *Estudios de historia de España*, 12, 1, 2010, pp. 93–116; H. Casado Alonso, 'Crédito y comercio en las ferias de Medina del Campo en la primera mitad del siglo XVI', in *Il mercato del credito in età moderna.* Reti e operatori finanziari nello spazio europeo, eds. E.M. García Guerra, G. De Luca, Franco Angeli, Milan 2010, pp. 21–48; H. Casado Alonso, 'El Duero oriental a finales de la Edad Media y principios del siglo XVI crecimiento económico y transformaciones', *Biblioteca: estudio e investigación*, 25, 2010, pp. 25–37; D. Igual Luis, 'Valladolid y sus círculos económicos de relación (1475–1520)', Edad Media Revista de Historia, 15 (2014), pp. 97–114; H. Lapeyre, *Une famille de marchands, les Ruiz. Contribution à l'étude du commerce entre la France et l'Espagne*, A. Colin, Paris 1955; R. Rodríguez González, *Mercaderes castellanos del Siglo de Oro*, Secretariado de publicaciones, Universidad de Valladolid, Valladolid 1995; E. Lorenzo Sanz, 'Los Ruiz Embito en el comercio con Sevilla y América', in

opportunity to open a company there. The decision to do so was primarily motivated by a desire to tap into in the substantial monetary flow of the Castile fairs which were of course closely linked to those of Lyon. Wide-ranging exchange activity contributed to invigorating and supporting the transfer of cash in different European markets, leveraging these gatherings. In the documents, we find frequent exchange triangulations between the French city and at least one in Castile: Valladolid, Medina del Campo or Villalón.[129] It was an opportunity the Botti did not want to miss. Moreover, it was often the case that companies or groups of merchants, in temporary business partnerships, used those fairs to move capital of varied provenance and set up business ventures that sometimes transformed into true expeditions.

Although Matteo wrote from Florence: 'now you have the Genoese over there, who, so I've heard, run most of the exchange that is done there',[130] the 'House of Castile' was nevertheless set up in September 1542.[131] In February of that year, Gherardo Bartolini had proposed to Matteo the idea of setting up a company in Valladolid, taking advantage of the presence of Giovanbattista Bellotti, who had just ended his partnership with the Bertini. Battista had already been in the region for a few months, as the first stop on his return trip to Italy. And so, Matteo proposed to his brother and Bellotti to put in the sum they thought best. They all participated together this time as well, since Francesco contributed, with some friends, 7000 ducats and Iacopo 6000. The company was to operate for three years under the name Botti and Bellotti. It could be liquidated with six months' notice, after which it would be tacitly considered renewed for the following year. Among the various options, the Eldest advised against a *società per via d'accomandita* since that would have made it necessary to publish the company's status, leaving it more exposed to raids by the tax authorities. The managerial approach entailed the diversification of

---

Historia de Medina del Campo y su tierra, eds. E. Lorenzo Sanz, Ayuntamiento de Medina del Campo y Consejería de Educación y Cultura de la Junta de Castilla y León, Medina del Campo 1986, pp. 393–436.

[129] On the Castille fairs, see B. Bennassar, *Valladolid au siècle d'or*; M.-T. Boyer-Xambeau, G. Deleplace, L. Gillard, *Moneta e credito nell'Europa del Cinquecento*, Einaudi, Turin 1991; D. Carvajal de la Vega, 'Intermediación financiera en las ferias castellanas a inicio de la Edad Moderna. Las cartas de poder,' in *El laberinto del crédito en la Edad Moderna: instrumentos, agentes y mercados*, eds. M. Cachero Vinuesa, N. Maillard Álvarez, Sílex Ediciones, Madrid 2023, pp. 15–46; H. Casado Alonso, 'Comercio y flujos financieros en los negocios de Simón Ruiz', in *Simón Ruiz y el mundo de los negocios en Europa en los siglos XVI y XVII*, ed. H. Casado Alonso, Ediciones Universidad de Valladolid, Valladolid 2017, pp. 139–163; H. Casado Alonso, 'Comprar y vender en las ferias de Castilla durante los siglos XV y XVI', in *Faire son marché au Moyen Âgee:* Méditerranée occidentale, XIIIe-XVIe siècles, eds. J. Petrowiste, M. Lafuente Gómez, Casa de Velázquez, Madrid 2018, pp. 111–132.

[130] ASF, *Miscellanea*, 107, fascicolo 3, Florence-Valladolid, Matteo Botti to Giovanbattista Botti (personal), 25 May 1542, c. 184v.

[131] ASF, *Miscellanea*, 107, fascicolo 3, Florence-Seville, Matteo Botti to the Botti company, 15 September 1542, c. 198v.

activity and monitored, prudent management, alongside and supported by the austerity of the partners, who were careful to limit superfluous expenditures and Spanish luxuries.[132]

Giovanbattista had resolved a few initial perplexities about the failures, protests and complications of the last fair. The Eldest, for his part, highlighted the advantages and usefulness of the venture, saying that Battista had found Valladolid to be a place where one could live 'happily' and with good profit. Iacopo, in case of need, could still count on the presence of his brother, who was living relatively close to Seville. And, lastly, Bellotti gained a suitable and advantageous occupation right when he found himself alone.[133]

The partners divided up the roles for the management of the venture, combining exchange with intense trade activity. From Florence, Matteo sent gold silk, other silks, frieze, cloth for stockings, camlet and spun gold to Valladolid.[134] Keeping the shop well stocked made it possible to do good business and thereby compensate for the risks of the financial manoeuvres. The experience was largely positive. The unwavering commitment of Battista and Bellotti, joined by Francesco in the summer of 1543, kept the business profitable and running smoothly. This continued until at least March 1545, when Castile became mired in a difficult period caused by another series of problems and failures that struck numerous Florentine merchants.[135] The Botti decided to close down and needed to settle their accounts, beginning a long process of liquidation. In August, the capital shares were repaid,[136] while the profits were distributed in October, during the Villalón fair. The Eldest had asked Francesco to convert his share into goods: 60 crates of sugar, 1000 Barbary hides, 800 *cantari* of lead[137] and 30 crates of sugar from New Spain.[138] Simone instead preferred coins, cash and *juros*.[139] In the end, they decided on a cash

[132] ASF, *Miscellanea*, 107, fascicolo 3, Florence-Valladolid, Matteo Botti to Giovanbattista Botti, 5 April 1542, c. 171v.

[133] ASF, *Miscellanea*, 107, fascicolo 3, Florence-Valladolid, Matteo Botti to Giovanbattista Botti, 25 May 1542, c. 183v.

[134] ASF, *Miscellanea*, 107, fascicolo 3, Florence-Valladolid, Matteo Botti to Giovanbattista Botti (personal), 25 May 1542, c. 186r.

[135] ASF, *Miscellanea*, 107, fascicolo 4, Florence-Valladolid, Matteo Botti to Giovanbattista Botti and Giovanbattista Bellotti and partners, 10 January 1545, c. 66v.

[136] ASF, *Miscellanea*, 107, fascicolo 4, Florence-Castille, Matteo Botti to the Botti company, 27 August 1545, c. 137r.

[137] One Cádiz or Seville *cantaro* = 4 *rove* = 100 pounds = 46 kg. A. Martini, *Manuale*, p. 322.

[138] ASF, *Miscellanea*, 107, fascicolo 4, Florence-Valladolid, Matteo Botti to Giovanbattista Botti, 14 March 1545, c. 73v. The Viceroyalty of New Spain included much of the central-western part of what is now the United States, Mexico and almost all Central America.

[139] ASF, *Miscellanea*, 107, fascicolo 4, Florence-Valladolid, Mattei Botti to Giovanbattista and Francesco Botti, 20 April 1545, c. 85r.

distribution.[140] All the brothers' shares were transferred to Seville with standard bills of exchange, from where, it seems, they chose to remit them to Rome.[141]

In February of the following year, the warehouse stock was still on hold; the liquidation was taking a long time. Between the end of 1547 and early 1548, Francesco and Giovanbattista left Valladolid, leaving Bellotti to settle the final accounts and complete any still open transactions. The company's profits were not very high. We do not know the exact figures, but Matteo's judgement is clear: it was enough to 'save the capital' and that was something to be happy about.[142]

[140] ASF, *Miscellanea*, 107, fascicolo 4, Florence-Castille, Matteo Botti to Giovanbattista and Francesco Botti, 12 August 1545, cc. 126v.-127r.

[141] ASF, *Miscellanea*, 107, fascicolo 4, Florence-Valladolid, Matteo Botti to the Botti company, 18 September 1545, c. 141v.

[142] ASF, *Miscellanea*, 107, fascicolo 4, Florence-Castille, Matteo Botti to the Botti company, 17 October 1545, cc. 147v.–148r.

Chapter 5
Intercultural Trade: Spread and Cross-fertilise

The Italians have been in the habit of creating, in the shade of their bell towers, beautiful things that please the world since the Middle Ages.

(Carlo Cipolla)

5.1 A Story About Pragmatic Choices

5.1.1 The Places of Trade

Apart from trade with New World markets, mediated through Seville, Fig. 5.1 shows the cities where the Botti did business.

They relied on numerous correspondents in these cities, most of whom fellow Florentines. This was a networking mechanism that proved to be especially effective in the world of Florentine trade. An ensemble of dynamic relationships that guaranteed information exchange and reciprocal support for their activity. While it is true that the traders' success depended on the performance of their companies, it also resulted from the geographic and quantitative aspects of their interrelations. This simple fact reveals the existence of a complex network with a composition and function that went well beyond the number of people and companies with which one corresponded. It was a vast network understood as an ensemble of dyadic connections based on different elements, such as business relationships, kinship, knowledge and friendship, among others.[1]

In Venice, the Botti family did business with Pandolfo Attavanti and the Bartolini. Venice was of special interest to the group which, as noted above, sent Matteo there for a few years. In Pisa, when they closed their company, they were doing business

[1] The bibliography on social networks, concentrating on methodology and applications for historical research, is vast. For a summary of the main studies on the subject, see A. Orlandi, 'Le prestazioni di una holding'.

A. Orlandi, *Money, Culture, Beauty. The Botti Family*,
https://doi.org/10.1007/978-3-032-00453-6_5

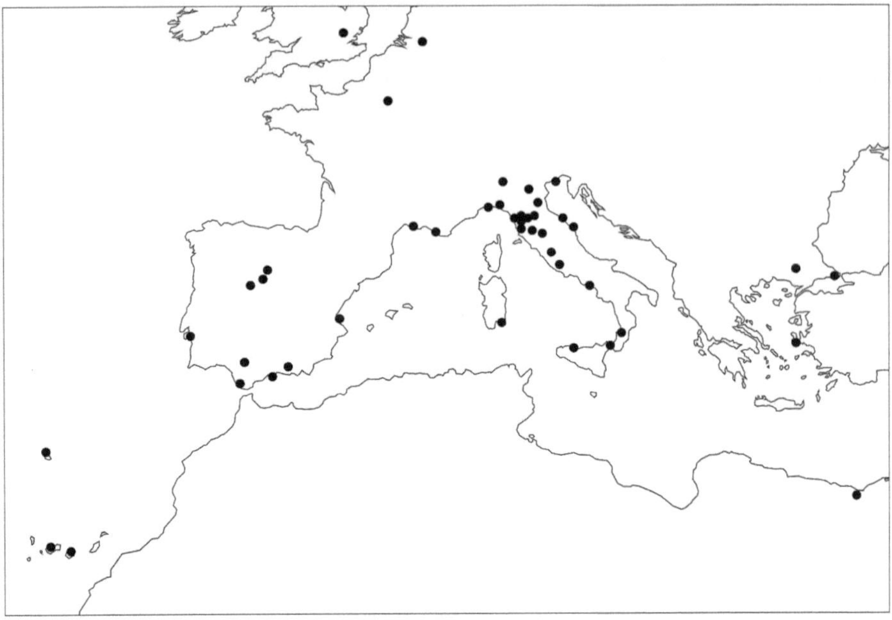

Fig. 5.1 The Botti family's main trading centres (The cities marked on the map are: Adrianople, Alexandria, Ancona, Antwerp, Bologna, Cádiz, Chios, Cagliari, Gran Canaria, Constantinople/Pera, Genoa, Granada, Lyon, Lisbon, Livorno, London, Lucca, Madeira, Málaga, Mantua, Marseilles, Medina del Campo, Messina, Milan, Monteleone, Montpellier, Naples, Palermo, Paris, Pesaro, Pescia, Pietrasanta, Pisa, Pistoia, Rome, Salamanca, Savona, Siena, Seville, Tenerife, Valencia, Valladolid, Venice, Vibo Valentia, Villalón, Viterbo and Volterra. The picture would be even more crowded if we had the correspondence sent from Seville, Cádiz and Valladolid, where the Botti had companies)

with the Capponi, the Salviati[2] and Carlo Nozzolini. In Genoa, we find the Gentile, the Spinola, the Negro and Antonio Palmieri, while in Savona they worked with Giovanni di Castro Delfino. In Siena, they had connections with the company of Giulio Santi, while in Rome they relied mostly on Filippo Del Bene, Bastiano da Montaguto and Battista Puccini. In the south, their contacts in Naples were Tommaso Ginori, Francesco and Miquel Blanco, Simone Corsi, the Capponi and the Biffoli; in Messina, Bernardo Corsi, Pantaleo Cinigo,[3] Signorini and Santacroce, Soldani and del Forese and, lastly, in Palermo, Lionardo della Seta and Francesco Ciragi. The southern cities were important supply markets for grain, legumes and feed in general. But our traders also knew how to move locally in search of other products.

[2]The economic links between Botti and Salviati also emerge in the documents of Alamanno Salviati. As we read in a book of memoirs, for example, in early 1541, his company in Pisa had sent the Botti in Cádiz 50 bales of gall for Iacopo and Giovanbattista to sell. Scuola Normale Superiore, *Archivio Salviati*, III, 22, c. 10r. I would like to thank my friend and colleague Heinrich Lang for pointing this out to me.

[3]ASF, *Libri di commercio*, 713, Florence-Messina, Matteo Botti to Pantaleo Cinigo, 28 June, c. 38v.

One example is Bartolomeo Steccuti and Larione Brandolini, two Tuscans who were asked to buy silks in little Monteleone, now Vibo Valentia.

Outside Italy, in Marseilles, the group relied on Alberto Temperani and Domenico Bonaccorsi to organise buying up mercury and cinnabar in Alexandria. In Montpellier, they could depend on the Dini, in Lyon the Bene, Bini, Beni, Dei, Strozzi and Bernardo Bellini, to whom they sent mostly frieze, silks, cloth and spun silk, raw material that was essential for internal production. And of course we must not forget that Giovanbattista himself lived there for seven years.

In Antwerp[4] and London, their main correspondents were the Guicciardini and Vernacci company and the Gondi and Giacomini company, with whom they traded gall and cloths from northern Europe and Florentine textiles. As we have noted, the Tuscan sources are incomplete. What emerges, for example, from the notarial contracts preserved in Cádiz is that Iacopo was shipping goods to England, giving them to merchants from the island who were there in Andalusia. In one case, more than 26 quintals of alum were sold to Duarte Hueldon, Ricardo Moz, Huyt Hamon and Hilu Titon.[5]

They also had contacts in the Near East. Guglielmo da Sommaia and Niccolò Gerini were active in Constantinople and Pera, supplying the group with cloth, wheat and much more.

We will not go into the complex relationships in the Iberian Peninsula that we looked at above, examining their companies in more detail. We will limit ourselves here to noting the Florentine merchant Giovanni Morelli in Lisbon. In the Canaries, where Iacopo had a few properties, the link was ensured by a number of people.

The goods they dealt in were highly varied. For the sake of concision, we will categorise in terms of area of provenance. From northern Europe: woollen cloth, metal, leather and hides, herring, salmon; from Atlantic Europe: tuna, anchovies, sardines, leather and hides, sugar; from Mediterranean Europe: woollen cloth, silks, raw materials for textiles, grain, feed, wine, oil, sugar and, lastly, from America: novel products and the sea of silver that was flooding the Old World. During the entire period studied for this volume, the Botti shifted more than 150 different types of goods, from the most refined and costly to the simplest for everyday use.

A system of trade that was, as we have established, run from Florence. A good proportion of their activity was driven by the Spanish companies, and it could not have been otherwise, given the effects of the discovery of America, the great event that Francisco López de Gomara described in his *Historia general de las Indias* as 'La mayor cosa despues de la creación del mundo, sacando la encarnación y muerte del que lo crió'.[6]

[4]As we have seen, Francesco lived in that city in the duchy of Brabant for some time.

[5]AHPC, *Protocolos notariales de Cádiz*, Oficio XIX, 4336, 24 September 1547, cc. 222–224.

[6]A. Orlandi, 'Fiorentini alla ricerca del Nuovo Mondo', p. 131.

5.1.2 The Spanish Branches and the Allure of New Worlds

> And we have seen that a ship went past the Strait of Magellan and was exploring in the direction of Peru, and this is good news and they will need to return to the Maluku where they will get lots of spices which, if they do it, will be very profitable and it is not chance that Magellan found them. This way they will be able to do things in a better and more modern way and just as God caused us to lose our old places he will cause us to discover modern ones.[7]

Matteo's account shows that Spain was no longer and merely the touchstone of the traditional system of trade that had engaged so many operators since the dawn of the trade revolution. Major change was expanding the peninsula's economic role and increasing its appeal. Until then it had been the link between the Mediterranean and the countries in Northern Europe, and it was now the one between the Old World and the New.[8] He wrote this account 20 years after the circumnavigation of the Tierra del Fuego (Land of Fire). In it, Botti uses the term 'modern' twice, with reference to phenomena that were almost not of his time, almost as if this extraordinary event were becoming the prerogative of his descendants. Extraordinary and

[7] 'E aviamo visto come una nave avea passato per lo Stretto dil Maghaglano e andava schoperendo per la volta dil Peri che è bona nova e doverranno ritornare a quelle Maluche di dove trarranno molti spezi che, se lo faranno, sarà di gran profitto e non l'ànno a caso che 'l Maghagliano le trovò luj. Così potranno fare li modernj e meglio e a questo modo da che Dio ci fa perdere li nostri lochi antichi ci farà ritrovare de' moderni.' ASF, *Miscellanea*, 107, fascicolo 3, Florence-Seville, Matteo Botti to Iacopo and Giovanbattista Botti, 16 September 1541, c. 123r.

[8] On the presence of Italian merchants in Andalusia in the sixteenth century, there are many essays in the following volumes that are still of interest: *La presenza italiana in Andalusia nel Basso Medioevo, Atti del secondo convegno, Roma, 25–27 maggio 1984*, eds. A. Boscolo and B. Torres, Cappelli editore, Bologna 1986; *Presencia italiana en Andalucía siglos XIV-XVII, Actas del I Coloquio Hispano-Italiano*, eds. B. Torres Ramírez and J.J. Hernández Palomo, Escuela de Estudios Hispano-Americanos de Sevilla, Seville 1985; *Presencia italiana en Andalucia siglos XIV-XVII, Actas del III Coloquio Hispano-Italiani, Escuela de Estudios Hispano-Americanos de Sevilla*, eds. Eds. B. Torres Ramírez and J.J Hernández Paolomo, Seville 1989. After these studies, and especially in the 1990s, a lot of research was done on the Genoese and the Florentines. See in particular the research of Enrique Otte, Consuelo Varela and others (E. Otte, *Sevilla y sus mercaderes a fines de la Edad Media*, Universidad de Sevilla-Fundación El Monte, Seville 1996; C. Varela, *Colombo e i fiorentini*). Here, we will limit ourselves to listing the most recent literature on Tuscan businessmen in particular. This research often looks at the mechanisms of their integration and subsequent entry into the local nobility: J.J. Iglesias Rodríguez, *El árbol de sinople. Familia y patrimonio entre Andalucía y Toscana en la Edad Moderna*, Universidad de Sevilla, Seville 2009; J.J. Iglesias Rodríguez, 'Los Fantoni'; J.J. Iglesias Rodríguez, 'Redes familiares y élites mercantiles internacionales en la Andalucía atlántica moderna (Cádiz, siglos XVI y XVII)', in *Familias, élites y redes de poder cosmopolitas de la Monarquía Hispánica en la Edad Moderna*, eds. F. Sánchez-Montes, J. Lozano, A. Jiménez Estrella, Comares, Granada 2016, p. 143–170. Also see some of the essays in *Mercaderes y redes mercantile*; J. Cartaya Baños, *Mayorazgos. Riqueza, nobleza y posteridad en la Sevilla del siglo XVI*, Editorial Universidad de Sevilla, Seville 2018. For the early seventeenth century, see J.L. Guasch-Tomás, 'Agents of Globalisation: An Approximation to Santi Federighi's Commercial Network, c.1620–1643', in *Merchants and Trade Networks in the Atlantic and the Mediterranean. Connectors of Commercial Maritime Systems*, eds. M. Herrero, K. Kaps, Routledge, New York 2016, pp. 130–144.

exceptional not only for the immensity of the spaces and remoteness of the territories, but also and most importantly for the new opportunities it offered.

Trade activity along the western routes and attempts along those of the east were leaving a mark on the economic situation in the Iberian Peninsula. The intense flow of trade moving in these two directions, along with the still vital Mediterranean traffic, allowed the country to become rich and impose itself across Europe.[9]

Our documents are pervaded by the family's natural bent for business and curiosity about discovering and experimenting with the new: 'please send me news about where you are and the things in India so I can share it with lots of my friends',[10] wrote Giovanbattista, who had continued to maintain relationships with traders and acquaintances in the Andalusian markets even after his return to Florence. The letters of the Tuscan companies and in particular the Florentine ones played an important informational and cultural role, contributing to the broad spread of information about the Americas. In them, economic and financial news mixes with varied descriptions of unknown plants and animals and the military activity of the conquistadores.

The letters were followed by the first, curious novelties, like the 'galli d'India' (Indian cocks)[11] that Francesco Botti shipped to Florence 1547 and the 'semi nuovi' (new seeds), probably maize, that his brother asked for in Seville.[12]

Pistachios in America

While trying to sell a shipment of Madeira sugar in the narrow streets of Venice, Matteo gave proof of his strong entrepreneurial spirit with an attempt to grow pistachios in America.

In 1533, he sent an invoice with some goods on their way to Andalusia. In it, he listed a long series of goods: camel hair fabrics, small wicker baskets, bellows, needles from Damascus and fine paper painted with 'the Inferno according to Dante'. And among these items, we also find, almost unbelievably, a bag of pistachios. Specifically, 'two pounds of pistachios produced by a big tree similar to the walnut in Syria or Egypt and they are excellent. They are sold for ducats per hundred pounds. I am sending them to you so you can try and see if they grow in the Indies like other things. It would be good to be able to grow them.'[13]

[9] During that period, 'trading with Spain in the broadest sense of the term was inevitable'. R. Carande, *Carlo V*, p. 148.

[10] ASF, *Libri di commercio*, 716, Florence-Seville, Giovanbattista Botti to Lorenzo del Rosso, 31 March 1563, c. 60v.

[11] That is what turkeys were called. And there is an interesting story about the Botti family's attempt to raise turkeys in Florence. Matteo described the episode in a letter, explaining that the animal had arrived in Florence with something wrong with his eyes. It was treated according to the instructions sent from America, but it died. It was thought that it was a problem caused by the Tuscan air. Four chicks hatched, however, and were sent to the country house where they could be raised by a woman specifically assigned to their care. ASF, *Miscellanea*, 107, fascicolo 5, Florence-Seville, Matteo Botti to Iacopo Botti (personal), 6 October 1547, c. 106r.

[12] ASF, *Libri di commercio*, 716, Florence-Seville, Giovanbattista Botti to Lorenzo del Rosso, 30 September 1562, c. 7v.

[13] '2 libbre di pistachi quali fano in uno albero grande come il nocie yn Soria o in Egitto e sono pregiati. E si ven dono IIIJ ducati il cento che gli mando per si metta prova se facessino all'Indie, come fanno l'altre coxe che saria bono mettervene seme.' ASF, *Libri di commercio*, 734, c. 119v.

> Mentioned in Genesis and available in the Middle East for thousands of years, they were considered a delicacy. Owning a pistachio plantation was a true status symbol. According to legend, pistachios were one of the Queen of Sheba's favourite foods. The 'green hazelnut' landed in Greece with the arrival of Alexander the Great and reached the western Mediterranean in 37 BCE thanks to Lucius Vitellius, who had brought it from Syria.[14] Arab domination substantially expanded to areas of cultivation and the Crusades contributed to increasing its trade. Venice, which had strong trade relations with Syria, contributed to spreading it throughout central Europe and the north.
>
> Matteo, with its value in mind, decided to send a pound or two to his brothers in Spain. Just as the new seeds that were so intriguing to Europeans were arriving from the Americas, they could attempt the reverse. As far as we know, it was a four-century wait. It was not until the 1930s that the botanist William E. Whitehouse proposed growing them in the Central Valley in California. Thus began the complex distribution of the rich nut that the enterprising Botti had imagined so far in advance![15]

One big novelty was cochineal, an American pigment that produced crimson and scarlet shades and was enchanting everyone everywhere. It was stirring up a lot of interest, and the Spanish, who wanted it to remain exclusive, kept it shrouded in mystery. Matteo Botti wrote to his correspondents in Seville:

> And we would greatly appreciate it if you could find out, if possible, if in the place where its harvested it is born on grass or on plants, or if it is a grub or something else, how it is harvested and if there are big ones.[16]

The clarifications he received were a disappointment. The information he received was too generic, what he wanted to know instead was 'if the product is made with the eggs of this animal, if it lives and walks on a tree and how much and how they harvest it and other small details about this beautiful secret of nature'.[17]

Books that described the Americas were also of interest. It is not difficult to find letters like the one written by Filippo Strozzi in June 1535, asking Francesco Lapi to send a printed book on the conquest of Peru from the city of Guadalquivir.[18] In

---

[14] G.B. Lanfranchi, 'Prestiti alimentari nelle tradizioni greca e romana', in *Atlante dell'alimentazione e della gastronomia. I, Risorse, scambi, consumi*, eds. M. Montanari, F. Sabban, Utet, Turin 2004, pp. 78–86, p. 84.

[15] D. Geisseler, W.R. Horwath, *Pistachio Production in California*, 2016, https://apps1.cdfa.ca.gov/FertilizerResearch/docs/Pistachio_Production_CA.pdf Also see R. Pearson, 'W.E. Whitehouse Dies. Pistachio Nut Developer', *The Washington Post*, 23 October 1982, https://www.washingtonpost.com/archive/local/1982/10/24/we-whitehouse-dies/db64936b-0343-4222-bd7d-14bb43061666/

[16] 'E aremo a ccaro molto, v'informassi, se gliè a voj possibile, se nel paese che la si coglie voi intendete che la sia materia che naschi in su erbe o piante, opure se è materia di bacherozzoli o quello sia, o come si raunj et se ve n'è gran quantità o come si facci. Non ci mancate che ci viene a proposito.'

[17] A. Orlandi, 'Zucchero e cocciniglia dal Nuovo Mondo, due esempi di precoce diffusione', in *Prodotti e tecniche d'Oltremare nelle economie europee. Secc. XIII-XVIII', Atti della "Ventinovesima Settimana di Studi" 14–19 aprile 1997*, ed. S. Cavaciocchi, Istituto Internazionale di Storia Economica "F. Datini" Prato, Le Monnier, Florence 1998, pp. 477–487, p. 485.

[18] F. Melis, 'Il commercio transatlantico di una compagnia fiorentina stabilita a Siviglia a pochi anni dalle imprese di Cortes e Pizarro', in F. Melis, *I mercanti italiani nell'Europa medievale e rinascimentale,* ed. L. Frangioni, Le Monnier, Florence 1990, pp. 45–134, p. 79.

June 1546, the Eldest wrote to Valladolid to find out 'if the second book about India has come out … which we think is much better than the one that has been in circulation up until now'.[19]

The search for new routes and discovery of rich mineral deposits is also found in their letters. We will limit ourselves to two examples. When, in May 1536, Francisco Pizarro offered a prize of 4000 ducats to the first ship to make it to the coast of Peru passing through the Strait of Magellan, the news spread quickly to Florence through a missive from Francesco Lapi to his majority partner.[20] Ten years later, Matteo Botti wrote from Florence:

> We heard that a ship arrived in Seville from the Terra Firma with gold and silver and the news that some soldiers who left for Peru three years ago were back and that new lands had been discovered rich in gold and silver. When you can get news from the Indies give me detailed information about it because I have some good friends who are asking me about it every day. Always send me as many details as you can.[21]

This need for knowledge also concealed a pragmatic attempt to assess the real opportunities, trying to avoid being overly influenced by celebratory, often exaggerated, descriptions of the riches of those still so distant lands. One the other hand, the news arriving in Europe was not always encouraging. In September 1526, 'our Florentine, Vespuccio' had returned to Seville 'from the Indies and with little profit'.[22]

In any case, the Botti helped finance voyages to new lands for the purpose of trade and discovery on more than one occasion. In May 1525, Iacopo, together with Francesco Rucellai, Zanobi[23] and Daniello,[24] 'wanted to go to the Indies':[25] 400 ducats jointly with the three partners financed an adventure to the American coasts. In 1526, the Cádiz house repeated the experiment, with, it seems, a share of 32%.[26] That year, Botti, with Zanobi Guidacci, Giovanni Morelli and Iacopo Fantoni, also

---

[19] ASF, *Miscellanea*, 107, fascicolo 5, Florence-Valladolid, Matteo Botti to the Botti company, 26 June 1546, c. 11v.

[20] ASF, *CSVS*, 1207, in F. Melis, *Documenti per la Storia Economica*, p. 214.

[21] 'E s'è inteso come in Sibilia stava arivato una nave di Terraferma con oro et argiento e come dava nuova che certi soldati ch'erono partiti dil Perù, III anni sono, stavano tornati e davono nuove come gli avevono scoperto nuove terre riche d'oro e d'argiento. Piacciavi quando potete havere d'esse nuove di l'Indie darmene aviso particulari che tengho cierti dilli boni che ongni dì me ne dimandano, mandatemi senpre più particulari potete'. ASF, *Miscellanea Medicea*, 107, fascicolo 5, Florence-Valladolid, Matteo Botti to the Botti company, 26 June 1546, c. 11v.

[22] ASF, *Acquisti e Doni*, Registro Galletti, 286/3, Valladolid-Florence, Francesco Gucci to Giovanni Balducci, 17 September 1526, c. 30s. This is a reference to Giovanni Vespucci, nephew of Amerigo and *piloto real* from May 1512 to 18 March 1525. C. Varela, *Colombo e i fiorentini*, pp. 86–96.

[23] This was probably Zanobi Guidacci.

[24] They were all Florentines.

[25] ASF, *Libri di commercio*, 711, Florence-Cádiz, Matteo Botti to Iacopo Botti (personal), 20 May 1525, c. 46v.

[26] ASF, *Libri di commercio*, 711, Florence-Cádiz, Matteo Botti to the Botti company, 14 July 1526, c. 103v.; ASF, *Libri di commercio*, 711, Florence-Cádiz, Matteo Botti to Giovanbattista Botti, 28 May 1526, c. 101r.

contributed 200,000 maravedís (about 533 ducats) to a mission led by Sebastiano Caboto.[27] And in 1544, the company in Guadalquivir contributed 175 ducats to fitting out another galleon headed to the New World.[28]

Attention to the departures and arrivals of the 'Armate de Indias' is a constant in all the correspondence. Both Matteo, in Florence, and Iacopo, in Andalusia, seized opportunities to participate. Their interest was not limited to the western route; they were also attentive to the eastern one. The 'fleets' heading to the Moluccas departed from Lisbon and our merchants made use of correspondents in that city, the Florentine company Sernigi-Morelli, to finance those voyages with their own funds. In October 1525 Iacopo paid 200 ducats[29] for a caravel headed to those islands. And he invested in another expedition the following year:[30] 'God willing they will return with the hoped-for profit ... [and] that we aren't working wonders to others' advantage'.[31] In October 1540, there is news of an armed ship heading to Calicut and the intention of Tommaso Marchi, a Florentine who had just returned to that region, to embark upon another venture to the East Indies.

The ventures were not always a success. In a few cases, the expense and risks outweighed the results, like on those occasions when the Eldest, with his proverbial prudence, wrote: 'in the long run it is always better to go slowly and calmly than to devote oneself to big, risky things, from which I aim to distance myself entirely'.[32] But these reflections were just temporary outbursts, if he wrote to his brother in 1554: 'Go ahead and invest money in the voyage of I don't know what he is called'.[33]

These investments, and not only those made by the Botti, explain why at least 50 Tuscan businessmen left Europe in the sixteenth century to try their luck in the

27 E. Otte, 'Los Botti', p. 47–86. Later research has revealed the precise amounts of their contributions: Iacopo Fantoni, 203,940 maravedís; Iacopo Botti, 203,940 maravedís; Zanobi Guidacci, 203,940 maravedís. They were joined by the Florentines Andrea Velluti with 101,970 maravedís and Iacopo Gualterotti who contributed, with Pandolfo Belachi, the same amount. J. Gil, 'Los armadores de Sebastian Caboto: un ingles entre italianos', in *Anuario de Estudios-Americanos*, XLV, Escuela de Estudios Hispano-Americanos, Seville 1988, pp. 3–65. Lastly, Federigo Melis noted a certain Piero Botti who in 1534 'fue con Pizzarro y Almagro a la conquista del Perù'. F. Melis, 'Gli italiani e l'apertura delle vie atlantiche', in *Mercaderes italianos en España Siglos XIV-XVI. (Investigaciones sobre su correspondencia y su contabilidad)*, Universidad de Sevilla, Seville 1976, pp. 169–175, p. 174.

28 G. Gribaudi, 'Navigatori, banchieri e mercanti italiani nei documenti degli archivi notarli di Siviglia (secolo XVI)', *Bollettino della R. Società geografica italiana*, LXX, LXXXIII, pp. 13–22, p. 21.

29 ASF, *Libri di commercio*, 711, Florence-Cádiz, Matteo Botti to Giovanbattista Botti, 28 October 1525, c. 66v.

30 ASF, *Libri di commercio*, 711, Florence-Cádiz, Matteo Botti to the Botti company, 30 October 1526, c. 117v.

31 ASF, *Libri di commercio*, 711, Florence-Cádiz, Matteo Botti to the Botti company, 18 March 1526, c. 135v.

32 ASF, *Libri di commercio*, 712, Florence-Cádiz, Matteo Botti to Iacopo and Giovanbattista Botti, 9 February 1529, c. 26r.

33 ASF, *Miscellanea*, 107, fascicolo 4, Florence-Seville, Matteo Botti to the Botti company, 29 November 1544, c. 53r. Iacopo Fantoni and Francesco Lapi also contributed to the voyage.

Americas. They were also little-known figures who left us accounts and descriptions of the places they saw and grappled with. They also brought culture and beauty to those regions.[34]

5.2 'Doing Trade' and Spreading Beauty

5.2.1 Tratan con 'todas las partes de la cristiandad y aun en Berbería'

Iacopo, Battista and Francesco often left Cádiz and Seville to buy goods where they were produced at more advantageous prices and get direct information about market trends. Battista often went to Lagos (Portugal) and Conil de la Frontera, even to help with the simple unloading of the tuna. Iacopo visited many breeders to personally buy up wool. Both closely monitored, sometimes going as far as Lisbon, the purchase of sugar from São Tomé and travelled to Granada for silks that were the most beautiful and best suited for Florentine manufacturers, to Barcelona to retrieve goods being held at the port and to Sanlúcar de Barrameda to strengthen ties with Duke of Medina Sidonia. This dynamism leads us back to our discussion of the diversity and breadth of their trade and the places where they were active.

To refresh our memory, we can turn to the Dominican Tomás de Mercado's reflections on the Andalusian ports:

> Tienen, lo primero, contratación en todas las partes de la cristiandad y aun en Berbería. A Flandes cargan lanas, aceites y bastardos; de allá traen todo género de mercería, tapicería, librería. A Florencia envían cochinilla, cue ros; traen oro hilado, brocados, seda y, de todas aquellas partes, gran mul titud de lienzos. En Cabo Verde tienen el trato de los negros, negocio de gran caudal y mucho interés. A todas las Indias envían grandes cargazones de toda suerte de ropa; traen de allá oro, plata, perlas, grana y cueros, en grandísima cantidad. Ítem, para asegurar lo que cargan, que son millones de valor, tienen necesidad de asegurar en Lisboa, en Burgos, en Lyon de Francia, Flandes, porque es tan gran cantidad la que cargan que no bastan los de Sevilla, ni de veinte Sevillas, a asegurarlo.[35]

As noted, the list of the goods they traded is long. It includes all the goods that were traded or monitored by their companies, with varying degrees of attention and in different quantities. Like most businessmen at the time, they were not specialised and remained open to bargaining for anything. But they certainly tended to prefer

[34] See the examples in A. Orlandi, 'New world villages and cities in the 16th century: cross-cultural influences between Italy and the Americas', in *Ciudades en expansión. Dinámicas urbanas entre los siglos XIV-XVI*, eds. M. Asenjo González, D. Alonso García, S.M. Pérez González, Dykinson, S.L., Madrid 2022, p. 331–348.

[35] T. de Mercado, *Suma de tratos y contratos*, 1523–1575.
https://www.cervantesvirtual.com/obra-visor/suma-de-tratos-y-contratos%2D%2D0/html/feec322c-82b1-11df-acc7-002185ce6064_4.html#I_51_ accessed 25 June 2024.

some products over others. They had more targeted interests, more attentive to the conditions and requirements of consumers, who they nevertheless tried to influence.

Matteo not only indicated the line of conduct the brothers needed to follow in their management of their companies, he also gave short-term instructions laying down the highest prices to adhere to for purchases. To supply the Tuscan market, he also speculated on the minimum quantities to buy up: and so, the 180 *cantari* of sugar per year needed to be from Madeira or the Canaries and not the lower quality sugar from São Tomé or the Indies. The 10/15 barrels of fatty tuna in brine and the 800/1.000 barrels of anchovies needed to have carefully marked staves. And he also specified 10/15 *lastri*[36] of Irish leather and 300/400 *lastri* of leather from Seville. When he then turned to the subject of English woollen piece goods, from Essex or Southampton, he not only indicated the acceptable cost but also specified the hues, recommending choosing those of 'good length'.[37]

The scale of the group's trade in a few products like sugar, salted fish and leather led to some specialisation. For preserved fish, categorised as *salumi*, shipments were often organised based on the capacity of a caravel and divided as follows: 50/60 barrels of smoked sardines, 500/600 barrels of *tarantellata* tuna in brine, 600/800 barrels of anchovies, 100/150 dozen cod and 10/12 barrels of Tinker mackerel prepared on Gibraltar. The main supplier was the duke of Medina Sidonia, who owned the tuna nets in Zahara and Conil and traded with the Botti mainly in exchange for brocades and cloth from San Martino. Between 1524 and 1528 they bought almost 7000 tons of tuna in brine,[38] which was then sold for about 240,000 lire. In 1531 alone, they traded 1226 quintals of it.[39] Their outlets were in Tuscany, Sardinia, Liguria, Lazio and Campania.

Local hides, especially from Cordova and other areas, were available across Andalusia. The ones from Barbary, Alexandria, Normandy, Ireland and America

---

[36] The *lastro* was a unit of measure for leather.

[37] ASF, *Libri di commercio*, 712, Florence-Antwerp, Matteo Botti to the Guicciardini and Vernacci company, 22 July 1531, c. 137v.

[38] 17,000 barrels which equalled 6902 quintals (1 barrel = 40.6 kg).

[39] According to a few sixteenth-century estimates, 100,000 tuna were fished a year in Conil and Zhara. J.M. Bello León, 'Almadrabas andaluzas a finales de la Edad Media. Nuevos datos para su estudio', Historia. *Instituciones. Documentos*, 32 (2005), pp. 81–113; María I. Pérez de Colosía, A. Sarriá Muñoz, 'Las almadrabas del duque de Medina Sidonia en Tarifa', *Baetica. Estudios de Arte, Geografía e Historia*, 13, 1991, pp. 241–254. Also see D. Florido del Corral, *Evolución histórica y cultural de las almadrabas en el litoral atlántico meridional (siglos XVI-XX)*, Barcelona, 2005; J.J. Iglesias Rodríguez, 'Ciudad y fiscalidad señorial: las rentas del Condado de el Puerto de Santa María en el siglo XVI', in *Actas del VI Coloquio Internacional de Historia Medieval de Andalucía*, Málaga, 1991, pp. 215–224; M.Á. Ladero Quesada, 'Las almadrabas de Andalucía (siglos XIII-XVI)', *Boletín de la Real Academia de la Historia*, CXC, Madrid, 1993, pp. 345–354; M.Á. Melón Jiménez, 'La trastienda del gran comercio. "Fraudes tolerados o no entendidos" en el Reino de Sevilla a finales del antiguo régimen', in *Comercio y cultura en la Edad Moderna*, eds. J.J. Iglesias, R.M. Pérez y M.F. Fernández, Universidad de Seville, Seville 2015, pp. 801–814; D. Ríos Toledan, *El mundo de la pesca en la Andalucía atlántica a fines de la Edad Media, Pensando Andalucía: Una visión transdisciplinar*, eds. J. Córdoba Toro, P. González Zambrano, Diputación de Cádiz, Cádiz 2019, pp. 214–227.

also arrived in Seville. The Botti bought them in large quantities, sometimes in partnership with other Tuscans and Spaniards. In the 1520s and 30s, the group bought almost 150,000 hides, mostly from Ireland and Barbary, buying up even close to 10,000 pieces at a time.

The sugar trade was the one that more than any other opened the path to specialisation. Sugar cane arrived from the Canaries, Madeira, Barbary, São Tomé and the New World, especially Mexico and Hispaniola.[40] The Florentines in Cádiz and Seville were extremely interested in it. According to our sources, they shipped 12,000 crates of it to Italy and the Netherlands in seven years (1524–1533). In one notable episode, a Portuguese gentleman by the name of Luis di Atouguia bought, with the Botti's companies in Andalusia, more than 102 tons of Madeira sugar, earmarked for Venice. As noted above, Matteo moved to the Lagoon to sell it, and made a profit of almost 20%.[41]

---

[40] Among the numerous studies on the production and distribution of sugar in the sixteenth century, see in particular Herrera, R. 2021. "De los ciclos de no espacialización a la era de azúcar: elementos de Historia de Cuba en un largo período (1492-1492) - Parte 1." International Journal of Cuban Studies 12, 2: 183-212; *Tropical Babylons. Sugar and the Making of the Atlantic World, 1450–1680*, ed. Stuart B. Schwartz, Chapel Hill, London, 2004; L. da Cunha Pinheiro, 'A produção açucareira em São Tomé ao longo de Quinhentos', in *Actas do Colóquio Internacional São Tomé e Príncipe numa perspectiva interdisciplinar, diacrónica e sincrónica*, Instituto Universitário de Lisboa, Lisbon 2012, pp. 27–46; F. Fernández-Armesto, *Las Islas Canarias después de la conquista. La creación de una Sociedad Colonial a principios del siglo XVI*, Ediciones del Cabildo Insular de Gran Canaria, Las Palmas de Gran Canaria, 1997; *La Empresa Azucarera en Canaria. Siglos XV-XX*, eds. S. de Luxán Meléndez, A. Viña Brito, Destilerías Arehucas, Las Palmas de Gran Canaria, 2009; M. Lobo Carrera, 'Los mercaderes italianos y el comercio azucarero canario en la primera mitad del siglo XVI', in *"«Aspetti della vita economica medievale»"*. Atti del Convegno di Studi nel X anniversario della morte di Federigo Melis, Florence-Pisa-Prato, 10–14 March 1984, Università degli Studi di Firenze, Florence 1985, pp. 268–282; L.E. Lopez y Sebastian and J.L. Del Rio Moreno, 'El Azúcar en Canarias y la Española: sistemas de explotacion y efectos en el comercio del siglo XVI', *AULA Revista de Humanidades y Ciencias Sociales*, 60, 5–6, 1996, pp. 53–77; L.E. Lopez y Sebastian and J.L. Del Rio Moreno, 'Comercio y transporte en la economía del azúcar antillano durante el siglo XVI', *Anuario de Estudios Americanos*, 49, 1992, pp. 55–87, V. Rau, 'O açúcar de S. Tomé no segundo quartel do século XVI', in *Elementos do História de Ilha de S. Tomé (Em comemoração do V Centenário do Descobrimento),* Centro de Estudos de Matinha, Lisbona 1971, pp. 7–69, pp. 7–9; G. Rodríguez Morel, 'The Sugar Economy of Española in the Sixteenth Century', in *Tropical Babylons*, pp. 85–114; A. Vieira, *As ilhas do Açúcar-A Economia açucareira da Madeira e Canárias nos séculos XV a XVI,* Funchal (https://silo.tips/download/as-ilhas-do-aucar-a-economia-aucareira-da-madeira-e-canarias-nos-seculos-xv-e-xv accessed 25 June 2024); A. Vieira, 'Canaviais, açúcar e aguardente na Madeira. Séculos XV a XX', *Revista de Historia Industrial*, 27, 2005, pp. 221–224; A. Vieira, 'Sugar Island. The Sugar Economy of Madeira and the Canaries, 1450–1650', in *Tropical Babylons. Sugar and the Making of the Atlantic World, 1450–1680*, ed. S.B. Schwartz, Chapel Hill, London: University of North Carolina Press, 2004, pp. 42–84.

A. Viña Brito, M. Ronquillo Rubio, 'El primer ciclo del azúcar en Canaria. Balance historiográfico', in *XVI Coloquio de Historia Canario-Americana,* ed. F. Morales Padrón, 2006, pp. 1673–1696 (https://accedacris.ulpgc.es/bitstream/10553/59048/1/8655-Texto%20del%20art%C3%ADculo-9134-1-10-20140506.pdf accessed 25 June 2024).

[41] ASF, *Libri di commercio*, 734.

Within this context, the scarcity of information about the slave market would seem to be emblematic.[42] Although Iacopo sold slaves for the Americas, there was little demand for them on the Florentine market. It is also true that the brothers never lost an opportunity to find out the prices for and ways of purchasing any good. Proof of this is found in the mention of a case of ostrich feathers 'for making crests for helmets', which would have fetched a good price in those bellicose years, a 'nautical chart' and the '*Triumphs* of Petrarch with a commentary in Castilian', just to cite two sophisticated Andalusian items that could have been appreciated in Tuscany.

While the Botti were exporting mostly raw materials from Spain, a clear sign of the country's economic backwardness, in the case of imports their attention was necessarily concentrated on finished products. What emerges is the prevalence of Florentine silks and woollen cloth, fabrics from Rouen, velvets from Modena, voile from Bologna, cloth from Perpignan, the Netherlands and Flanders and tabbies and camlets from the East and Tuscany. We can only imagine the quality and richness of these goods. Laces and net made by nuns from the convent of Ripoli (who preferred to make only the finest ones), gold and silver thread that the Florentine gold beaters wound onto spools and shipped in little wooden boxes,[43] paintings made by artists who were by then even known in Spain, Venetian glass, majolica, pottery from Montelupo Fiorentino, prayer books, musical instruments, rugs, jewelled buttons and much more. Some of these goods were sent to the Americas along with others like taffeta from Granada, wine, quince jam and small objects.

[42] In September 1548, for example, Lorenzo del Rosso, who was already working with the Botti at the time, received a license in Seville to transport 35 slaves to the Indies. Archivo de Indias de Sevilla (henceforth AGI), *Indiferente*, 424, L. 21, cc. 241v.–242v.

[43] In the sixteenth century in particular, the big Florentine merchants who had silk textile mills also produced their own gold and silver leaf for making damask and brocade. B. Dini, 'I battilori fiorentini del Quattrocento', in *Medioevo, Mezzogiorno, Mediterraneo: studi in onore di Mario Del Treppo*, Liguori, Naples 2000, pp. 139–161; B. Dini, 'Una manifattura di battiloro nel Quattrocento', in *Tecnica e società nell'Italia dei secoli XII-XVI, Atti dell'undicesimo Convegno Internazionale di studio tenuto a Pistoia nei giorni 28–31 ottobre 1984*, Centro Italiano di Studi di Storia e d'Arte-Pistoia, Editografica, Bologna 1987, p. 83–11. This process of growth was already starting to emerge in the first half of the fifteenth century. Extra-thin gold leaf, fashioned by skilled artisans, was transformed by the hard-working hands of the 'cloistered women' into fragile thread that, wrapped around silk, was used to weave especially fine fabrics.

Our merchants received precious metals when the galleons returned from the West Indies.[44] They also received hides, dyestuffs,[45] raw silk, wool, pearls and other little-known products that were for this reason in higher demand in Europe. A royal note signed in December 1530 gave permission to Raffaello Acciaiuoli, resident in Valladolid, to ship one pound ten ounces[46] of a balm 'que se ha descubierto en las nuestras Indias que es provechoso para les heridas y otras enfermedades de los cuerpos humanos'. Acciaiuoli, who sold it at 8 *reali* an ounce, stored it in glass containers to help preserve it as long as possible.[47]

New Goods to Try: Silk and Wool from the Americas

In November 1540, Matteo wrote to the company in Seville: 'And people have seen that they have started sending silk from India'.[48] He had not heard this news from his brother and was irritated by this. Two months later, he returned to the subject, calling attention to the fact that 'no good' would come of being the last to get in on the new.[49] He was therefore asking for the prices for that fibre and a bundle of it to try out. Iacopo was not of the same view. He had reported the arrival of the ships returning from the New World, but it would seem that he had not sent so much as a 'sample' to Tuscany. The Eldest sent letter after letter repeating his request, which continued to be ignored. In the end, he seemed to resign himself, perhaps because Calabrian and Sicilian silk was starting to look profitable. In February 1548, he went back on the attack and turned to Francesco: he wanted 40/50 pounds of it at 850 maravedís a pound. It did not matter to him that the American fibre was less luminous than that from Almería, what he had in mind was 'a test' and so he was willing to spend a bit more.[50]

Wool also started to arrive from the West Indies. News of it came later than that for silk. The first mention dates to December 1547, when five ships had returned to Seville loaded with precious metals, cochineal, hides and wool. In his letter, Matteo described it is 'new

[44] Archivo General de Indias (henceforth AGI), *Contratación*, 202, B.N. 17. With the exception of a brief period at the beginning, trade with the Americas was subject to rigid controls and only Spanish subjects were allowed to traffic. Foreigners had two possibilities: either become recognised as Spanish subjects or obtain a special royal permit. The process was often complicated. People came up with various ploys to get around the difficulties posed by the prohibitions. The most frequent was to send goods in the name of Spanish traders. To give one example, in the autumn of 1570, Lorenzo del Rosso appealed against the Casa de la Contratación, which had sequestered two bars of silver that he had received in exchange for five friezes earmarked for the New World. The Florentine was demanding the return of the metal, arguing that the sale of the cloth had been finalised in Seville and not in the Americas. Whereas the authorities held that since the price was double the going rate, the transaction had been completed in American territory. AGI, *Justicia*, 897, 5.

[45] On dyestuffs and cochineal in particular, see A. Orlandi, 'Zucchero e cocciniglia'.

[46] In today's weight, the balsam was just over 600 g.

[47] 'Since it was discovered in our Indies to be effective for wounds and other illnesses of the human body'. Acciaiuoli was tasked with bringing some of the balm to a few people who had been prescribed it by the doctor in Aragon. AGI, *Indiferente*, 422, L. 14, 10 December 1530, c. 151*r.*

[48] ASF, *Miscellanea*, 107, fascicolo 3, Florence-Seville, Matteo Botti to the Botti company, 25 November 1540, c. 35r.

[49] ASF, *Miscellanea*, 107, fascicolo 3, Florence-Seville, Matteo Botti to the Botti company, 25 Janaury 1541, c. 58r.

[50] ASF, *Miscellanea*, 107, fascicolo 5, Florence-Seville, Matteo Botti to Francesco Botti, 24 February 1548, c. 173v.

merchandise' for testing out.[51] We do not know if and when the brothers sent it to Tuscany. What we do know is that 'try' and 'test' were words that our merchants repeated ad nauseam. Expressions that embody their curiosity and appetite for risk.

5.2.2 An Example of Intercultural Exchange: Elegant Cloth

The Botti family's trade activity lends itself to drawing out a further aspect of our reflections overall. Their work in the exchange of goods underpinned the spread of beauty and taste. Subtle but important mechanisms that left their mark on local society and influenced the economic processes themselves.

Interacting with distant peoples and contexts, and so with different customs, habits and tastes, had a beneficial effect on intercultural trade and hence positive cross-fertilisation that could transmit the existential and aesthetic models that emerged from the quality and type of products. It goes without saying that the Botti propagated the taste and 'design thinking' of Renaissance Florence through their trade activity.

It was easy enough to do in Europe at the time, which was captivated by an almost irresistible love for luxury, to the point that every aspect of everyday life acquired highly specific meaning and symbolic value. Rooms were decorated with Flemish tapestries, Cordova leather panels, painted chests and gilded chair backs. Dining tables were set with broad-rimmed bowls, platters for carved meat and little plates for napkins. And garments embellished with silk and jewels, shirts decorated with black silk collars and *piombini* of white twist and stockings tied with shiny black and red ribbons were worn almost every day. The customs of this period became increasingly refined and the appetite for dazzling display intensified in every context. In the account books, the entries that the merchants made for 'day-to-day personal expenses' became increasingly common, and examination of individual purchases reveals a greater number of valuables. The repeated prohibitions laid down by the systematically evaded sumptuary laws were of little use.

The most direct symbol of social standing was clothing. Use of expensive woollen cloth and cloth of silk and gold took on the function, more than anything else, of a status symbol. It was therefore no coincidence that the Botti paid particular attention to these goods, which were clearly defined in terms of taste and style, and even turned their hand to manufacturing them.

[51] ASF, *Miscellanea*, 107, fascicolo 5, Florence-Seville, Matteo Botti to Iacopo Botti, 10 December 1547, c. 149v. We are unable to say whether the wool reported by Matteo was from sheep (possibly introduced by the Europeans into the New World) or the native vicuña or llama. J. Clutton-Brock, *A Natural History of Domesticated Mammals*, Cambridge University Press, Cambridge 1987, pp. 121–129; R.M. Nowak, *Walker's Mammals of the Word*, The Johns Hopkins University Press, Baltimore-London 1991, pp. 1353–1357.

The cloths produced by the Florentine Wool Guild were highly varied, including old and new types or, to cite Francesco Ammannati, 'revisitations of old types':[52] cloth from San Martino[53] and Garbo[54] and for the use of Perpignan,[55] twills,[56] *stametti,*[57] *accordellati,*[58] camlets, *rovesci*[59] and friezes. The *sopramani*[60] were of higher quality, in contrast to the *corsivi,*[61] which were ordinary and of less value. The San Martino and Garbo cloth was of good quality. The *rovesci*, *accordellati*, *stametti* and *perpignani* were more common fabrics. Twill was a thin, light fabric that could also be made in a heavy version, while camel-hair *cammellotto* was little suited to the Andalusian market.[62]

Stametti, twills and *perpignani* were used in various ways. Reading about the different ways of using these types of cloth in so many letters reveals our merchants' deep knowledge of local production. The former, Matteo wrote, were good for

[52] F. Ammannati, *Per filo e per segno*, pp. 79–80. The history of the Florentine Wool Guild between the fourteenth and sixteenth centuries has been widely studied. Besides Francesco Ammannati's updated volume, see F. Franceschi, *Oltre il «Tumulto». I lavoratori fiorentini dell'Arte della Lana fra Tre e Quattrocento*, Olschki, Florence 1993; R.A. Goldthwaite, *L'economia della Firenze rinascimentale*, pp. 365–466; H. Hoshino, *Industria tessile e commercio internazionale nella Firenze del tardo Medioevo*, eds. F. Franceschi and S. Tognetti, Olschki, Florence 2001; H. Hoshino, *L'Arte della lana in Firenze nel basso Medioevo. Il commercio della lana e il mercato dei panni fiorentini nei secoli XIII-XV*, Olschki, Florence 1980; H. Hoshino, *L'industria laniera fiorentina dal Basso Medioevo all'Età Modera: abbozzo storico dei secoli XIII-XVII*, Rome 1978. For a more general reading, see F. Franceschi, 'Woollen Luxury Cloth in Late Medieval Italy', in *Europe's Rich Fabric. The Consumption, Commercialisation, and Production of Luxury Textiles in Italy, the Low Countries and Neighbouring Territories (Fourteenth-Sixteenth Centuries)*, eds. B. Lambert, K.A. Wilson, Ashgate, Farnham-Burlington 2016, pp. 181–204; J.H. Munro, 'The Rise, Expansion, and Decline of the Italian Wool-Based Cloth Industries, 1100–1730: A Study in International Competition, Transaction Costs, and Comparative Advantage', *Studies in Medieval and Renaissance History*, 9, 2012, pp. 45–207, 114–20.

[53] Fabric made with the finest English wool. H. Hosino, *L'industria laniera*, p. 3.

[54] This was the term for fabrics produced using Mediterranean wool. H. Hosino, *L'industria laniera*, p. 3.

[55] A light fabric originally from Southern France and Catalan-Aragonese Spain. F. Ammannati, *Per filo e per segno*, p. 79.

[56] A fabric with remote origins that became a heavy, fine fabric in the sixteenth century. F. Ammannati, *Per filo e per segno*, p. 79.

[57] A fabric made using fine carded wool. *Ibid.*

[58] A fabric that derived from a type made in Lucca in the early fourteenth century. It was usually made with Castilian wool. H. Hoshino, *L'Arte della Lana*, p. 125.

[59] 'A kind of wool cloth with the long hair on the reverse.' N. Tommaseo, E. Bellini, *Dizionario della lingua italiana scritta e parlata,* Rizzoli Editore, Milan 1977.

[60] Made using a wool from Castile called 'lana sopramano'. H. Hoshino, 'Alcuni aspetti del commercio dei panni fiorentini nell'Impero Ottomano ai primi del '500', in *Industria tessile e commercio internazionale nella Firenze del Tardo Medioevo*, Olschki, Florence 2001, pp. 125–135, p. 133.

[61] A low-quality fabric. H. Hosino, *L'industria laniera*, p. 6.

[62] ASF, *Libri di commercio*, 711, Florence-Cádiz, Matteo Botti to Iacopo Botti (personal), 14 December 1524, c. 32v.

summer stockings,[63] but he preferred twill. In an exchange with his brother Iacopo, who was doubtful, he advised consulting with a *calzettaro* (stocking maker), but he was convinced that, in the end, when the Andalusian 'gentlemen' tried it they would give up 'the *stametti*, because of its different vigour, breadth and goodness' (see Footnote 63).

Our merchants traded Florentine woollen cloth in both the East and the West. Sales in both directions were closed for the most part in-house, less frequently on commission and even more rarely jointly. Matteo worried from Florence about the well-packed fabrics arriving at the different market outlets. To get an idea of the growth of their trade activity, in 1524, they traded 96 *pezze* of cloth, in 1526, 161 and in 1531 almost 300. To find a market for them, routes were created that went from Florence to Constantinople and Pera in the east, Lisbon in the west and Antwerp in the north, passing through the Andalusian, Castilian and Moroccan markets. All of this without neglecting the Italian centres, from the biggest markets like Genoa, Pisa, Ancona, Rome and Naples to the smaller ones such as Volterra and Pescia.

The Levant had been the most thriving market since the 1520s.[64] In 1524, more than 70% of the textiles went to Pera and in 1527 that percentage went up to 85%. When the eastern markets became less receptive, the Botti's attention turned, almost automatically, to the west, specifically southern Spain. On the other hand, when the capacity for absorption in Constantinople, Pera and Adrianople increased, fewer shipments were sent to Andalusia. In any case, Iacopo and Giovanbattista also sent Florentine cloths as needed to Barbary in exchange for wool and to Lisbon for silver.

In the 1530s, when the sultan was trying to stem the haemorrhaging of gold, Florentine interests in the East dimmed.[65] Matteo also started to devote more attention to the Northern European textile trade. The increasing quantity of those fabrics can be partly attributed to the problems caused by the siege of 1529, as well as the gradual rise of English and Netherlandish woollen piece goods. Both had their weight. On the other hand, the Wool Guild was also going through a difficult patch between 1530 and 1535, freeing up market quotas in favour of more common but less expensive products.[66] And then there was a marked upturn starting in 1540.[67] In the meantime, there was a type of fabric that was drawing all the wool producers' attention: the new frieze, which provided work for at least 30 years.[68] Initially

[63] ASF, *Libri di commercio*, 711, Florence-Cádiz, Matteo Botti to Iacopo and Giovanbattista Botti, 28 October 1525, c. 70v.

[64] On the capacity for absorption of eastern markets in the first decades of the sixteenth century, also see B. Dini, 'Aspetti del commercio'; H. Hoshino, 'Alcuni Aspetti del commercio dei panni'.

[65] A. Orlandi, 'Oro e monete'.

[66] The siege forced Florentines to produce less woollen cloth, but the 23,000 pieces of 'garbi' reported in the customs logs in Ragusa (Dubrovnik) in 1531 show that textile production was still thriving. H. Hosino, *L'industria laniera*, p. 4.

[67] As noted above, it reached its apex between 1550 and 1580. H. Hosino, *L'industria laniera*, p. 4–5.

[68] The examined documents stop at 1566. But it is highly probable that it continued to be produced until 1580.

developed as a relatively common cloth, it became lighter, more sophisticated, extremely fine and in high demand in the sixteenth century.[69] Thanks to this cloth, the rustle of shuttles and flapping of beaters could still be heard along the streets of sixteenth-century Florence.

In 1541, Matteo wrote: 'a lot of it is going from here to Castile and it seems to me that they really love it. What is certain is that according to the women there is nothing better. Today, all the men are using it for habits, cloaks and stockings'.[70] In short, it was a versatile fabric and this is how it was also seen by the Florentines, both men and women. Moreover, according to the Eldest it was perfect for making cloaks in the Spanish style[71] and was becoming a necessity in warmer regions.[72] If these were the ways it could be used, knowing this helped avoid mistakes like that of the Andalusian gentlemen who tried to use frieze to make stockings.[73] To 'enjoy them', Botti added, 'they need to be made wide and comfortable',[74] but he was still convinced that the most suitable fabric was twill.

Matteo bought the best pieces of cloth in Florence from skilled woolmakerss, the 'fine',[75] '*cappate*' ones 'of Spanish wool and not mixed with *matricina* (local wool) like people do today',[76] finished with silk tassels of an intense black with not so much as a hint of red.[77] Very rarely, they were the white ones that were mostly used for the 'stockings of Grand Masters' and garments for nuns and friars.[78] It yielded high profits ranging from 33% to 45%, which is why the Botti devoted ever greater amounts of attention to it.

---

[69] F. Ammannati, *Per filo e per segno*, p. 79; P. Chorley, 'Rascie and the Florentine Cloth Industry During the Sixteenth Century', *The Journal of European Economic History*, XXXII, 3, 2003, pp. 487–527; H. Hoshino, *L'industria laniera*, p. 4.

[70] ASF, *Miscellanea*, 107, fascicolo 3, Florence-Seville, Matteo Botti to the Botti company, 1 August 1541, c. 112v.

[71] ASF, *Miscellanea*, 107, fascicolo 3, Florence-Seville, Matteo Botti to Giovanbattista Botti, 9 January 1542, c. 151r.

[72] ASF, *Miscellanea*, 107, fascicolo 3, Florence-Seville, Matteo Botti to Giovanbattista Botti, 16 September 1541, c. 120r.

[73] ASF, *Miscellanea*, 107, fascicolo 3, Florence-Seville, Matteo Botti to Giovanbattista Botti, 9 January 1542, c. 151r.

[74] ASF, *Libri di commercio*, 711, Florence-Cádiz, Matteo Botti to the Botti company, 18 March 1527, c. 138r.

[75] Making it using 'thin yarn is the important thing'. ASF, *Miscellanea*, 107, fascicolo 5, Florence-Cádiz, Matteo Botti to the Botti and Peri company, 28 January 1548, c. 165r.

[76] ASF, *Libri di commercio*, 715, Lyon-Valladolid, Giovanbattista Botti to Carlo Martelli, 15 April 1561, c. 89v.

[77] ASF, *Libri di commercio*, 715, Lyon-Florence, Giovanbattista Botti to Vincenzo Manovelli, 29 December 1559, c. 39v. Frieze usually measured 3 *braccia* (1.74 m) wide by 59 (34.22 m) long. On just one occasion, an order was made for pieces of cloth one *braccio* wider than usual, for an additional cost of 3 *scudi* each. This is the arithmetic mean worked out based on the measurements in the documents.

[78] ASF, *Miscellanea*, 107, fascicolo 4, Florence-Seville, Matteo Botti to the Botti company, 2 January 1545, c. 59v.

The trading reached its apex in the decade between 1560 and 1570. This was the period during which the shop of Vincenzo Manovelli, Elisabetta's son, was opened. In order to help his nephew, Giovanbattista, in Lyon, started ordering increasingly large quantities, starting in August 1559. Two hundred fourteen pieces arrived between 1561 and 1563.[79] From that point forward, our merchants mainly supplied the family shop, which almost seemed specialised in this type of good. The possibility of turning to Vincenzo's shop not only made it possible to trade the best pieces of cloth but also to fetch better prices than the current ones.[80] The outlets for frieze were numerous and diverse: 'all of Spain appreciates it and here its being sent every day to places where it hadn't been going before … and Rome, Naples, Messina and Palermo are consuming a lot of it, France, too.'[81] The Botti, however, had a clear preference for the Spanish markets and wealthy Castilian gentlemen, especially Andalusian. Seville and Valladolid were the most thriving markets where this cloth was making inroads. For that matter, it was years before Spanish manufacturers were able to produce a fabric that could complete with that of Florence. In May 1548, Matteo wrote: 'they are starting to make it over there and although for now they are not making it like ours, they will in time'.[82]

5.2.3 *The Magnificence of Silks*

Brocades, damasks, silks embellished with gold and silver, velvets and taffetas were used with increasing frequency. This drove, starting in the mid fifteenth century, the proliferation of silk and gold-beater's workshops, which achieved a high level of professionalism in the sixteenth century.[83] The Italian textile centres that had long linked their activity to the Wool Guild, began to concentrate more intensely on silk starting in the mid sixteenth century. As Ruggero Romano observed, 'All Italy

[79] ASF, *Libri di commercio*, 724, 725.

[80] ASF, *Libri di commercio*, 716, Florence-Valladolid, Giovanbattista Botti to the Martelli company, 23 November 1562, c. 20r.

[81] ASF, *Miscellanea*, 107, fascicolo 5, Florence-Seville, Matteo Botti to Iacopo Botti, 14 November 1547, c. 135v.

[82] ASF, *Miscellanea*, 107, fascicolo 5, Florence-Cádiz, Matteo Botti to Iacopo Botti (personal), 8 May 1548, c. 197v.

[83] For an interpretation of the relationship between the Silk Guild and the city government, see F. Franceschi, 'Big Business for Firms and States: Silk Manufacturing in Renaissance Italy', *Business History Review* 94, 1 (2020), pp. 95–123.

seems to have become a civilisation of silk'.[84] And the number of people working in this industry increased significantly in Milan, Venice, Genoa and Florence.[85]

It had been a long process. In the fourteenth century, the Florentine silks that were being traded on the European market were of good quality, but could not stand up to comparison with the refined weaves made in the East that arrived in Italian cities from Constantinople. In the early fifteenth century, the situation was already changing. According to the account of someone who had accompanied the diplomatic mission of Henry III of Castile to the court of Tamerlane, Florentine products were circulating in Samarkand.[86] And it all crescendoed from there. In 1422, another Florentine delegation visited the sultan of Egypt, bringing as gifts not only 25 lengths of wool but also fine silks. The decision to offer textiles to someone who already had a long tradition in that industry was a sign of awareness of the high quality of their own production. Another diplomatic trip was organised in 1488: for this mission, the gifts included not cloth of silk and gold only but also inlaid wood, bone and ivory.[87] Products that were made with a higher level of skill and a keener sense of taste in Florence.

To conclude, as we noted above, Bonsignore Bonsignori wrote in 1492 that Florentine silks were more beautiful than the ones from Bursa.[88]

---

[84] R. Romano, 'La storia economica. Dal secolo XIV al Settecento', in *Storia d'Italia. Dalla caduta dell'Impero romano al secolo XVIII*, eds. R. Romano, C. Vivanti, Giulio Einaudi editore, Turin 1974, 6 vols., II, pp. 1813–1934, p. 1186–1187. On this theme more generally, see *La seta in Europa. Secc. XIII-XX, Atti della Ventiquattresima Settimana di studi dell'Istituto Internazionale di Storia Economica «F. Datini» di Prato (Prato, 4–9 maggio 1992)*, ed. S. Cavaciocchi, Istituto Internazionale di Storia Economica "F. Datini" Prato, Le Monnier, Florence 1993, in particular B. Dini, 'L'industria serica in Italia', in *La seta in Europa*, pp. 108–121*; La seta in Italia dal Medioevo al Seicento. Dal baco al drappo*, eds. L. Molà, R.C. Mueller, C. Zanier, Marsilio, Venice 2000; L. Molà, 'A Luxury Industry: The Production of Italian Silks 1400–1600', in *Europe's Rich Fabric*, pp. 205–234. Also see F. Franceschi, 'Big Business' and S. Tognetti, 'I drappi di seta', in *Il Rinascimento italiano e l'Europa. Vol. 4: Commercio e cultura mercantile*, eds. F. Franceschi, R.A. Goldthwaite, R.C. Mueller, Fondazione Cassamarca, Treviso-Vicenza 2007, pp. 143–170.

[85] Among the numerous studies concentrated on specific contexts, we will cite F. Edler De Roover, *L'arte della seta a Firenze nei secoli XIV e XV*, Olschki, Florence 1999; P. Massa, *La "Fabbrica" dei velluti genovesi. Da Genova a Zoagli*, Scheiwiller, Milan 1981; P. Massa, *Un'impresa serica genovese della prima del Cinquecento*, Giuffrè, Milan 1974; L. Molà, *The Silk Industry in Renaissance Venice*, The Johns Hopkins University Press, Baltimore-London 2000; S. Tognetti, *Un'industria di lusso*. On Bolognese voile, see A. Orlandi, 'Impalpabili e trasparenti: i veli bolognesi nella documentazione datiniana', in *Il velo in area mediterranea fra storia e simbolo*. Tardo Medioevo-prima Età moderna, eds. M.G. Muzzarelli, M.G. Nico Ottaviani, G. Zarri, il Mulino, Bologna 2014, pp. 307–324.

[86] D. Catellacci, 'Diario di Felice Brancacci, ambasciatore con Carlo Federighi al Cairo per il Comune di Firenze (1422)', *Archivio storico italiano*, S. IV, VIII, 1881, pp. 157–188.

[87] These objects, described as 'Damascene', were imitations of objects that had been typical, which is not to say exclusive, in those regions in the past.

[88] G. Nigro, M. Spallanzani, 'Intrecci mediterranei tra economia e arte', in *Intrecci Mediterranei. Il tessuto come dizionario di rapporti economici, culturali e sociali*, Museo del Tessuto, Prato 2006, pp. 16–41; A. Orlandi, 'Oro e monete da Costantinopoli'.

In the sixteenth century, silk and gold thread was woven to create the most elegant and expensive silks on the market. Using the best raw materials, like silk from Almeria and Granada, and choosing the most expert artisans ensured excellent results. The production process was complex and required experience and skill. Working the loom was extremely tricky, but in the end warp and weft were woven into damasks, brocades and velvets that were so lavish and splendid as to justify the greatest care. As Matteo wrote about one valuable brocade, 'keep it far from humidity and from all odours, good or bad. Handle it carefully so that it is not ruined.'[89]

The silks were shipped everywhere: in the East, to Constantinople, Adrianople and Bursa; in the West, to southern Italy, the Iberian Peninsula, Flanders, England and Germany. In the 1530s, the eastern markets started to become saturated, so the Botti family turned its attention to those in Spain, which, thanks to the arrival of American silver were seeing the demand for luxury goods soar. Our merchants were well aware of this and, as early as 1524, started experimenting with new hues, expanding the traditional palette of reds, blacks, greys and yellows to include two unusual colours: 'true' crimson and a 'rich, beautiful' Spanish green.[90] 'I think they will be a success because they are cheerful like you say' (see Footnote 90), the Eldest observed, referring to the hues best suited to Andalusian taste.[91]

With the same spirit that had distinguished the brothers since the beginning, they tried to find a market for it in the New World as well: red damasks, lightweight silks, taffeta for stockings, colourful satins and cloth of gold and of silver. As early as 1525, Iacopo was writing to Florence for information 'to give the friend who trades in India and the kinds of cloth he would like and the prices he wants to pay'[92] and sometime later he was thinking about trying brocatelles and velvets in the Americas.

In 1531, when they opened the Silk Guild workshop, Matteo consulted with his brothers in order to orient its production to Spanish tastes: 'tell us the ones you want and if they need to be cloths or brocades with fur or with loops or gold tabby or

[89] ASF, *Miscellanea*, 107, fascicolo 3, Florence-Seville, Matteo and Simoni Botti to the Botti company, 25 November 1540, c. 34v.

[90] ASF, *Libri di commercio*, 711, Florence-Cádiz, Matteo Botti to Iacopo Botti (personal), 15 October 1524, c. 21v.

[91] B. Dini, 'L'industria serica in Italia', in *La seta in Europa*, pp. 91–123, p. 116.

[92] This is the full passage: 'I saw the note you sent me for supplying the friend who trades in India and the kinds of silks he would like and the prices he wants to pay. To which I would say that if he is happy with ordinary silks like the ones I recently sent you we could make him happy as to the price'. ('Ho visto la nota mi mandi per fornire l'amicho che tratta in 'Ndia e la sorte drappina che lui vorrebbe e li pregi che lui vole dare. A che ti dicho che quando si contentassi di drappi ordinari chome di quella sorta buona mandatoti utimamente che mi pare pure che ne alleghi per paragone qualchuno, chome tu say, far conto ancora tu a' pregi già datoti ci salveremo benissimo.') ASF, *Libri di commercio*, 711, Florence-Cádiz, Matteo Botti to Iacopo Botti (personal), 20 January 1525, c. 48r.

thread or whatever they need to be so that we can do it for you'.[93] When he later sent silks made 'in our workshop', he did so with ill-disguised pride.[94]

At this point, it was Iacopo's turn to try to master the trade. It was not always easy to satisfy Andalusian gentlemen. The *hidalgo* chose fabric with care, asked for its price and promised to pay at some later time, leaving the seller with a fair bit of anxiety. For that matter, it was clear that those fabrics could only have a clientele of high lineage:[95] nobles and very wealthy ecclesiastics. And so, when the news arrived of Charles V's wedding in Seville, the correspondence was full of apprehension: 'sell them for as much profit as possible, which we don't think will be difficult since everything will sell out with the arrival of the emperor and his wedding'.[96]

Magnificence was achieved right on the shores of Guadalquivir, thanks to the prelates of the great Christian cathedral. In July 1541, the Botti ordered a white damask for them in Florence,[97] the pattern for which had been chosen in Seville. When the order arrived in Tuscany, the silk weavers took out 'a few big mistakes';[98] their professionalism made them sensitive to the even the smallest technical issues and, most importantly, changing tastes. It is no coincidence that they were always up to date about the best silks for religious vestments. In the middle of the sixteenth century, for example, fashionable silks included 'cloth of gold with the patterns they want, silks for churches with a pattern that changes like gold does' and with 'artichoke flowers', the thistle motif.[99]

Three weavers were employed in Florence, and they worked on the order for five months. Matteo, as promised, paid 30 or 40 *scudi* a week and received three pieces

---

[93] ASF, *Libri di commercio*, 712, Florence-Cádiz, Matteo Botti to Iacopo and Giovanbattista Botti, 15 July 1531, c. 129v.

[94] ASF, *Libri di commercio*, 721, Florence-Cádiz, Francesco Botti to the Botti company, 29 October 1533, c. 176v.

[95] A. Manikowski, *'Il secolo della seta. Conseguenza del boom della seta nel Seicento per le trasformazioni sociali e politiche in Europa', in La seta in Europa*, pp. 839–853, p. 852; A.M. Piuz, 'La soie, le luxe et le puovoir dans les doctrines françaises (XVIe-XVIIe s.)', in *La seta in Europa*, pp. 817–837, p. 818.

[96] '[I]ngegniatevi cavarci di cotesty con più profitto possete, la qualcosa stimiamo che non v'abbi a manchare, massime venendo lo 'Nperadore.' ASF, *Libri di commercio*, 711, Florence-Cádiz, Matteo Botti to Iacopo and Giovanbattista Botti, 30 December 1525, c. 80v.

[97] This fabric 'is usually made in two ways: poor, half covered with gold, and rich, entirely covered with gold. Since it is for such an important church, we will have the rich kind made by a friend who already made one for the bishop of Verona that cost 3 scudi per *braccio*. And since we need to provide something that will last for a long time and for wealthy people, we will have it made as if it were for us'. ('si costuma fare di quello povero a oro mezo coperto e di quello a oro tutto coperto, perché a servire a tanta grande chiesta lo fareno fare tutto ricco a uno amico che llo fe' a' dì passatj per il Veschovo di Verona quale costò a scudi iii il braccio et perché à servire a cosa che à durare anni domini e per persone riche fare no come vorremo fare per noj') ASF, *Miscellanea*, 107, fascicolo 3, Florence-Seville, Matteo Botti to Iacopo and Giovanbattista Botti, 14 June 1541, c. 95r.

[98] ASF, *Miscellanea*, 107, fascicolo 3, Florence-Seville, Matteo Botti to the Botti company, 14 July 1541, c. 104v.

[99] A. Orlandi, 'Note su affari e devozione nei documenti di alcuni mercanti fiorentini (1450–1550)', *Storia Economica*, 3, 13, 2010, pp. 319–344, p. 326.

of cloth in November that were 153.5 *braccia* in length.[100] The damask was about 2.5 ducats for one *braccio*, an excellent price since similar weaves had cost more than 3 ducats. For the payment of the total, almost 408 ducats, a bill of exchange was issued with a deadline of 30 days after sight, at an exchange rate of 370 maravedís per ducat.

The Andalusian canons were so satisfied that two months later they sent a new order to Tuscany for cloth of silk and gold, valued at around 1500 ducats. The cost was particularly high, but, as the Eldest wrote, after the prelates had seen the vestments they would be convinced 'that their local supply is nothing [...] and it will seem to them they've never had anything so rich.'[101] A hundred ducats worth of silks was added to these shipments, sent as a sample to the vicar of the archbishopric of Seville, a respected client and not to be neglected since the churches under him were obliged to adhere to his choices. As noted, besides the ecclesiastics, there were often also the dukes of Medina Sidonia.

Clients from Valladolid started to arrive in the middle of the 1540s. The Castilian city was enjoying a period of major growth at the time. A sizeable demographic increase and the consequential building expansion were giving it a monumental appearance. Economically, the tertiary sector was advanced and flourishing.[102] Merchants, bankers, notaries and courtiers were the backbone of its prosperity.[103] In this case as well, wealth was on full display. Noblemen, ladies and the wealthy middle class flaunted jewels, brocade clothing embellished with costly satins, velvets and taffetas.

As we know, Matteo had a workshop in Florence with a gold beater, Bartolomeo Carnesecchi. In September 1542, he sent two crates of cloth of silk and gold to the Botti and Bellotti company in Valladolid: they were 'the crème de la crème'.[104] It was the beginning of a 'joint silks venture', and the Eldest committed to sending two or three crates of assorted silks and four to six pieces of gold cloth for every fair. In truth, the Castilian company was not convinced of the advisability of trading in cloth of silk and gold, but the Eldest responded to this uncertainty: 'we don't want to disappoint a friend who wants to test the region and is the man who is ahead of everyone else in trading this type of cloth'.[105] And in the end, there turned out to be a good market for those fabrics in Valladolid. Whenever they were unable to sell them in Cádiz, Seville and environs, Lisbon was a good alternative.[106]

---

[100] The Florentine *braccio* was equal to 0.583 metres. A. Martini, *Manuale*, p. 206.

[101] A. Orlandi, 'Note', p. 326.

[102] B. Bennassar, *Valladolid au siècle d'or*, p. 141.

[103] Ibid, p. 219.

[104] ASF, *Miscellanea*, 107, fascicolo 3, Florence-Valladolid, Matteo Botti to the Botti and Bellotti company, 4 December 1542, c. 208v.

[105] ASF, *Miscellanea*, 107, fascicolo 3, Florence-Valladolid, Matteo Botti to the Botti and Bellotti company, 17 February 1543, c. 234r.

[106] ASF, *Libri di commercio*, 711, Florence-Cádiz, Matteo Botti to Iacopo Botti (personal), 9 September 1525, c. 61r.

Their trade on the non-Iberian markets was handled directly from Florence.[107] In 1545, an opportunity presented itself in Lyon: the wedding of an illegitimate daughter of Charles V and an Orleans, which could not be missed.[108] Matteo sprang into action, drawing on the support of the Panciatichi.

Even the northern markets benefited. The Botti family's correspondents in London and Antwerp, the Guicciardini and Vernacci and, later, the Gondi and the Giacomini, were able to find a market for silks in Flanders, the Netherlands and England.

The silks traded by the Botti were almost all made in Florence, in part because Matteo did not like the ones from Lucca, which he found 'full of water, with little silk and in unappealing hues'.[109]

5.2.4 A Doll Dressed in Silk

In 1558, an elegant dress was made for a doll out of fine satin by one of the most important Florentine silk weavers. It might be the most telling example of this love for beauty and luxury. Iacopo had asked for one from his brother Simone, wanting to give it as a present to his youngest daughter, Ginevra. The toy was the handiwork of a group of specialized artisans. Simone chose the best, guided by his own artistic sensibilities and the close contacts his family had, as we have seen, with some of the greatest artists of the time. The first artisan involved was the carpenter Antonio Particini, who the family knew through Vasari, who called him a 'rare master wood carver' who 'merits the highest praise'.[110] We know that this praise was founded on direct knowledge, since the architect from Arezzo noted in his diary on 1 November 1534 that the carver had commissioned a portrait from him in exchange for some wooden items.[111] We have multiple sources for his activity, as he also worked on the San Niccolò gate when the duke was at war with Siena and determined to strengthen the city's gates. For that project, he was chosen along with Benvenuto Cellini to work on Porta al Prato and Porticciuola d'Arno.[112] He is also referred to as among those who presented the duke with a project for the Salone dei Cinquecento in

---

[107] A important example was Lyon where, in the sixteenth century, 80% of imported silks came from Italy. See A.M. Puiz, 'La soie, le luxe et le pouvoir', p. 818.

[108] ASF, *Miscellanea*, 107, fascicolo 4, Florence-Valladolid, Matteo Botti to Giovanbattista and Francesco Botti, 20 April 1545, c. 84v. The wedding was called off, but even just the anticipation of it was a boon for the sale of silks.

[109] ASF, *Libri di commercio*, 721, Pisa-Cádiz, Francesco Botti to Lorenzo Grazia, 28 May 1534, c. 209v. On silk production in Lucca, see I. del Punta, M.L. Rosati, *Lucca una città di seta*.

[110] C.L. Ragghianti, *Critica d'arte*, volume 20, Vallecchi, Florence 1977, p. 71.

[111] G. Vasari, *Ricordanze*, c. 6v. (www.memofonte.it accessed 24 June 2024).

[112] *Le opere di Benvenuto Cellini arricchite di note ed illustrazioni*, introduction by Francesco Tassi, Società Editrice Fiorentina, Florence 1843, p. 293, available on Google Books.

Palazzo Vecchio.[113] Antonio was not successful on this occasion, but the prestige of both task and client shows that he could compete at the highest level. Antonio Particini was paid the considerable sum of 18 lire and 10 soldi to carve the doll's body. We do not know whether the doll had jointed limbs but, judging by the sum paid, it is likely that it did.

The finely carved figure was then painted by a certain 'Gian Iacopo', who was paid 2 lire for the work. This was probably Gian Iacopo Mattoncini da Castrocaro, who was Lorenzo di Credi's student and had inherited his workshop.[114] Mattoncini never developed a clear artistic personality of his own and was heavily influenced by Credi. But he was in any case a well-known artist, and Simone paid him to paint the doll's wooden parts using 'the colour of flesh'. Although it was a simple task, a true painter, who had been mentioned by Vasari and influenced by Perugino and Leonardo, had been nevertheless wanted for the job. We do not know with certainty, but it is likely that Gian Iacopo also designed the doll's features, which we like to imagine resembled those of Caterina Sforza, as painted by Lorenzo di Credi in the *Lady of the Jasmine*.

Once made, the doll needed to be dressed. The tailor modelled the doll's clothing on the rich wardrobe of the elegant Eleonora of Toledo, who was a trend setter in sixteenth-century Florence. A 'grammar of dressing' was emerging in sixteenth century Italy, offering a theory of fashion and the clothed body that attributed clothing with an important role in economic, political and cultural change.[115]

The duchess's style was based on the petticoat-surcoat combination,[116] and this was the outfit chosen for the pretty doll. One and a quarter *braccia* of yellow satin was needed for the petticoat and one and two-thirds *braccia* of green damask for the surcoat.

---

[113] As we read in a notebook: 'When Duke Cosimo I decided to the great hall in Palazzo Vecchio built on designs by Giorgio Vasari, the piecework list drawn up on 12 April 1563 was given to four master wood carvers: Batista di Baccio Botticelli […] Antonio Particini […], Antonio Crocini […], Filippo di Baccio d'Agnolo, all four of them woodworkers and master wood carvers.' ('Avendo pensato il Duca Cosimo Primo a fare il Salon grande di Palazzo Vecchio col. disegno di Giorgio Vasari, fu dato la listra del cottimo del dì 12 Aprile 1563 a quattro maestri di legname che furono Batista di Baccio Botticelli […] Antonio Particini […], Antonio Crocini […], Filippo di Baccio d'Agnolo, tutti e quattro legnaiuoli e maestri d'intaglio') ASF, *Minute di lettere e Registri*, 14,028, inserto 1, April 1563. On the Salone dei Cinquecento, see U. Muccini, *Il Salone dei Cinquecento in Palazzo Vecchio*, Le Lettere, Florence 1990, p. 77.

[114] I would like to thank my friend and colleague Andrea del Grosso who helped me to identify the doll's painter. Without his expertise, Gian Iacopo would have remained an unknown decorator. G. Vasari, *Le vite dei più eccellenti pittori*, cit., p. 389, consultable at www.liberliber.it.

[115] E. Paulicelli, 'Geografia del vestire tra Vecchio e nuovo mondo di Cesare Vecellio', in *Moda e moderno. Dal Medioevo al Rinascimento*, Meltemi, Rome 2006, pp. 129–153, pp. 132–133, p. 135; also see E. Paulicelli, *Writing Fashion in Early Modern Italy. From Sprezzatura to Satire*, Ashgate, Burlington 2014.

[116] R. Orsi Landini, 'Lo stile di Eleonora', in R. Orsi Landini, B. Niccoli, *Moda a Firenze, 1540–1580. Lo stile di Eleonora di Toledo e la sua influenza*, Pagliai Polistampa, Florence 2005, pp. 23–45, p. 23.

According to women's fashion at the time, the surcoat needed to be generous, rich, well decorated and preferably in a heavy fabric,[117] all features included by the tailor. To create a play of light and colour, the yellow petticoat was finished off at the hem with green velvet and the green surcoat with white velvet. The decorative combination of silk and velvet, fabrics with different sheens, was very common.[118] To finish off this colour contrast, pieces of white and green fringe were purchased for additional decoration.[119] These fabrics cost 28 lire, almost 40% of the total expenditure (Fig. 5.2).

The surcoat was decorated with 28 buttons embellished with piping,[120] while *vernice di seta* and silk twist (double threads of silk or precious metal) were used to decorate the bands along the neck line, the bust, the lower hem and other parts of the petticoat and surcoat.[121] Volume was an important component of sixteenth-century costume, and 1 lira and 15 soldi were spent for the cloth and felt needed to support the hems and keep the petticoat and surcoat flared.

The cost and aesthetic value of women's clothing were the two factors that made it a luxury.[122] Alongside the tailor's skill in interpreting and innovating the most fashionable models, it was the beauty of the fabrics which counted, as well as the silk, silver and gold embellishments and the addition of pearls or precious stones. Their richness was the central feature of a fashion that was the fruit of both consumer taste and the skill of those who made it, artisan workshops which were by this point able to shape taste and fashion in even the most exclusive European courts (Fig. 5.3).[123]

Our doll's costume displayed many of these distinguishing characteristics. There was nothing accidental about the fact that the yellow satin used for the petticoat was

---

[117] R. Levi Pisetzky, *Il costume e la moda nella società italiana*, Giulio Einaudi editore, Turin 1978, pp. 208–209; R. Orsi Landini, 'I singoli capi di abbigliamento', in R. Orsi Landini, B. Niccoli, *Moda a Firenze*, pp. 77–170, p. 96.

[118] R. Orsi Landini, 'Lo stile di Eleonora', p. 28.

[119] Eleonora's role a trend setter is revealed by the fact that prior to the latter half of the sixteenth century her wardrobe did not include garments with colour contrasts, which made their first appearance precisely in the years in which our doll's clothing was made. R. Orsi Landini, 'Lo stile di Eleonora', p. 28.

[120] R. Orsi Landini, 'I singoli capi di abbigliamento', p. 111.

[121] R. Orsi Landini, 'I singoli capi di abbigliamento', p. 90.

[122] On how the symbolic value of clothing has changed over time, see C.M. Belfanti, *Civiltà della moda*, Il Mulino, Bologna 2008, pp. 12–45.

[123] E. Polidori Calamandrei, *Le vesti delle donne fiorentine nel Quattrocento*, Multigrafica Editrice, Rome 1973, p. 66. More generally on the subject of consumption models and the conception of luxury among Florentine merchants in the late Middle Ages and early modern period, see the work of Richard A. Goldthwaite. In particular, R.A. Goldthwaite, *Private Wealth in Renaissance Florence*; R.A. Goldthwaite, *Ricchezza e domanda*. An interesting example concerns the Lusitanian court. For the wedding of the infanta Maria, Florentine silks were purchased together with fabrics from Lucca and Venice. A. Jordan Gschwend, 'Sartorial Elegance at the Lisbon Court. Shopping for luxury fabrics in Florence, Lucca, and Venice', in *Textile and Fashion-Venice etc. Rintracciare Studiare Divulgare. Per Doretta Davanzo Poli*, ed. Paola Venturelli, Palermo University Press, Palermo 2023, pp. 205–214.

Fig. 5.2 Example of a surcoat and petticoat worn by Eleonora of Toledo. Agnolo Bronzino, *Portrait of Eleonora of Toledo and Francesco de' Medici* (c. 1549), Cincinnati Art Museum, Cincinnati

bought from Zanobi da Filicaia. His work was of the highest quality, and his silks were purchased for the duke's house. In 1567, he was paid 18 *scudi* for cloth for Isabella, Cosimo and Eleonora's third born and by then wife of Paolo Giordano Orsini and duchess of Bracciano.[124] Domenico della Luna, who supplied the green damask for the surcoat, was also from a family of well-known silk manufacturers.[125]

Our doll passed from the tailors into the hands of the Augustinian nuns of Santa Monica. Simone must have known them well; their convent was in Albergaccio, an area between the Carmine church and Via Serragli. The nuns' task required precision and patience. They were entrusted with finishing the figure, including the head, and with making the ruff, the white pleated collar which was to encircle the doll's neck.

The toy cost 70 lire and 15 soldi, not including the cost of packing it up and shipping it to Spain. It was quite a sum, equal, for the purpose of comparison, to more than 4 months' wages earned by Giovanni Vespucci (Amerigo's nephew), who was

[124] ASF, *Mediceo del Principato*, 221, Florence-*, Tommaso di Iacopo de' Medici to Giovanbattista de' Servi, 2 February 1567, c. 29r.

[125] F. Edler De Roover, *L'arte della seta a Firenze*, pp. 19–20.

Fig. 5.3 Little girl with a sixteenth-century doll, although different from the Florentine one. Daniël van den Queborn, *Luise Juliane von Oranien-Nassau* (c. 1582), Siegerlandmuseum, Siegen

a royal pilot in Seville at the time.[126] The doll was clearly a luxury object that the daughters of wealthy Sevillian gentlemen would have yearned for.

5.2.5 Marketing Experiments

The doll is an interesting example that reveals a desire to transmit a taste for beauty, in part to strengthen commercial trade. There are other examples in the Botti papers that feature similar strategies, which we might even describe as marketing.

This was the case for a dress that was sent to Maddalena Botti, the beloved first-born of Iacopo, who wrote to Matteo: 'your niece has received everything you sent and we were pleased to see the new fashion from over there, which wasn't around in my time and is very different'.

The dress had been stitched with pleats that started below the bosom, a style that made 'the woman seem pregnant even not being so'. Neither Iacopo nor his wife liked the shape. It was not in fashion in Seville. The little girl's mother wanted to alter the dress rather than reject it, adapting it to the local style. But Iacopo, who felt the tie with his country and was most importantly a talented merchant, chose a

[126] Vespucci's annual salary was 10,000 maravedís, equal to 27 ducats. C. Varela, *Colombo*, p. 90.

different path. The dress was unusual, and he wanted to make it become fashionable in Seville as well! It would become an object of desire, like every luxury good. And so he asked his brother Matteo to have one or two works made for him 'in the Flemish style', depicting the city's churches, palazzos of the important families, even 'that big dome', streets and bridges dotted with more women than men, all of the former 'wearing what is fashionable there'. Iacopo suggested in particular the church of Santa Trinita, the bridge of the same name with the palazzos of the Berti and the Spini, just like the fresco by Van der Straet in the museum of Palazzo Vecchio (Fig. 5.4).[127]

The plan was to attach the paintings to a wooden board and hang them on the walls of the house. Iacopo knew that when his friends visited and looked at those paintings their initial amazement would quickly turn into a desire to imitate the style of the Florentine women. It was a brilliant idea. And certainly a good marketing ploy and effective way of spreading taste.

Another, albeit less sensational, case is that of the leather clothing that Iacopo was having sent from Florence. Heavy jackets, doublets, fur-lined tunics and *coietti*, clothing made from goatskin, the softest and finest ones. Colourful 'cordovan' was used for fashionable boots and shoes, while black leather was preferred for everyday footwear. The most eloquent example is that of the *coietti*. Francesco, who was in Pisa, ordered four skins tanned with sumac from Iacopo. He wanted them for two

Fig. 5.4 Jan van der Straet, *Ponte Santa Trinita* (1555), Museo di Palazzo Vecchio, Florence

[127] ASF, *Miscellanea*, 107, fascicolo 2, Cádiz or Seville-Florence, Iacopo Botti to Matteo Botti, 6 June 1541.

coietti with sleeves, as was the fashion. When that garment in the latest style arrived in Seville, it would, like the doll and the dress, spread the taste for the beautiful and well-made.

These strategies worked elsewhere as well. One example is Lyon, the financial capital of the sixteenth century where, as we know, Giovanbattista lived for seven years.[128] During that long sojourn on the banks of the Rhône and the Saône, he participated in the social life of the city, discussing business and more frivolous matters as well as news from the court. Through interacting with others, he contributed to the development of habits and taste. It all often unfolded in the luxurious homes of his fellow Florentines. The double row of balconies and Florentine-style loggias had also arrived in the French city and embellished the residence of the Guadagni and those of other merchant-bankers who had transferred the features of Tuscan architecture to their new homes.[129]

Giovanbattista's papers also reveal his contribution to cultural cross-fertilisation by circulating products from Lyon. In a letter to his brother Matteo in Venice about two gold bracelets sent as a gift to his sister-in-law, Lucrezia Tosinghi, he wrote:

> in a small box covered in black leather ... I sent a gift of two gold bracelets that weigh 3 ounces 22 *danari* and 10 *grani d'oro*. Let me know that they have been received by them. Although it is a small gift, my desire to serve is great. I don't know if they are in fashion there, all the women wear them here.[130]

The bracelets were an immediate success and a few months later the Eldest asked his brother to send more just like them.

Although austerity constraints were increasingly tenuous, Battista's status required a high standard of living and his account books give us an idea of some of his personal expenditures and their nature. There are quite a few entries in the account for 'day-to-day expenses' and 'furnishings'. It is likely that he kept up the Florentine style, especially in the case of clothing. His wardrobe was quite rich and frequently updated. One of his tailors was a fellow Florentine, Niccolaio Conisigli.

---

[128] On the Florentine nation in Lyon, see J. Boucher, *Présence italienne à Lyon à la Renaissance*, LUGD, Lyon 1994; M. Cassandro, *Le fiere di Lione, e gli uomini d'affari italiani nel Cinquecento*, Baccini e Chiappi, Florence 1979, pp. 33–42; A. Orlandi, 'Affaires et petites vanitas'; A. Orlandi, *Le Grand Parti*, pp. 43–48. The Florentine quarter was between the right bank of the Saône and the slopes of the Fourvière, and its architecture was heavily influenced by the Florentine style. G. Iacono, S.E. Furone, *Les marchands banquiers florentins et l'architecture à Lyon au XVI*e *siècle*, Publisud, Paris 1999, pp. 241–258; É. Picot, *Les Italiens en France au XVI*e *siècle*, Vecchiarelli, Rome 1995.

[129] Giovanbattista Botti's stay in Lyon is described in A. Orlandi, 'Affaires et petites vanités', pp. 341–357.

[130] '[D]rento [...] un cassettino copertto di coio nero [...] mandai a donare dua braccialletti d'oro quali pesorno once 3 danari 22 grani 10 d'oro. Harò caro intendere li habbia ricieuti et se bene el presente è piccolo, la volontà è grande in servirla. Non so se costà si usano, qua tutte le donne le portano.' ASF, *Libri di commercio*, 715, Lyon-Venice, Giovanbattista Botti to Matteo Botti, 12 May 1559, c. 12v. In Florence, one ounce was equal to 24 *denari* and one *denaro* equalled 24 *grani*. One ounce weighed 28.29 g. If the units of measurement were French, one ounce would have been equal to 30.59 g. A. Martini, *Metrologia*, pp. 207, 473.

Together, they chose the fabrics, patterns, shapes and finishing touches for each garment. We cannot be certain, but it is likely that the long camel-hair mantles lined with black and red fox fur, short capes for going horseback riding with sleeves embellished with velvet and silk jackets lined with taffeta presented Florentine fashion to Lyon, albeit with a few features of the French style.

This intercultural exchange was in any case widespread. From Venice, where there was a significant number of Florentines, Matteo shipped, far and wide, refined, fragile glasses with a gilded foot, embroidery books bound in gold, feather fans, bags, sword belts, silver baskets, ivory combs, offices of the Virgin, porcelain and musical instruments.

In 1533, a shipment of more than 1000 pieces of porcelain made by master potter Gasparo da Pesaro arrived in Cádiz along with 440 glasses by Filippo Serena, a Murano glassmaker.[131] In 1534, 12 glass mirrors in cases made by the talented Vincenzo Gallo arrived in Andalusia.[132] The following year, the sound of cornets, crumhorns and flutes made by Alvise Bassano,[133] son of Jeronimo, the head of a famous family of musicians, filled the palace of the dukes of Medina Sidonia. Some of Bassano's siblings had moved to the court of Henry VIII in England, while he was still in Venice in 1535 and making musical instruments worthy of the lords of Andalusia.[134]

The cross-fertilisation of taste and beauty moved in both directions, however. And once again, the Botti were behind it. Here, our example concerns the Spanish tradition of treating and working embossed and coloured leather. Cordovan, or *guardamacil*, was used everywhere and throughout the sixteenth and seventeenth centuries for wall coverings, bed coverings, screens, backrests, trimming, small boxes, binding and more. The leather was embossed using wooden stamps in various designs.[135] Coloured leather was made in Florence as well; it was acceptable and cost less than that of Andalusia. The gold ones were of good quality and the red hues seem to have been even more beautiful than the Spanish ones. But the blues and greens could not stand up to comparison with the ones made in Cordova. And so, Matteo asked his brothers for 'the recipe for dying leather blue'.[136] Battista sent

[131] ASF, *Libri di commercio*, 734, cc. 121v.–122v.

[132] ASF, *Libri di commercio*, 734, c. 57s. Also see M. Spallanzani, *I fiorentini e il vetro veneziano (ca. 1450–1550). Fonti*, Olschki, Florence 2023, pp. 91–93.

[133] D. Lasocki, R. Prior, *The Bassanos. Venetian Musicians and Instrument Makers in England, 1531–1665*, Routledge, London-New York 2016; G.M. Ongaro, 'New Documents on the Bassano Family', *Early Music*, vol. 20, 3, 1992, pp. 409–413; A. Ruffatti, *'Italian Musicians at the Tudor Court—Were They Really Jews?, Jewish Historical Studies*, 3, 1996–1998, pp. 1–14; A., Ruffatti, 'La famiglia Piva-Bassano nei documenti negli Archivi di Bassano del Grappa', *Musica e Storia*, 6, 2, 1998, pp. 349–368. ASF, *Libri di commercio*, 725, c. 136r.

[134] ASF, *Libri di commercio*, 734, c.136r.

[135] J.V. Waterer, 'Cuoio', in *Storia della tecnologia. Le civiltà mediterranee e il Medioevo circa 700 a.C.-1500 d.C.*, eds. C. Singer, E.J. Holmyard, A.R. Hall, T.I. Williams, Editore Boringhieri, Turin 1981, 5 vols., II., pp. 150–192, p. 182.

[136] ASF, *Miscellanea*, 107, fascicolo 5, Florence-Castille, Matteo Botti to Giovanbattista and Francesco Botti, 26 June 1546, c. 11v.

the instructions soon after, but the recipe was 'so fragmentary that no conclusions can be drawn from it and whoever wrote it doesn't seem to understand the principle. We need to know everything from A to Z'.[137] '... [T]hey can't say you dye it with indigo, they need to say how to prepare the indigo, which mordant is needed, whether they do it hot or cold. We are in the dark here about everything.'[138] For our merchants, the method remained a mystery, but not for the artisans of Florence, who are still producing leather of the highest quality even today.

[137] ASF, *Miscellanea*, 107, fascicolo 5, Florence-Valladolid, Matteo Botti to Giovanbattista and Francesco Botti, 4 December 1546, c. 36v.

[138] ASF, *Miscellanea*, 107, fascicolo 5, Florence-Valladolid, Matteo Botti to Giovanbattista and Francesco Botti, 24 February 1547, c. 59r.; *Miscellanea*, 107, fascicolo 5, Florence-Valladolid, Matteo Botti to Francesco Botti, 14 September 1547, c. 101v.

Chapter 6
From a Taste for Beauty to Pleasure in Money

Si con el dinero podría ganar, también podría perder.

(Luis de Molina) (This quote is cited in F. Gómez Camacho, 'La teoría monetaria de los doctires españoles del siglo XVI', Moneda y Crédito Revista de Economía, 172, 1985, pp. 55–92, p. 70.)

6.1 Financial Activity: Calculated Risk

6.1.1 Playing with Money or Dedication to Trade?

In the second half of the sixteenth century, despite the arrival of large quantities of precious metal, the Jesuit theologian Luis de Molina observed that 'no existe tanto dinero legal como sería necesario para realizar el volumen de negocios que se practica'.[1] His observation was rooted in trends that were creating frequent monetary scarcity and providing incentive for using various kinds of financial and credit instruments.[2] Among them, merchants readily resorted to the *instrumentum ex causa cambi*, as well as overdrafts, endorsements and discounts. As we know, it was broad use of the bill of exchange that had, for more than three centuries, made up for lack of liquidity, facilitating the expansion of trade.

[1] L. de Molina, *De Iustitia et Iure*, Cuenca 1597, Tomo II, col. 496, B. Also see F. Gómez Camacho, 'La teoría monetaria', p. 66.

[2] The growth and diversification of credit and financial instruments began in the fourteenth century. F. Melis, 'La grande conquista trecentesca del "credito di esercizio" e la tipologia dei suoi strumenti fino al XVI secolo', in F. Melis, *La banca pisana e le origini della banca moderna*, ed. M. Spallanzani, Istituto Internazionale di Storia Economica "F. Datini" Prato, Le Monnier, Florence pp. 307–324. During the sixteenth century, these means underwent only minor improvements, their functioning remaining largely unchanged. M. Cassandro, 'Strategia degli affari dei mercanti-banchieri italiani alle fiere internazionali d'Oltralpe (secoli XIV–XVI)', in «*Aspetti della vita economica medievale*», Atti del Convegno di Studi nel X anniversario della morte di Federigo Melis, Firenze-Pisa-Prato, 10–14 marzo 1984, Università degli Studi di Firenze, Florence 1985, pp. 140–150, p. 145.

A. Orlandi, *Money, Culture, Beauty. The Botti Family*,
https://doi.org/10.1007/978-3-032-00453-6_6

In its most typical form, it resembled today's money transfer, an international payment made without the physical circulation of money. The sender transferred local money to the recipient, who received the equivalent in his city's currency. The operation involved two intermediaries, a payee and a drawee, and the parallelism of their roles made it possible over time to strengthen their reciprocal positions as debtor and creditor, as determined by the exchange contracts between them.[3]

Bills could be used as credit instruments. A loan was made and repaid by sending the bill back and forth. Whenever possible, the contracting parties, engaging in 'dry exchange', agreed the exchange rate both outgoing and incoming. As one can imagine, this practise was harshly condemned by the Church, because the parties were hiding the interest rate in the difference.

How to Conceal the Interest Rate

In the Second Letter to the Corinthians (2 Cor. 6:10), St Paul wrote that Christians needed to behave as subjects 'nihil habentes et omnia possidentes'. Similarly, the application of interest created more than a few problems: 'Mutuum date, nihil inde sperantes', wrote Luke (6:35), a concept commonly interpreted in connection with the condemnation of usury and, hence, the obtainment of any form of profit. The exegesis of the position on accumulated wealth and charging interest developed over a long time, in a lengthy, contradictory process that we cannot go into here. We will limit ourselves to noting that, thanks to the contribution of the minor orders and, later, the humanists, the legitimacy of wealth attained through trade had been long recognised. It seems significant that Matteo Botti wrote in a letter to Iacopo that it was basically useless to ask the opinion of theologians, since, in his view, making a lot of money should not weigh too heavily on one's conscience. It was up to the merchant to choose the correct conduct, looking inward, paying attention to the motivations behind his activity and considering the profit that is 'ordinarily made by merchants where they are running more than a little risk'.[4]

The ban on charging interest was far more effective and was imposed on the more traditional types of loans, which had less of a connection to the motivations and conduct determined by the complex system of doing business. The ban was still so fully felt that sometimes the interest rate was hidden in the loan terms. There were many different ways of doing this, but the main one was to state the amount to be repaid but not the amount lent. Our documents have also revealed another way of concealing this illegal practice: a fake sale with an extended payment. In this case as well, the Eldest explains in abundant detail how it could work, in a letter written in 1544 to Borsio Botti, a relative who lived in Bagnacavallo:

'I see that you would like me to lend you 150 scudi for two years with interest, to buy a house that you lack that amount of money for. To which I would reply that there is no one here who gives money for a price and especially for so much time. When someone from here wants to ask for money he finds a way to buy goods with an extended payment deadline of one year and then he resells them for cash. Doing this is very costly, since 150 scudi

[3] R. De Roover, *L'évolution de la lettre de change (XIVe-XVIIIe sieclès)*, Librairie Armand Colin, Paris 1953; F. Melis, *Documenti per la storia economica*. Among the first scholars to study these themes, also see A. Sapori, *Libro giallo della Compagnia dei Covoni*, Cisalpino, Milan 1970; A.E. Sayous, *Els mètodes comercials a la Barcelona medieval*, Editorial Base, Barcelona 1975. The payee received the money to be transferred and issued the payment order; the drawee received the order and saw to paying the amount to the recipient of the bill of exchange.

[4] ASF, *Libri di commercio*, 713, Florence-Seville, Matteo Botti to the Botti company, 11 May 1540, c. 160v.

for one year would cost him more than 24. This seems to me to be high interest, but there is no other way to do it here. I wrote about this to Simone in Rome, and he tells me that people can do contracts like these there. I do not have cash like I did in the past; if I had some, I would give you my money without interest, because people do not lend with interest to anyone since it would not be a legal contract.'[5]

That was for loans. It was also forbidden for businesses to apply a higher price for goods sold with an extended payment. But that ban was regularly evaded. Again, it is Matteo who explains: 'since if we pay attention to the details, we will not have to sell with an extended payment deadline, nor do other things that merchants do on a daily basis. And so, let's behave honestly and put our trust in God and be satisfied.'[6]

In other words, the rigour of the theologians was an abstraction largely in conflict with peacefully accepted reality and everyday practice.

The third possible function of a bill of exchange was speculative, in the form of triangulations involving at least three different cities. They were bought and resold from one market to another, making money on the variation of exchanges rates.[7] It was a method that led Luis de Molina to observe: 'si con el dinero podría ganar, también podría perder'.[8] In these cases it was in fact fundamental to have good knowledge of their variations. There was no guarantee of profit and this uncertainty, which could result in a loss, was reason enough for avoiding condemnation by the Church. And so, Matteo explained the reasons for accepting the illegalities of the agreed upon exchange: 'it is only because they are done in dry exchange that they are almost free from the risk of loss'.[9]

The processes that led to an increasing number of bill traders at the trade fairs, gradually transforming from mercantile to financial, are well known.[10] For the Botti,

---

[5] 'Vegho come desiderate vi faciessi qui credito per dua anni di scudi 150 ad interesso per comperare una possessione a che vi mancha tal somma. A che vi dicho che qui non si trova nis suno che costumi dare dinari a costo et maxime per tanto tenpo, in però quando uno qui vuole fare danari costumano conprare qualche merchantia per termine d'uno anno, di poi la rivendono per danari contanti et a tal modo se ne fa una gran perdita talché 150 scudi per uno anno gli co steranno più di 24, il che mi pare uno grande interesse ed. altro modo qui non ci è. Io n'ò scripto a Roma a Simone perché mi avisi come quivi vi saria modo, perché colà usano più di questi con tratti che qui [...]. Io non sono in dinari come già ero, se io vi fussi vi serviria di mia dinari sanza premio nissuno, perché mai usano darne a costo a nissuno perché non sono contratti liciti.' ASF, *Miscellanea*, 107, fascicolo 4, Florence-Bagnacavallo, Matteo Botti to Borsio Borsi, 28 November 1544, c. 52r.

[6] ASF, *Libri di commercio*, 713, Florence-Seville, Matteo Botti to the Botti company, 11 May 1540, c. 160v.

[7] These were what was known as *cambi con ricorsa*. G. Mandich, 'Fiere cambiarie concorrenti (genovesi, fiorentine, veneziane) nel 1622–1652', in *La repubblica internazionale del denaro tra XV e XVII secolo*, eds. A. De Maddalena, H. Kellenbenz, Istituto trentino di cultura, Il Mulino, Bologna 1986, pp. 123–151, pp. 147–151.

[8] F. Gómez Camacho, 'La teoría monetaria', p. 70.

[9] '[C]he se avessimo a guardare per minu to non aremo a vendere a tenpo, né fare altre cose che cotidianamente fanno li mercanti; in però attendiamo all'onesto e rimettiamoci in Dio e basti.' ASF, *Miscellanea*, 107, fascicolo 3, Florence-Seville, Matteo Botti to Iacopo and Giovanbattista Botti, 14 June 1541, c. 96v.

[10] G. Mandich, 'Fiere cambiarie concorrenti', pp. 123–151; C. Marsilio, *Exchange Fairs and the Money Market in Early Modern Italy (1630–1650)/Fiere di cambio e mercato monetario nell'Italia di Età Moderna (1630–1650)*, Città del Silenzio, Genoa 2018.

the main fairs were the ones in Lyon and Castile.[11] There were also many transactions that relied on other Spanish, French and Italian markets.[12] But the two most frequent were Seville and Florence.[13]

Seville was one of the most enterprising.[14] Thanks to its central role in trade with the Americas and the arrival of large quantities of precious metals, it enjoyed decisive weight in the sixteenth-century credit and monetary system. This could result in big profits which, according to Matteo, could even reach 30% in Andalusia.[15] Florence did not have a fair but, as we know, it moved significant amounts of money.

The network of the financial markets was very well coordinated. One exemplary case is that of a complex transaction that the Botti arranged in February 1542. On instructions from the Eldest, Bellotti ordered the issue of a bill of exchange, from the Castile fairs, for the Strozzi in Lyon. The latter issued a second one for the Salviati in Antwerp, who 'returned it back' to the French city for Palla Strozzi who,

---

[11] F. Bayard, 'Les Bonvisi, marchands banquiers à Lyon, 1575–1629', *Annales. Économies, Sociétés, Civilisations*, XXVI, 1971, pp. 1234–1269; M.-T. Boyer-Xambeau-G. Deleplace-L. Gillard, *Moneta e credito*; M. Cassandro, 'Banca e commercio fiorentini alle fiere di Ginevra nel secolo XV', *Rivista Storica Svizzera*, XXVI (1976), pp. 567–611; M. Cassandro, 'Economia e politica nelle città di fiera: Ginevra e Lione (secoli XIV-XVI)', in *Strutture del potere ed élites economiche nelle città europee dei secoli XII-XVI*, ed., G. Petti Balbi, Liguori, Naples 1996, pp. 291–310; M. Cassandro, 'I forestieri a Lione nel '400 e nel '500: la nazione fiorentina', in *Dentro la città. Stranieri e realtà urbane nell'Europa dei secoli XII-*XV, ed. G. Rossetti, GISEM, Liguori, Naples 1989, pp. 163–175; M. Cassandro, 'Le élites internazionali a Ginevra e Lione nei secoli XV-XVI', in *Sistema di rapporti ed élites economiche in Europa (secoli XII-XVII)*, ed. M. del Treppo, Liguori, Naples 1994, pp. 231–248; M. Cassandro, *Le fiere di Lione*; M. Cassandro, 'Strategia degli affari'; B. Dini, 'I mercanti banchieri italiani e le fiere di Ginevra e Lione', in *L'Italia alla fine del Medioevo. I caratteri originali nel quadro europeo*, vol. I, ed. F. Salvestrini, Centro di Studi sulla civiltà del tardo Medioevo San Miniato, FUP, Florence 2006, pp. 433–456; R. Gascon, *Grand commerce et vie urbaine au XVIe siècle. Lyon et ses marchands (environs de 1520–environs de 1580)*, SEVPEN, Paris 1971; R. Gascon, 'Nationalisme économique et géographie des foires, la querelle des foires de Lyon, 1484–1494', *Cahiers d'Histoire*, III (1956), pp. 253–287; R. Gascon, 'Un siècle du commerce des épices à Lyon, fin XVe-fin XVIe siècle', *Annales. Économies, Sociétés, Civilisations*, XV, 1960, pp. 638–666; C. Marsilio, 'La lunga avventura delle fiere di cambio: da Lione a Novi', in *Libri italiani del Seicento nel fondo antico della Biblioteca Civica di Novi Ligure*, eds. A. Sisti, M. Balbi, Città del silenzio edizioni, Novi Ligure 2011, pp. 83–90; N. Matringe, *La Banque en Renaissance. Les Salviati et la place de Lyon au milieu du XVIe siècle*, Presses Universitaires de Rennes, Rennes 2016; I. Melani, *«Di qua» e «di là da' monti». Sguardi italiani sulla Francia e sui francesi tra XV e XVI secolo*, volume I, FUP, Florence 2011, p. 245; A. Pallini-Martin, *Banque, négoce et politique. Les Florentins à Lyon au moment des guerres d'Italie*, Classiques Garnier Numérique, Paris 2018; É. Picot, *Les Italiens en France*.

[12] F. Ruiz Martín, *Lettres marchandes, échangées entre Florence et Medina del Campo*, S.E.V.P.E.N. Paris 1965, pp. lxxxii–lxxxiii.

[13] The indispensable intermediation of the Lyon and Castile fairs is understood.

[14] E. Otte, 'Il ruolo dei Genovesi nella Spagna del XV e XVI secolo', in *La repubblica internazionale del denaro tra XV e XVII secolo*, eds. A. De Maddalena, H. Kellenbenz, Istituto trentino di cultura, Il Mulino, Bologna 1986, pp. 17–56, p. 28.

[15] ASF, *Miscellanea*, 107, fascicolo 3, Florence-Seville, Matteo Botti to the Botti company, 11 November 1542, c. 205r.

once he received the sum, needed to choose, based on the going exchange rates, whether to return it to Giovanbattista Bellotti in Villalón or the Capponi and Biffoli in Naples or the Salviati in Antwerp.[16]

When making decisions about transactions, one assessed monetary scarcity and abundance, which was heavily influenced by the quantities of precious metals in circulation. When American gold and silver was unloaded in Seville, it was then scattered across Europe. Quickly when handled by businessmen, more slowly in the case of spending set by governments. And so, while the arrival of precious metals meant an abundance of cash in Spain, this surplus spread quickly from the Iberian Peninsula to cities in Italy, Germany, France and Flanders.[17] In short, it was well known that the periodic arrival of metal from the New World corresponded to money flowing like water: 'You say you feel deeply that the quantity of money will be decreasing soon, but there is no sign of it now. And it cannot even be envisaged, since a huge fortune has arrived in Seville from Peru and New Spain, which is to say Mexico. A bigger amount was expected and so as soon as everything arrives in gold and silver, they will need to transfer it to all the markets in Italy.'[18]

The Botti were well aware of those mechanisms. And so the levels of exchange via bill were also heavily influenced by the volume of trade: 'when the goods don't flow, the exchange doesn't fly'[19] and 'for the little faith we have in the market there will be a lot of money'.[20] On the other hand, the large quantities of wheat imported from Puglia and Sicily to Spain could contribute to creating a lack of liquidity in Seville, especially if the grain was paid for in cash. At the same time, the emperor's visits, the arrival of the Genoese galleys in Andalusian ports, ready to load products bound for Italy, and the sizeable war expenditures ordered by Charles V in those years stirred up trade and therefore facilitated bill-based transactions.[21]

The money market being so elastic, traders were keen to exploit the opportunity to speculate and 'profit from abundance and scarcity'. All this required a network of agents and correspondents who could provide detailed information about financial trends.

In the everyday circulation of money, the unexpected was always just around the corner and could change the normal course of business. Getting saddled with 'bad'

[16] ASF, *Miscellanea*, 107 fascicolo 3, Florence-Lyon, Francesco Botti to Palla Strozzi, 25 February 1542 c. 168v.

[17] F. Ruiz Martín, *Lettres marchandes*, p. lxxxv.

[18] ASF, *Libri di commercio*, 716, Florence-Venice, Giovanbattista Botti to the Attavanti company, 28 July 1565, c. 167r.

[19] ASF, *Miscellanea*, 107, fascicolo 3, Florence-Seville, Matteo Botti to Francesco Botti, 10 June 1541, c. 92r.

[20] ASF, *Miscellanea*, 107, fascicolo 3, Florence-Caesarean Court of Spain, Matteo Botti to Luigi dei Mozzi, 9 January 1542, c. 148v.

[21] Matteo's reflections on the effects of the major loans requested by the emperor to finance his wars in 1542 are revealing. All the Spanish kingdoms 'will feel the effects of the big expenditures of the lords and hidalgos but they will have money problems and those who have debt will not repay it willingly'. ASF, *Miscellanea*, 107, fascicolo 3, Florence-Valladolid, Matteo Botti to the Botti and Bellotti company, 4 December 1542, c. 210r.

money was, for example, not so rare. This is what happened in November 1547 when they had some Spanish *scudi* tested in Florence and the *campsores* found them to be 'worse than ours by 1 ½% which is a huge loss and a disgrace for those who coin money. If this mint were in Italy, they would all be banished like happened a few days ago in the case of 10 milanesi that someone brought here and were found to be 2 ½% worse, and therefore confiscated.'[22]

6.1.2 *Moving Money and Playing with Exchange Rates*

The method used for transferring money between Tuscany and Andalusia is fairly clear in the Botti documents. Matteo described the group's decisions in detail. Their actions depended on the fact that there was no exchange between Florence and Cádiz or Seville or Valencia or 'any place in Spain at all',[23] and so the only solution was to go through Lyon or Rome. In the case of Lyon, the group worked with various bankers who represented important Florentine families – Panciatichi, Del Bene, Bini, Guadagni and Strozzi – active in the French city. Once the funds were received there, they were transferred to Seville, for the Botti, through the Ricasoli or Jacopo Fantoni. If, as often happened, 'good receivers' for Andalusia could not be found in Lyon, the transfer was made through the Castile fairs. In this case, the bill was issued to Valladolid, where the payees could be the Botti and Bellotti or the companies of the Martelli or the Affaitadi and Giraldi, who then transferred the funds to Seville. Alternatively, Iacopo, once informed that the funds were available, would sometimes issue a bill directly to the depositaries.

The other possible route went through Rome, where the Montaguti, Casi, Detti and Altoviti were active, receiving funds from Florence and Pisa. From Rome, the journey continued on to Spain, following the exact same route along the banks of the Rhône.

These were the most common triangulations used by Tuscan merchants working in Andalusia. It would, however, be rash to view these practices as rigid and fixed. What we have just described is attested by a letter from Francesco in which he writes that the 'proceeds' from the leather sold in Pisa on behalf of Giovanni Nadal[24] were sent to Spain, choosing from among possible recipients in Barcelona, Valencia, Seville or even Naples.[25]

---

[22] '[P]eggio che nostri 1 ½ per cento che è una gran falta et vergognia di chi batte; che se cotesta zecca fussi qua in Italia stariano tutti sbanditi come ferno a' giorni passati a' milanesi che uno mercante ne portò x qui et come gli trovorno peggio 2 ½ per cento gliene tolsono.' ASF, *Miscellanea*, 107, fascicolo 5, Florence-Seville, Matteo Botti to Iacopo Botti, 14 November 1547, c. 135v.

[23] ASF, *Libri di commercio*, 712, Florence-Cádiz, Matteo Botti to Lorenzo Gratia, 10 June 1531, c. 118r.

[24] A merchant active in Cádiz.

[25] The following is the list of operators they could involve, depending on the market chosen for the money transfer: Giovanni Clarete in Barcelona; Francesco Forcadel in Valencia; Bernardo and Perotto Forcadel and the Ricasoli and Ridolfi in Seville and Francesco Blanco in Naples.

The return trip to the Italian peninsula was not much different from the outgoing journey. From Seville, Valencia and the Castile fairs, the monetary flow stretched to Tuscany, passing through Lyon or Rome. In this case, it would seem that Valencia began to play a more important role starting in the 1530s,[26] since it was increasingly considered as a potential intermediary stop.

The exchange rate influenced the route chosen in both directions. The family's extensive network of financial markets even stretched as far as the Canaries, with which Iacopo had close business relations, as discussed above. It would seem, in fact, that at least 14 bills of exchange were issued from the Seville company to those islands during the period at hand.[27] As is well known, the sole exception was the Levant, which did not use this important financial instrument. Money was moved physically in special containers between the Near East and Europe, transferred by land and sea with all the attendant risks of each.[28]

All these methods were used by the Botti with revealing casualness. That said, they tried to avoid the purchase of money as much as possible. The Eldest suggested using internal surpluses, urging his brothers to secure the needed funds relying on Lyon, Rome and Florence, which he would then replenish. He also urged them to organise purchases carefully with the available funds.[29]

We have tried to reconstruct the magnitude of the transactions made between 1524 and 1559. The documents provide a lot of information, but since they are mostly letters, it is less precise and detailed than that in account books. This is why it was difficult to identify the vertices of the bills of exchange, their value, the rates used and the markets involved.

Moreover, in a few cases the generic nature of the information does not allow us to establish the amount of the bill or transfer, its destination or the fairs used for the operation. In short, the extent of exchange with Florence, to which we have limited ourselves, is undoubtedly underestimated. This is confirmed by the intensification of activity between 1546 and 1548 documented in the only exchange notebook that has come down to us (Table 6.1).

---

[26] In the early sixteenth century, the bank of Valencia was already being used for financial transactions with Italy. M.Á. Ladero Quesada, 'El banco de Valencia, los genoveses y la saca de moneda de oro castellana. 1500–1503,' *Anuario de Estudios Medievales*, vol. 17 (1987), pp. 571–594, p. 575. E. Otte also noted a gradual increase in the issue of bills of exchange from Valencia to Italy between 1494 and 1506. E. Otte, 'Sevilla y Valencia a fines de la Edad Media', in *Lluís de Santàngel i el seu temps (Congrés Internacional. Valencia, 1987)*, Ayuntamiento de Valencia, Valencia 1992, pp. 283–297.

[27] E. Otte, 'Canarias: plaza bancaria europea en el siglo XVI', in *IV Coloquio de Historia Canario-Americana, 1980,* Ediciones del Excelentísimo Cabildo Insular de Gran Canaria, Gran Canaria 1982, Tomo I, pp. 157–173, p. 164.

[28] ASF, *Libri di commercio*, 712, Florence-Pera, Matteo Botti to Antonio Gerini, 27 February 1531, c. 72r. On the process for transferring coins from the Near East to Florence, see A. Orlandi, 'Oro e monete da Costantinopoli', pp. 981–1004.

[29] ASF, *Libri di commercio*, 712, Florence-Cádiz, Matteo Botti to Iacopo and Giovanbattista Botti, 10 January 1531, cc. 49v.-50r.

Table 6.1 The Botti's bill of exchange activity (1524–1559)[a]

Bills of exchange sent to Florence		Bills of exchange sent from Florence	
Provenance	Value in ducats	Destination	Value in ducats
Seville	15,963	Seville	37,228
Cádiz	4326	Cádiz	14,306
Medina del Campo	10,000	Valladolid	15,822
Salamanca	31	Villalón	417
Valencia	695		
Valladolid	8835		
Total	39,850	Total	67,773

[a] Twenty-three years are sufficiently documented

Looking at this table, we find intense levels of exchange activity that often exceeded the head office's available funds. More detailed analysis of the data reveals that in the 1540s, amounts were sent ranging between 5000 and 8000 ducats per year.

During the entire documented period, our traders moved 67,773 ducats to Spain: of these, more than 37,000 went to Seville and 14,306 to Cádiz. Moreover, when Valladolid opened up in 1541, we find a gradual increase of transfers to Castile which, from 1541 to 1559, reached 15,800 ducats.

These funds were not only used to finance trade, but also for speculation. It is not always possible to identify the purposes, since the correspondence only rarely explains the reasons for the transfer or bill. In any case, the brothers tried to profit from the movement of bills of exchange independent of the reason they were issued. They also chose the most opportune moment to shift the funds needed to support exchange. And so, when Matteo transferred 2000 scudi to Francesco in Valladolid, he asked: 'see to it that it makes a profit and send it to the fairs over there or in Lyon or in Rome'.[30]

The flow from Spain to Italy was smaller. From Spain, any liquidity that wasn't transferred was transformed into products, examples including the large quantities of tuna in brine, sugar and leather shipped to Florence. Between 1524 and 1559, almost 16,000 ducats left Seville headed for Tuscany, while almost 19,000 were shifted from the fairs of Castile.

Overall, the reconstructed financial transactions totalled 100,000 ducats, very large sum, especially considering that it is underestimated. And this underestimation is not only due to the incomplete documentation, but also because some of the brothers' activities are not found in our documents at all. To take one example, when Francesco was in Antwerp in March 1555, it was deemed opportune to 'invest something in England', since it was very convenient to exchange with London and Venice from Flanders.[31]

---

[30] ASF, *Miscellanea*, 107, fascicolo 5, Florence-Valladolid, Matteo Botti to Giovanbattista and Francesco Botti, 24 January 1547, c. 58v.

[31] ASF, *Libri di commercio*, 723, Florence-Seville, Giovanbattista Botti to Iacopo Botti, 11 August 1554, c. 58v.; *Libri di commercio*, 723, Florence-Valladolid, Giovanbattista Botti to the Affaitadi and Giraldi company, 14 August 1554, c. 59v.; *Libri di commercio*, 715, 15 March 1555, c. 24v.

We have seen the group's immense diligence, although even this was a source for practical Matteo's complaints. Always worried about speculative activities, he said that although in some cases their exchange activity won them entry 'into the book of the very rich',[32] far more often it led to disastrous failures. Commerce was of course less risky, but it also yielded lower profits than financial speculation. The Botti were adept at combining the two activities, although they were of course not easy to keep separate, especially for Florentines, merchants and bankers par excellence.

6.1.3 Assessing Risk: Insurance Activity

'All the risks are run on this ship: God, the sea, people and every other form of accident and fortune'.[33] This is an excerpt from an old policy drawn up in Pisa on 26 January 1385 to protect five parcels of cloth, one of fustian and ten of iron materials on the journey from Porto Pisano to Palermo.[34] At the end of the fourteenth century, the introduction of differentiated freight and the construction of larger ships, with the subsequent expansion of trade, stimulated the growth of the insurance market.[35] This expansion continued, gradually and without interruption, from the fifteenth to the sixteenth century, when the practice, by this point well known to all, received a further boost from the opening of the Atlantic routes.[36] Because the journey to the

[32] ASF, *Miscellanea*, 107, fascicolo 5, Florence-Seville, Matteo Botti to the Botti company, 5 March 1547, c. 64v.

[33] F. Melis, *Origini e sviluppi delle assicurazioni in Italia (secoli XIV-XVI), Le fonti*, Istituto Nazionale delle Assicurazioni, Rome 1975, p. 191.

[34] The term *mercie* was used for metal objects and materials.

[35] F. Melis, 'Werner Sombart e i problemi della navigazione nel Medioevo', in F. Melis, *I trasporti e le comunicazioni nel Medioevo*, ed. L. Frangioni, Istituto Internazionale di Storia Economica "F. Datini" Prato, Le Monnier, Florence 1984, pp. 3–68.

[36] Among the numerous studies on transatlantic insurance, see A.M. Bernal Rodríguez, 'La aseguración marítima de la Carrera de Indias: seguros, crédito y actividad financiera (ss.XVI-XVIII)', in *VI Congreso de la Asociación Española de Historia Económica*, Gerona 1997, pp. 1–15; A.M. Bernal Rodríguez, 'Sobre los seguros marítimos en la Carrera de Indias, siglo XVI', in *Actas del V Centenario del Consulado de Burgos*, eds. F. Ballesteros Caballero, H. Casado Alonso, A.C. Ibáñez Pérez, S. Escolar Díez, Diputación Provincial de Burgos, Burgos 1994, pp. 501–527; H. Casado Alonso, 'El seguro marítimo en la Carrera de Indias en la época de Felipe II', in *Comercio y cultura en la Edad Moderna. Actas de la XIII Reunión Científica de la Fundación Española de Historia Moderna. Comunicaciones*, eds. J.J. Iglesias Rodríguez, R.M. Pérez García, M.F. Fernández Chaves, Universidad de Sevilla, Seville 2015, pp. 1253–1270; O. Cruz Barney, *El riesgo en el comercio hispano-indiano. Préstamos y seguros marítimos durante los siglos XVI a XIX*, Universidad Nacional Autónoma de México, Mexico City, 1998; H. Casado Alonso, 'Insuring Life, Insuring Debt: Life Insurance in Sixteenth-Century Spain, Pedralbes. *Revista d'historia moderna*, 40, 2020, pp. 75–95; M. Garzón Pareja, 'El riesgo en el comercio de Indias', *Revista de Indias*, 35 (1975), pp. 187–191.

Indies was so risky, shipowners and merchants often protected themselves, insuring hulls, equipment, artillery and cargo.

Every decision about whether to undersign a policy was based on careful risk assessment. Choosing the ship was a delicate process, requiring information about the type of craft and the crew, the nationality of the shipowner and the captain, their ability to handle the dangers of the sea, the voyages they had made and any accidents and damage suffered.[37] Risk assessment also extended to the safety of the seas, based on political developments and pirate activity. And so, if the ship was not reliable or if ill-intentioned French or English or 'Turkish or Moorish ships'[38] were disturbing navigation, Matteo advised his brothers to postpone the shipments or insure the cargo.[39] If a boat instead offered good guarantees and the voyage seemed relatively safe, they kept costs down by insuring only part of the hold or shipping the goods without taking any precautions at all. On the other hand, Matteo wrote, 'these high freight charges and insurance fees are breaking us',[40] and he was well aware of the option to take out a policy in a location other than that of the departure of the goods or make do with an alternate route. And so, in reference to a bag of pearls, he observed that 'if they could be shipped via Lyon that would be the best route of all due to the high cost of insurance'.[41]

Contractual methods and procedures were another source of worry. Preparing a contract correctly guaranteed its validity and its enforceability against insurers. In Florence, the matter was rigidly regulated by a law passed in 1524 that required using a broker, who was the only one authorised to prepare policies.[42] As we learn from Matteo, the general, universal *scritta*[43] had to include 'the name of the ship, the owner, the place where it will be loaded and where it is going'[44] and 'only one ship may be indicated and a maximum of two ports and so if one wants more ports one needs to prepare two contracts and say: insurance from Rio to Cádiz for X amount for that ship and X amount for the ship from Cartagena to Alicante'.[45]

[37] F. Melis, 'Sulla realtà dell'assicurazione nei trasporti marittimi (secoli XIV-XV)', in F. Melis, *I trasporti*, p. 234.

[38] ASF, *Miscellanea*, 107, fascicolo 4, Florence-Valladolid, Matteo Botti to the Botti company, 18 September 1545, c. 144r.

[39] ASF, *Libri di commercio*, 711, Florence-Cádiz, Matteo Botti to Iacopo Botti (personal), 31 October 1524, cc. 28r.–29r.

[40] ASF, *Libri di commercio*, 711, Florence-Cádiz, Matteo Botti to Iacopo and Giovanbattista Botti, 13 September,1525, c. 63r.

[41] ASF, *Libri di commercio*, 711, Florence-Cádiz, Matteo Botti to Giovanbattista Botti, 3 August 1525, c. 58v.

[42] On the role of the Florentine insurance market, see G. Ceccarelli, *Risky Markets: Marine Insurance in Renaissance Florence*, Brill, Leiden 2020.

[43] F. Melis, *Origini e sviluppi*, p. 234. A *scritta* was the model used for drawing up contracts.

[44] ASF, *Libri di commercio*, 711, Florence-Cádiz, Matteo Botti to Iacopo Botti (personal), 9 September 1525, c. 60v.

[45] ASF, *Libri di commercio*, 712, Florence-Seville, Matteo Botti to Iacopo Fantoni, 22 February 1528, c. 9r.

In Seville, on the other hand, a private document containing the general conditions of the contract was all that was needed. In 1552, this practice was declared invalid by the Casa de la Contratación and it became obligatory to publish the contract. A specialised intermediary, the *corredor de lonja*, had to transcribe the contents of the documents into a special book and certify that they were signed by the interested parties in his presence.[46] The process became even more rigid four years later, a change justified by frequent disputes between insurer and insured and, consequently, by the by-then extremely widespread use of this institution (Fig. 6.1).[47]

Insuring goods shipped from Venice to Cádiz in Florence

The Seville insurance market was the most dynamic in Andalusia, but Florence also played an important role and was sometimes able to offer policies with more advantageous conditions. It was not by chance that Matteo advised his brothers and clients to have contracts drawn up in Florence even though it was not the departure city. And so, in August 1525, he reminded his Spanish correspondents that 'when we would have had time to do them here [in Florence] it would have been a good thing because they would not have cost more than 8 or 9 per cent. When you think you have time, you can let us know, since 15 per cent is a bit too much'[48] He did the same in Venice to insure the voyage of the Santo Antonio, a Portuguese galleon commanded by Bartolomeo Alfonso di Portinam of Villanuova, which was leaving from the lagoon for Cádiz. He loaded a bit of everything onto that big ship. Along with cumbersome, less valuable items like loads of steel, planks of Candia fir, sacks of orpiment, sword blades and fabric of every kind, the cargo hold was also carrying the cream of what was being produced in Venice at the time. And so, Andalusia was being sent baskets made of silver wire, iridescent laces in a range of hues, glasses, coolers, porcelain, elegant fans made of ostrich feathers, a special powder for cleaning mirrors, leather bags and even a recently printed book on the life of Christ by a poet from Mantua. The value of the cargo is unknown, but we know it was insured for 2600 ducats, a sizeable sum covered by twenty-three insurers including the most important Florentine merchant-banker families of the time. The cost of the policy, equal to 12% including the commission for the Botti, was 325 ducats.[49]

We only have sporadic information about the premiums charged. The data is so fragmentary that we are unable to make any observations about their levels or variability, which, as we know, depended on numerous factors, including the length of the trip.

The Botti were expert insurers active in Florence, Cádiz and Seville. In the most complex and risky cases, they partnered with others, often Florentines. Research by Federigo Melis revealed that, in the period 1524–1526, Matteo and his brothers

[46] Documents lacking this certification were declared void. A. García y Sanz, 'El seguro marítimo en España en los siglos XV y XVI', in *Actas del V centenario del Consulado de Burgos*, ed. F. Ballesteros Caballero, H. Casado Alonso, A.C. Ibáñez Pérez, S. Escolar Díez, Diputación Provincial de Burgos, Burgos 1994, pp. 445–498.

[47] A.M. Bernal Rodríguez, 'Sobre los seguros marítimos'; M. Garzón Pareja, 'El riesgo en el comercio'.

[48] ASF, *Libri di commercio*, 711, Florence-Cádiz, Matteo Botti to Giovanbattista Botti, 3 August 1525, c. 58v.

[49] ASF, *Libri di commercio*, 734, c. 126v.

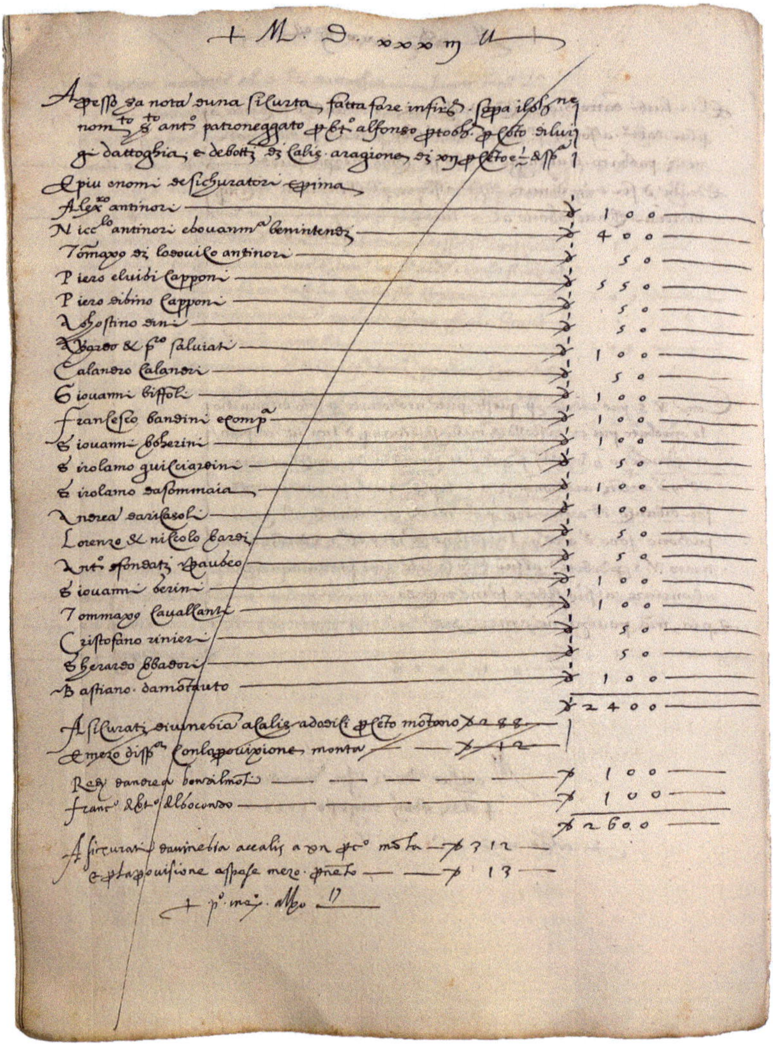

Fig. 6.1 *Book of debtors and creditors*, c. 126v. ASF, *Libri di commercio*, 734

drew up 89 contracts in Florence, collecting almost 6300 florins in premiums.[50] The intensity of this activity is attested by the fact that in the autumn of 1525, the Eldest, in temporary partnership with Piero and Luigi Capponi, wrote to Cádiz asking to

[50] F. MELIS, *Origini e sviluppi*, p. 285. In the first year, they sold 19 policies for 1092 florins; the second year, 46 policies for 3100 florins, in the third year, 24 policies for 2100 florins. On the Botti family's Florentine insurance activity, also see G. CECCARELLI, *Risky Markets*, pp. 178, 180, 214, 215.

'insure' all the ships leaving for Flanders or Livorno up to 20–25 ducats,[51] committing 150 to the company in Seville under the same terms.[52] For these reasons, he urged keeping the account for the partnership with the Capponi clearly separate from that of the group.[53]

Their most intense activity started in the 1540s. In 1541, again in partnership with the Capponi, they concluded a number of transatlantic contracts. That same year, Iacopo paid 50 ducats 'for damage to the ship San Giovanni della Polla that was going to Nombre di Dio'.[54] And in October 1544, when peace between the emperor, the French crown and England seemed imminent,[55] Botti ordered the Seville company to underwrite policies in partnership with Capponi and Carnesecchi for every ship headed to England, up to 150 gold ducats.

The document that sheds the most light on this activity is the debit side of a current account, in the section relative to damages. It does not provide information about successful policies. That said, the information unearthed by Federigo Melis and the data that emerges from this document reveal that the family's insurance activity was for the most part positive, despite Matteo's anxieties. As we learn from the document, between September 1544 and December 1545, our merchants partnered with the company of Giovan Francesco Bini and Palla Strozzi of Lyon to insure trips all over the world. From Seville to Nombre de Dios, from São Tomé to Flanders, from Ayamonte to London, from Cádiz to Rouen, from Sicily to Andalusia, from Venice to Candia.[56] The information that we have reconstructed is presented in Tables 6.2, 6.3, 6.4, 6.5, 6.6, 6.7 and 6.8.

The fragmentary nature of the available data allows us to offer only a rough idea of our merchants' insurance activity. It shows how variable the damage was from one voyage to the next, and unfortunately we do not know how many contracts were successfully completed. We know only that in this case Iacopo had to pay damages of 4000 ducats on a total of 25,525 relative to 92 policies. Damages of 15%, which could have been more than the premiums collected.

The clients were for the most part local, but we also find Genoese merchants (Centurioni, Spinola, Cattani, Lomellino, Marini, Grillo, among others), French (Julio, Leonardo and Batista di Bringnie), German (Domingo aleman) and the

---

[51] ASF, *Libri di commercio*, 711, Florence-Cádiz, Matteo Botti to Iacopo Botti (personal), 22 June 1525, c. 53r.

[52] ASF, *Miscellanea*, 107, fascicolo 4, Florence-Castile, Matteo Botti to the Botti company, 25 October 1544, 38r.

[53] ASF, *Libri di commercio*, 711, Florence-Cádiz, Matteo Botti to the Botti company, 18 March 1527, c. 135v.

[54] ASF, *Miscellanea*, 107, fascicolo 3, Florence-Seville, Matteo Botti to the Botti company, 14 July 1541, c. 105v.

[55] ASF, *Miscellanea*, 107, fascicolo 4, Florence-Valladolid, Matteo Botti to the Botti company, 25 October 1544, c. 38r.

[56] ASF, *CSVS*, 1090. In this account, the amounts reimbursed are expressed in maravedís, which we converted into ducats. Considering the period in question, we used the exchange rate 1 ducat = 375 maravedís.

Table 6.2 Reimbursements for voyages overseas (1544–1545)

Trip	No. contracts	Value (in ducats)	
		Insured	Reimbursed
Seville-'New Spain'	2	300.00	100.00
Seville-Nombre de Dios	1	300.00	2.72
Seville-Cartagena de Indias	1	np	500.00
Seville-'Terra Firma'	2	1000.00	63.75
Sanlúcar de Barrameda-'New Spain'	1	350.00	350.00
Las Palmas de Gran Canaria or Tenerife-Santo Domingo	1	500.00	57.70
Cape Verde-'New Spain'	3	650.00	308.37
'New Spain'-Seville	8	1500.00	244.22
Nombre de Dios-Seville	1	200.00	11.00
Santo Domingo-Seville	3	500.00	339.73
Cape Honduras-Seville	2	450.00	3.61
Total	25	>5750.00	1981.10

Table 6.3 Reimbursements for voyages to Flanders (1544–1545)

Trip	No. contracts	Value (in ducats)	
		Insured	Reimbursed
Málaga-Flanders	12	3250.00	144.54
Dénia or Alicante-Flanders	1	100.00	np
São Tomé-Flanders	5	1125.00	342.09
'Villalon d'Algarve'-Flanders	1	250.00	4.72
Madeira-Flanders	5	1150.00	523.47
Lisbon-Flanders	2	600.00	103.22
Tavira-Flanders	2	540.00	74.37
Gran Canaria-Flanders	1	500.00	168.52
Las Palmas de Canaria-Flanders	1	100.00	3.34
El Puerto de Santa María-Flanders	1	150.00	8.25
Total	31	7765.00	>1372.52

Table 6.4 Reimbursements for voyages to England (1544–1545)

Trip	No. contracts	Value (in ducats)	
		Insured	Reimbursed
Rota-London	1	200.00	200.00
Ayamonte-London	1	200.00	189.60
Cádiz-London	2	300.00	4.67
Cádiz-Bristol	1	200.00	12.38
Total	5	900.00	406.65

Table 6.5 Reimbursements for voyages to and from Rouen (1544–1545)

Trip	No. contracts	Value (in ducats)	
		Insured	Reimbursed
Rouen-Seville	1	200.00	25.58
Rouen-Cádiz/Seville	2	660.00	272.05
Cádiz-Rouen	4	940.00	297.39
Total	7	1800.00	595.02

Table 6.6 Reimbursements for voyages to Sicily (1544–1545)

Trip	No. contracts	Value (in ducats)	
		Insured	Reimbursed
Sicily-Cádiz	1	500.00	268.33
Sicily-Seville	3	3220.00	82.75
Total	4	3720.00	351.08

Table 6.7 Reimbursements for voyages between Madeira and Andalusia (1544–1545)

Trip	No. contracts	Value (in ducats)	
		Insured	Reimbursed
Madeira-Cádiz	1	150	250
Madeira-Seville	1	300	30
Total	2	450	280

Table 6.8 Reimbursements for other voyages (1544–1545)

Trip	No. contracts	Value (in ducats)	
		Insured	Reimbursed
Tarragona-Seville	1	100.00	48.67
Candia-Venice	1	500.00	31.75
Tenerife-Cádiz	1	500.00	15.00
Ayamonte-Galicia	1	150.00	150.00
Sanlúcar de Barrameda-Naple	1	300.00	5.22
Faro-Marseilles	1	300.00	5.22
Gran Canaria-Venice	1	500.00	6.60
Seville-Biscay	1	250.00	250.00
Málaga-Civitavecchia and Rome	1	250.00	25.00
Cádiz-Naples	1	np	42.50
Cádiz-Barcelona	1	300.00	30.00
Cádiz-Livorno	4	1290.00	124.13
Cádiz-Civitavecchia	1	200.00	16.34
Alicante-Cádiz	1	np	400.00
'Capo da Guera'-Cádiz	1	500.00	22.16
Total	18	›5140.00	1172.59

group's own Seville company, which insured voyages to Livorno, Naples and Civitavecchia on more than one occasion. Their best client, however, was Francesco Nuñes Peres. That year, he turned to the Botti 16 times, for 4365 ducats on ships headed to Flanders.

The most frequent cause of damage was the capture of vessels by pirates. Sometimes, the ships sank, other times, storms or damage forced the captains to unload the cargo at the nearest port, with inevitable damage. Fortunes varied, and while the Botti's insurance account recorded a loss in 1545, in spring the next year the situation had reversed, even though Matteo had written that he expected 'more harm than good and God only knows how 1547 will go!'[57]

The surviving documentation also provides information about the activity of other Florentine companies. To take one example, in 1551 Cosimo Martelli in Seville paid 400 gold ducats to Bartolomé de Vizcarra, alcalde of Castillo de Triana, for the loss of the galleon San Juan during a voyage from Havana to Seville.[58] In Valladolid, the Martelli split their risks partnering with the Mannelli company in Lyon. In just four months, they drew up 14 contracts, two of which for New World routes. The insured party was Niccolò Cattaneo Stella, who had loaded 150 ducats worth of goods onto the ship Santo Spirito coming from Santo Domingo and another 150 ducats on the galleon San Julio departing from Cádiz for Veracruz.[59]

6.1.4 Lending to Sovereigns: A Probable Loss

Cities, monarchies and papacies facing extraordinary expenses or unexpected expenditures tried to secure the funds they needed through levies, loans and issuing currency.

Governments had long endeavoured to create taxation systems that could exploit every possible source of wealth. Research on European public finances in the Middle Ages and early modern period has clearly revealed that taxation methods were profoundly unequal and insufficient for growing financial needs. Cities and states soon started to run up debt with interest with or without reimbursement of capital. Levies and loans were not in conflict, even though indebtedness made it necessary to identify and in some cases institute new taxes to guarantee repayment. While, on the one hand, having a clear understanding of which sources of income

---

[57] ASF, *Miscellanea*, 107 fascicolo 5, Florence-Seville, Matteo Botti to Iacopo Botti, 6 October 1547 c. 107r.

[58] Archivo Histórico Provincial de Sevilla (henceforth AHP), *Protocolos Notariales de Sevilla*, Oficio XV, 9169 Libro II, Scrivania di Alonso de Cazalla, 14 November 1551 c. 1969v. The register was published in the Catálogo de los Fondos Americanos of the Archivo de Protocolos de Sevilla, Tomo IV, Siglo XVI, Instituto Hispano Cubano de Historia de América, Seville 2002 documenti 1487 pp. 397–398.

[59] ASF, *CSVS*, 1506 Valladolid-Lyon, Martelli company to the Mannelli company, 14 August 1556 c. 15s.

were pledged as security inspired creditors' confidence, this was also the only way to demonstrate financial stability and obtain, if necessary, more money.[60]

As we know, the process of public borrowing sharply accelerated in Europe in the first half of the sixteenth century. This was not only due to the drainage of resources to fund wars; the characteristics of the absolute state, with the expansion of its functions and indispensable bureaucratic apparatus, also made the sixteenth century a complex period for the fiscal and financial policies of countries dominated by the need for new income. Among them, Spain and France, embroiled in arduous wars over control of Italian territories, saw their debt swell. The Botti family became involved through the acquisition of *juros* and *tiletti.*

While Giovanbattista sent detailed news during his sojourn in Lyon, information about underwriting state debt is fragmentary. In the case of the Spanish crown, we know that Iacopo bought, in December 1547, *juros* for 12,000 scudi at 7.14%, and in 1581 he invested another 200,000 maravedís against the revenue of the 'Almojarifazgo Mayor'.[61] Of course he underwrote many more, as emerges indirectly from sources such as the wills of his wife and daughters, which list securities from the estate.[62] Francesco had put 10,000 scudi in 2 *juros* against the income of the Maestrazgo and Montazgo; Matteo seems to have been inclined to buy them for another 1500. For his part, Giovanbattista underwrote two *juros al quitar*: one of them came to 4300 ducats in 1566 and yielded 13%. Six years later, after he had moved back to Florence permanently, he asked Martelli in Valladolid to sell it.[63] The other security of more than 360,000 maravedís came to him in payment of a crate of Florentine cloth of silk and gold. It was guaranteed against the revenue of La Calahorra and other parts of Granada.[64]

Simone, who was in Rome in November 1547, bought *uffici* that paid 12%.[65] During his time in Antwerp, Francesco obtained 2200 gold ducats against the debt

---

[60] For a summary of the theme and an updated interpretation, see A. Orlandi, *La ricchezza del debito pubblico dal XII al XXI secolo*, Il Mulino, Bologna 2022.

[61] In 1559, Lorenzo del Rosso also purchased a *juro* of 11,288 maravedís against the revenue of Almojarifazgo de Indias. E. Vila Vilar, 'Partecipación de capitales italianos en la rentas de Sevilla en el siglio XVI', in *La presenza italiana in Andalusia nel Basso Medioevo.* Atti del secondo convegno, Rome, 25–27 May 1984, eds. A. Boscolo, B. Torres, Cappelli, Bologna 1986 pp. 85–102, pp. 92–94.

[62] AGS, *CME*, 270.20; AGS, *CME*, 300.27. Wills of Anna Francisca Fonte, Ana Paula Botti and Ginebra Botti.

[63] ASF, *Libri di commercio*, 716 Florence-Valladolid, Giovanbattista Botti to the Martelli company, 21 October 1562 c. 10v.

[64] ASF, *Libri di commercio,* 716, Florence-Madrid, Giovanbattista Botti to Vincenzo Ambrogi, 6 January 1564 c. 91r.; *Libri di commercio*, 726 Florence, 15 July 1565 c. 12s.; *Libri di commercio*, 727 Florence-Medina del Campo, Giovanbattista Botti to Vincenzo Ambrogi, 28 March 1566 c. 25r.; *Libri di commercio*, 727 Florence-Medina del Campo, Giovanbattista Botti to Vincenzo Ambrogi, 20 June 1566 c. 34r.; *Libri di commercio*, 727 Florence-Medina del Campo, Giovanbattista Botti to Vincenzo Ambrogi, 30 June 1566 c. 34v.

[65] ASF, *Miscellanea*, 107 fascicolo 5, Florence-Seville, Matteo Botti to Iacopo Botti, 14 November 1547 c. 135r.

secured by the revenue of Bruges and, as we have seen, joined a consortium for a loan to Philip II.

Giovanbattista Botti in Lyon and the Debt of Henry II, King of France

While he was living in France, Giovanbattista got directly involved in the crown's debt. It was a real adventure. In 1555, the year he arrived in Lyon, Henry II was heavily in debt and the heads of the banks were becoming increasingly concerned. Finding it impossible to procure the funds needed for paying interest and capital, the king decided to convert floating debt into medium- and long-term debt. This consolidation was called the Grand Parti. Most of the sovereign's debts were bundled into a single sum equal to about 3,500,000 livre tournois. If we consider additional small loans obtained primarily from Florentine bankers, the king's total debt had reached 5,150,000 livres tournois.[66] It was to be paid off in regular instalments of 5% quarterly that could be settled at each of the city's four fairs. For the first instalment, the capital share was equal to 1% and interest 4%. The whole transaction was to be concluded with the payment of the instalment at the fair of the Apparition in 1565. The contract temporarily reduced the extent of floating debt, but the treasury's endless needs transformed it into an open structure, ready to receive new creditors. The problems were clear from the beginning and the government was forced to stop making payments in 1558 after having paid only the first six instalments. The debt was dangerously approaching 9,000,000 livre. The creditors' attempts to secure some repayment were becoming frantic, but the death of the king rendered void what few partial agreements had been made and the lenders' anxiety only grew. Panic spread and a few banks failed. After a few meagre payments, the Grand Parti stood at about 8,700,000 livre. Some of the interest was settled by taking on new debt, but, in 1582, 4,000,000 still remained.[67] The whole operation, which had seemed extremely modern at first, ended in the worst possible way.

Botti went through this ordeal with filled with worry, since he had bought portions of the debt for himself, his brothers and third parties. The collected securities portfolio had an overall value of more than 13,200 scudi. In the end, the loss came to 60% of the capital and matured interest.

Our traders, like their compatriots in general, bought state debt not only for the promised interest; they knew full well that the treasuries might not fulfil their pledges. They got mixed up in this risky activity for its indirect advantages: positive relationships with the authorities and socio-political considerations made it possible to influence if not control many economic matters.

When thinking about the Botti family's activity in Andalusia, it is helpful to keep in mind that their banking activity also extended to the local nobility and colleagues. Among them, they had especially strong ties with the dukes of Medina Sidonia, important members of the Andalusian aristocracy. In 1538, the duke owed them 1,500,000 maravedís. The following year, Iacopo advanced him the revenue from the 'hierbas de la frontera' which guaranteed 4,330,000 maravedís a year.[68] And in 1545, Lady Teresa de Zúñiga, duchess of Béjar and Plasencia, marchesa of

[66] R. Doucet, 'Le Grand Parti de Lyon au XVIe siècle', *Revue Historique*, CLXXI, 1933, 3, pp. 473–513; R. Doucet, 'Le Grand Parti de Lyon au XVIe siècle (suite et fin)', *Revue Historique*, CLXXII, 1934, 1, pp. 1–41.

[67] A. Orlandi, *Le Grand Parti*, pp. 30–33. Also see the more recent H. Lang, 'Credito e insolvenza sovrana. I prestiti alla Corona francese di mercanti-banchieri toscani e tedeschi meridionali (1550–1559)', *Annali dell'Istituto Storico Italiano-Germanico in Trento* 41, 2015 pp. 12–38.

[68] A. Franco Silva, *La Isla de León*, p. 30.

Gibraléon, Ayamonte and Bañares, granted him the power to manage all her movable and immovable assets.[69]

Lastly, a real curiosity. He also provided loans against securities, albeit not professionally. This is found in his will, which reveals that there were two strongboxes in the 'cámara de la sala baja antes a la huerta'. One contained 5500 ducats that he was keeping on deposit and securities against loans. The other contained about 5000 ducats in reals.[70]

The Botti brothers' appetite for risk was in precarious balance with their aversion to loss, but not so much as to lead them to pass on possible profit and so the pleasure of money.

[69] AHP, *Protocolos Notarilaes de Sevilla*, Oficio XIX, 12320 Libro IV, 7 May 1545 c. 3839ff.
[70] AGS, *CME*, 300.27 c. 18v.

Chapter 7
To Conclude: Trade Is Not Just a Mechanical Art

'We heard that the ship arrived in Lisbon from Calicut with gold and spices, and the ones from the Indies with gold and goods'.[1] From the Far East to the Far West, the world was expanding its borders and Europe was discovering new civilisations, embracing hitherto unknown products and assimilating, albeit slowly, unusual customs. And so, the distances were getting shorter and different cultures were making each other's acquaintance. Long, perilous journeys across the Indian and Atlantic Oceans linking the Mediterranean to the rest of the world were becoming commonplace. Two major ocean routes connected Lisbon to the East Indies and Seville to the West Indies.

This was the context the Botti family worked in. Our merchants were fully involved in this fluid, dynamic scenario. Indeed, their decisions overlapped or, perhaps better still, went along with changing events, neither anticipating nor suffering them. In a certain sense, their decisions were guided by the great geographic discoveries and consequential economic change. In 1519, they were already active in the region with the best link to the Americas: Andalusia, where they took advantage of the opening of the Atlantic, while continuing to trade in the Mediterranean and northern Europe.

While the ocean opened new prospects, the old Mare Nostrum continued to be the centre of the western world. The geographic discoveries were not able to immediately push it to the side in the world of big trade. It continued to nourish rich, vital economic activity. The group's interests remained focused on the Italian markets, from Venice to Messina and from Naples to Milan, with varying intensity. The Mediterranean also meant contact with the Provençal coast from Aigues-Mortes to Marseilles, the Spanish shores from Alicante to Barcelona, Africa from Barbary to Alexandria and the Levant, including Adrianople, Constantinople, Pera and Chios. Our merchants were active in all these markets. In short, their activity was balanced

[1] ASF, *Miscellanea*, 107 fascicolo 5, Florence-Castile, Matteo Botti to Giovanbattista and Francesco Botti, 24 July 1546 c. 18r.

A. Orlandi, *Money, Culture, Beauty. The Botti Family*,
https://doi.org/10.1007/978-3-032-00453-6_7

between an Atlantic in a period of continuous growth and a still-flourishing Mediterranean.

They shipped everything in this expanded geographical space: as we have seen, more than 150 different types of goods were traded. Commercial activity that, rooted in medieval customs, was characterised by the diversity of the traded products, even though some more than others came to distinguish their trading, opening the road to specialisation.

A range of goods that the opening of the Atlantic routes was, among other things, further expanding. New kinds of leather, sugar, wood, dyes and pearls were arriving from the West Indies, but goods hitherto unknown were coming, as well. The Americas were a kaleidoscope of infinite possibilities. News, men and merchandise were coming from those lands, piquing merchants' curiosity.

Cádiz, Seville and Valladolid were, along with Florence, the drivers of the Botti family's activity, vantage points from which they could observe the flow of business without losing sight of new opportunities. That said, they were also active individually and in partnerships in other important economic centres (Pisa, Venice, Rome, Antwerp, Lyon).

They had a multi-city presence that, like that of other Florentine traders, made them very wealthy and the authors of a clearly intercultural form of trade. The branches and companies were managed by men who had learned the local language and customs without ever losing contact with their motherland. They ably presented and spread their ideas and culture, including through goods, especially ones that came from Florentine workshops.

This intercultural exchange was rooted in effective mediation between artisans and merchants. Renaissance values did not spread solely through the activity of artists and intellectuals who moved from one court to another, but also, to an important degree, thanks to traders like the Botti. This happened in both directions of their trade activity. The goods they sent to Florence provided local artisans with ideas and stimulus, while the ones they exported spread Florentine taste and style abroad.[2]

We have seen many examples of this. From silks in Seville with patterns corrected in Tuscany to embossed and painted leather *guardamaciles* admired along the banks of the Arno, from guidance on the correct sartorial use of certain fabrics or on the sophisticated style of dresses to simple leather jackets and from toys to jewellery. What seems even more interesting is their skill in spreading beauty, like in the case of the gold bracelets made in Lyon that quickly became fashionable in Venice.

All this underpins the fact that our merchants created an important trade and financial system through a dense network of economic and social connections. Running between the nodes of that network was the rich Florentine production of 'beautiful things that please the world'. The carefully monitored money was needed for intervening vigorously on the market but was also used for many other reasons,

[2]On these themes, see M. Belfanti, 'Renaissance et *made in Italy*'; F. Braudel, *Le modèle italien*; E. Pommier, *L'invention de l'art*; G. Nigro, 'Alle origini del fattore Italia'.

such as currency speculation and financing the debt of nascent state structures. The pleasure of money and love for beauty made them industrious merchants devoted to supporting artists in Florence and Seville.

Fellow Florentines returning to Tuscany from Spain spoke of their prestige. Matteo wrote that they extolled the 'great faculties' of Iacopo and Giovanbattista,[3] even painting Iacopo as a 'prince of the greats'.[4] The Eldest must have also been highly esteemed in his hometown. Not only for trade, not only for his relationship with artists, not only for his generosity to the poor. He was greatly appreciated by the city authorities for his wealth. It is no coincidence that when Cosimo I asked him for a loan of 5000 scudi, he could not and did not want to say no. Similarly, when the captain of the ship of the duke of Medina Sidonia came to Florence, Matteo gave him a letter of credit worth 9000 scudi to use in Naples to buy up grain.[5]

Simone also enjoyed high esteem. In 1558, the Grand Duke named him guarantor of 5000 scudi towards the large dowry of Lucrezia de' Medici, the betrothed of Alfonso II d'Este.[6]

Financial problems were clearly not the cause of the break-up of the group, which continued to remain united for many years after the separation. It was all a matter of internal family issues. Iacopo had not had any male children, Giovanbattista had returned to Florence and Francesco, Simone and Matteo had died one after the other. In short, it was a series of concomitant causes that prevented the continuation of the kind of striving that had distinguished a half century of trade and financial activity.

The space they left did not remain empty: Francesco de' Santis and Nerozzo del Nero in Cádiz and Lorenzo del Rosso in Seville continued Iacopo's legacy. And so, the goodwill of the most daring of the Botti brothers did not go to waste. When his brother died, Giovanbattista was certain that, 'working well', those three Florentines would build some 'excellent positive momentum'.[7]

The rich fruit of long, hard years of trade left its mark. In Seville, the beneficiaries were Iacopo's daughters, becoming part of the Andalusian nobility. And in Florence, young Matteo, son of Giovanbattista, by then titled, like many other Florentines, ended the adventure of his predecessors as a Medici ambassador. He had not learned the art of trading, but he had the taste for beauty, pleasure in collecting[8] and love for artists.

---

[3] ASF, *Miscellanea*, 107 fascicolo 4, Florence-Castile, Matteo Botti to Giovanbattista and Francesco Botti, 10 January 1545 c. 64r.

[4] ASF, *Miscellanea*, 107 fascicolo 5, Florence-Castile, Matteo Botti to Giovanbattista and Francesco Botti, 25 September 1546 c. 27r.

[5] ASF, *Miscellanea*, fascicolo 4, Florence-Seville, Matteo Botti to Giovanbattista and Francesco Botti, 30 January 1546 c. 185r.

[6] F. Point-Waquet, 'Les Botti', p. 695.

[7] ASF, *Libri di commercio*, 716 Florence-Cádiz, Giovanbattista Botti to Francesco de' Santis, 1 February 1563 c. 46r.

[8] His collection included 23 valuable timepieces. F. Point-Waquet, 'Les Botti', p. 695.

Monetary Note

The circulation of Florentine currency in the sixteenth century was highly complex, due to the constant variation of the gold and silver exchange ratio. In any case, starting in the late fifteenth century, the official gold coin was the *fiorino d'oro in oro*, or ducat.

In early 1531, Clement VII and the Florentines promised to pay the Spanish 300,000 gold ducats to stop the siege. In order to 'save' something, the mint reduced the weight, devaluing the coins by 3%.[1]

This devaluation made the gold ducat equal to a *scudo d'oro di sole*. The effects were soon felt on the market, and, to eliminate all doubt, an official announcement was made that legally ruled the equivalence of the gold ducat and the *scudo d'oro di sole*, with both equal to seven lire.[2]

The regulation was probably not immediately applied, creating some confusion among traders. For example, the Biscayan merchants would not accept scudi in place of ducats.[3]

The situation remained unstable. In February 1532, a ducat was worth 1 *scudo d'oro di sole* and 4 *soldi di piccioli.*[4] Twelve months later, a ducat equalled 1 *scudo*

[1] ASF, *Libri di commercio*, 721 Pisa-Cádiz, Francesco Botti to the Botti company, 30 January 1531 c. 3v.

[2] This is how the *scudo di sole* was described by the monetary authorities: 'and the *scudo Fiorentinum* of France, Venice and Genoa, which is popularly and commonly called *scudo di sole*, must and can be spent at seven lire for one of these coins'. ('et lo scudo Fiorentinum di Francia, di Vinetia et Genova, che vulgarmente et comunemente sono chiamati scudi di sole, si debba et possa spendere per libre septe di tal moneta l'uno.) M. Bernocchi, *Le monete della Repubblica Fiorentina. Il libro della Zecca*, I, Olschki, Florence 1974 pp. 475–476.

[3] ASF, *Libri di commercio*, 721 Pisa-Cádiz, Francesco Botti to the Botti company, 30 January 1531 c. 3v.

[4] ASF, *Libri di commercio*, 721, Pisa-Cádiz, Francesco Botti to the Botti company, 20 March 1532, cc. 41v.

A. Orlandi, *Money, Culture, Beauty. The Botti Family*,
https://doi.org/10.1007/978-3-032-00453-6

and 6 *soldi di piccioli*, which in turn equalled 7 lire and 9 soldi (149 soldi in total).[5] Businessmen in particular wanted a bit of clarity, but it was not until the second half of the sixteenth century that the 7-lire florin/ducat (140 soldi) and the 7.5-lire *scudo d'oro in oro* (150 soldi) became, along with the lira, stable money of account that merchants and bookkeepers could use without fear of error.[6]

As for Spain, besides the silver real that had been minted since the fourteenth century, the ducat was a gold coin minted since the time of the Catholic Kings (1497). It circulated internationally and equalled 375 maravedís. Due to its high gold content, Charles I replaced replaced the old coin in 1536 with the scudo equivalent to 350 maravedís. The ducat therefore became money of account widely used by merchant companies.

[5] ASF, *Libri di commercio*, 721 Pisa-Cádiz, Francesco Botti to the Botti company, 1 February 1533 c. 101r.

[6] R.A. Goldthwaite-G. Mandich, *Studi sulla moneta fiorentina (Secoli XIII-XVI)*, Leo S. Olschki, Florence 1994, pp. 64–65.

Manuscript Sources

Italian

ARCHIVIO DI STATO DI FIRENZE
FONDI

Acquisti e Doni, Registro Galletti, 286/3, Travel book and letter book.

Arte dei Medici e Speziali, Books of the dead, 248.
Arte dei Medici e Speziali, Books of the dead, 251.

Carte Strozziane, V Serie, 1090, Statement of account.
Carte Strozziane, V Serie, 1506, Letter book.

Diplomatico, Loose letters.

Decima repubblicana, 1842 arroti 37, Account book.

Libri di commercio e di famiglia, 710, Book of properties.
Libri di commercio e di famiglia, 711, Letter book.
Libri di commercio e di famiglia, 712, Letter book.
Libri di commercio e di famiglia, 713, Letter book.
Libri di commercio e di famiglia, 714, Book of properties.
Libri di commercio e di famiglia, 715, Letter book.
Libri di commercio e di famiglia, 716, Letter book.
Libri di commercio e di famiglia, 721, Letter book.
Libri di commercio e di famiglia, 723, Letter book.
Libri di commercio e di famiglia, 724, Book of debtors and creditors.
Libri di commercio e di famiglia, 725, Book of debtors and creditors.
Libri di commercio e di famiglia, 726, Memoir and letter book.
Libri di commercio e di famiglia, 727, Letter book.
Libri di commercio e di famiglia, 734, Book of debtors and creditors.
Libri di commercio e di famiglia, 742, Letter book.
Libri di commercio e di famiglia,743, Letter book and exchange book.

A. Orlandi, *Money, Culture, Beauty. The Botti Family*,
https://doi.org/10.1007/978-3-032-00453-6

Manoscritti, Carte dell'Ancisa DD, 351. Various scriptures.
Manoscritti, 594 I, sc. III, 26. Family tree.

Mediceo del Principato, 221, Register of letters.

Mercanzia, Libri delle accomandite, 10832.

Minute di lettere e Registri, 14028, Loose letters.

Miscellanea Medicea, 107, fascicolo 2, Loose letters.
Miscellanea Medicea, 107, fascicolo 3, Letter book.
Miscellanea Medicea, 107, fascicolo 4, Letter book.
Miscellanea Medicea, 107, fascicolo 5, Letter book.

Notarile antecosimiano, 13918, Notarial deeds.

Raccolta Ceramelli Papiani, 930. Family coat of arms.

Tratte, Book of ages, 81.

Ufficiali poi Magistrato della Grascia, 191.
Ufficiali poi Magistrato della Grascia, 192.
Ufficiali poi Magistrato della Grascia, 193.

BIBLIOTECA NAZIONALE CENTRALE DI FIRENZE
FONDI

Capponi, 9, Book of debtors and creditors.

SCUOLA NORMALE SUPERIORE (Pisa)
FONDI

Archivio Salviati, III, 22, Memoir.

Spanish Sources

ARCHIVO DE INDIAS DE SEVILLA
FONDI

Contratación, 202, Notarial deeds.
Indiferente, 422, 424, Royal note and licence.
Justicia, 897, Notarial deeds.

ARCHIVO GENERAL DE SIMANCAS
FONDI

Contaduría de Mercedes, 270.20, Will of Ana Francisca Fonte.
Contaduría de Mercedes, 300.27, Will of Iacopo Botti.
Contaduría de Mercedes, 300.27, Will of Ana Paula Botti.
Contaduría de Mercedes, 300.27, Will of Ginebra Botti.

Contaduría de Mercedes, 79.36, *Juro* for Luis Zapata.

ARCHIVO HISTÓRICO PROVINCIAL DE SEVILLA
FONDI

Protocolos Notariales de Sevilla, Oficio XV, 9169, Libro II, Notarial deeds.
Protocolos Notariales de Sevilla, Oficio XIX, 12320, Libro IV, Notarial deeds.

ARCHIVO HISTÓRICO PROVINCIAL DE CÁDIZ
FONDI

Protocolos Notariales de Cádiz, Oficio XIX, 4336, Notarial deeds.
Protocolos Notariales de Cádiz, Oficio XIX, 4339, Notarial deeds.

Bibliography

Acidini Luchinat, C. (1991). Il mecenatismo familiare. In F. Borsi (Ed.), *'Per bellezza, per studio, per piacere'. Lorenzo il Magnifico e gli spazi dell'arte* (pp. 101–124). Giunti.

Afonso, L. U. (2016). Patterns of artistic hybridization in the early protoglobalization period. *Journal of World History, XXVII/2*, 215–253.

Ajmar-Wollheim, M., & Molà, L. (2011). The global renaissance: Cross-cultural objects in the early modern period. In G. Adamson et al. (Eds.), *Global design history* (pp. 11–20). Routledge.

Ammannati, F. (2013). Un calzolaio del Quattrocento: Girolamo Talducci e la sua bottega in Porta Santa Trinita. *Prato Storia e Arte, 113*, 143–155.

Ammannati, F. (2020). *Per filo e per segno. L'arte della lana a Firenze nel Cinquecento*. FUP.

Andelson, C. (1983) Cosimo I de' Medici and the foundation of tapestry production in Florence. In *Firenze e la Toscana dei Medici nell'Europa del '500, III Relazioni artistiche. Il linguaggio architettonico europeo* (pp. 899–924). Olschki.

Angiolini, F. (1996). *I cavalieri e il principe. L'Ordine di Santo Stefano e la società toscana in età moderna*. EDIFIR.

Antoni, T. (1975). Le scuole di abaco a Pisa nel secolo XIV. In *Studi di ragioneria, organizzazione e tecnica economica. Scritti in memoria del prof. Alberto Riparbelli* (Vol. I, pp. 57–62). Cursi.

Antunes, C., Grafe, R., & Lamikiz, X. (2024). Trade and the colonial economies, 1500–1828. In P. Lains, L. Freire Costa, R. Grafe, A. Herranz-Locán, D. Igual Luis, & H. Vasconcelos Vilar (Eds.), *An economic history of the Iberian Peninsula, 700-2000* (pp. 409–442). Cambridge University Press.

Arévalo, R. G., & Ocaña, A. C. (2018). Hermanas. Relaciones entre la península ibérica y la península itálica, de la Edad Media a la Moderna. *eHumanista: Journal of Iberian Studies, 38*.

Bailyn, B. (1955). *The New England merchants in the seventeenth century*. Harvard University Press.

Bargellini, P. (1964). *La Splendida Storia di Firenze dal Duca d'Atene a Cosimo I*. Vallecchi Editore. 4 vols., II.

Barocchi, P. (1999). Sulla collezione Botti. *Prospettiva, 93–94*(II), 126–130.

Battista, G. (2024). *Le avventure di una famiglia di mercanti-banchieri fiorentini. Storia documentata dei Rinieri del Vaio di San Giovanni*. Aska Edizioni.

Bayard, F. (1971). Les Bonvisi, marchands banquiers à Lyon, 1575-1629. *Annales. Économies, Sociétés, Civilisations, XXVI*, 1234–1269.

Belfanti, C. M. (2008). *Civiltà della moda*. Il Mulino.

Belfanti, C. M. (2012). Renaissance et *made in Italy*: l'invention d'une identité culturelle pour l'industrie de la mode. In P. Minard, C. Maitte, & M. de Olivera (Eds.), *La gloire de l'Industrie, XVIIe-XIXe siècle. Faire de l'histoire avec Gérard Gayot* (pp. 145–162). Presses Universitiares de Rennes.

A. Orlandi, *Money, Culture, Beauty. The Botti Family*,
https://doi.org/10.1007/978-3-032-00453-6

Bellavitis, A., Frank, M., & Sapienza, V. (Eds.). (2017). *Garzoni. Apprendistato e formazione tra Venezia e l'Europa in età moderna*. Universitas Studiorum S.r.l.

Bello León, J. M. (2005). Almadrabas andaluzas a finales de la Edad Media. Nuevos datos para su estudio. *Historia. Instituciones. Documentos, 32*, 81–113.

Beloch, K. J. (1994). Introduction. In L. del Panta & E. Sonnino (Eds.), *Storia della popolazione d'Italia*. Casa editrice Le Lettere.

Bennassar, B. (1967). *Valladolid au siècle d'or, une ville de Castille et sa campagne au XVI siècle*. Mouton & Co.

Bennassar, B., & Bennassar, L. (1992) *1492 ¿Un mundo nuevo?* Nerea.

Bernal Rodríguez, A. M. (1994). Sobre los seguros marítimos en la Carrera de Indias, siglo XVI. In F. Ballesteros Caballero, H. Casado Alonso, A. C. Ibáñez Pérez, & S. Escolar Díez (Eds.), *Actas del V Centenario del Consulado de Burgos* (pp. 501–527). Diputación Provincial de Burgos.

Bernal Rodríguez, A. M. (1997). La aseguración marítima de la Carrera de Indias: seguros, crédito y actividad financiera (ss.XVI-XVIII). In *VI Congreso de la Asociación Española de Historia Económica*, Gerona (pp. 1–15).

Bernal Rodríguez, A. M., Collantes De Terán, A., & García-Baquero, A. (2008). *Sevilla, de los gremios a la indstrialización*. Ayuntamiento de Sevilla.

Bernocchi, M. (1974). *Le monete della Repubblica Fiorentina. Il libro della Zecca* (Vol. I). Olschki.

Berti, M. (1978). Aspetti dell'attività commerciale di Livorno all'inizio del regime di porto franco colti da un osservatorio significativo: la società di Giulio del Beccuto. In *Atti del Convegno "Livorno e il Mediterraneo nell'età medicea" 23-25 settembre 1977* (pp. 278–291). U. Bastogi Editore.

Berti, M. (2000). *Nel Mediterraneo ed oltre. Temi di storia e storiografia marittima toscana (secoli XIII-XVIII)*. ETS.

Bethencourt, F., & Egmond, F. (Eds.). (2007). *Cultural exchange in early modern Europe, III, correspondence and cultural exchange in Europe, 1400-1700* (pp. 80–103). Cambridge University Press.

Bisaha, N. (2004). *Creating east and west: Renaissance humanists and the Ottoman Turks*. University of Pennsylvania Press.

Black, R. (2011). *Humanism and education in medieval and Renaissance Italy*. Cambridge University Press.

Black, R. (2021). Maestri e insegnamento di grammatica allo Studio fiorentino nel XIV e XV secolo. In L. Fabbri (Ed.), *Studium florentinum: l'istruzione superiore a Firenze fra XIV e XVI secolo* (pp. 177–195). Edizioni di Storia e Letteratura.

Bocchi, F. (1591). *Le bellezze della città di Fiorenza dove a pieno di pittura, di scultura, di sacri tempii, di palazzi i più notabili artifizii et più preziosi si contengono*. Sermartelli. https://www.memofonte.it/files/2019/12/Bocchi_LE_BELLEZZE_DELLA_CITTA_DI-FIORENZA_1591.pdf

Borghini, R. (1584). *Del riposo in cui della pittura e della scultura si favella, de' più illustri pittori e scultori e delle più famose opere loro si fa menzione; e le cose principali appartenenti a dette arti s'insegnano*, libro IV. Giorgio Marescotti. https://www.memofonte.it/home/files/pdf/guide_borghini_4.pdf

Borlandi, F. (2012). *Discorso di inaugurazione dell'anno accademico 1962-1963 dell'Università di Genova* (pp. 223–230). Società Ligure di Storia Patria, Biblioteca digitale.

Boscolo, A., & Torres Ramírez, B. (Eds.). (1986). *La presenza italiana in Andalusia nel Basso Medioevo, Atti del secondo convegno, Roma, 25-27 maggio 1984*. Cappelli editore.

Boucher, J. (1994). *Présence italienne à Lyon à la Renaissance*. LUGD.

Boyer-Xambeau, M.-T., Deleplace, G., & Gillard, L. (1991). *Moneta e credito nell'Europa del Cinquecento*. Einaudi.

Braudel, F. (1974). L'Italia fuori dall'Italia. Due secoli e tre Italie. In R. Romano & C. Vivanti (Eds.), *Storia d'Italia. Dalla caduta dell'Impero romano al secolo XVIII. L'economia delle tre Italie* (pp. 2089–2248). Giulio Einaudi editore.

Braudel, F. (1989). *Le modèle italien*. Arthaud.

Braunstein, P. (1989). Réseaux familiaux, réseaux d'affaires en pays d'Empire: les facteurs des société Fugger (1380-1520). In F. Crouzet (Ed.), *Le négoce international, XIIIe-XXe siècle* (pp. 23–34). Economica.

Braunstein, P., & Franceschi, F. (2007). «Saperssi governar». Pratica mercantile e arte del vivere. In *Il Rinascimento italiano e l'Europa. Commercio e cultura mercantile* (Vol. IV, pp. 655–677). Colla Editore.

Brucker, G. A. (1962). *Florentine politics and society, 1343-1378*. Princeton University Press.

Brucker, G. A. (1969). *Renaissance Florence*. University of California Press.

Bucci, M., & Bencini, R. (1973). *Palazzi di Firenze* (Vol. IV). Quartiere di Santo Spirito.

Burckhardt, J. (1860). *Die Kultur der Renaissance in Italien*. Schweighauser'schen Verlagsbuchhandlung.

Burke, P. R., Clossey, L., & Fernández-Armesto, F. (2017). The global Renaissance. *Journal of World History, XXVIII/1*, 1–30.

Cantagalli, R. (1971). Matteo Botti. In *Dizionario Biografico degli Italiani* (Vol. 13). https://www.treccani.it/enciclopedia/matteo-botti_(Dizionario-Biografico)/

Capretti, E. (2004). *I Medici mecenati a Firenze: da mercanti a signori*. Polistampa.

Carande, R. (1987). *Carlo V e i suoi banchieri*. Marietti.

Cartaya Baños, J. (2018). *Mayorazgos. Riqueza, nobleza y posteridad en la Sevilla del siglo XVI*. Editorial Universidad de Sevilla.

Carvajal de la Vega, D. (2023a). Intermediación financiera en las ferias castellanas a inicio de la Edad Moderna. Las cartas de poder. In M. Cachero Vinuesa & N. Maillard Álvarez (Eds.), *El laberinto del crédito en la Edad Moderna: instrumentos, agentes y mercados* (pp. 15–46). Sílex Ediciones.

Carvajal de la Vega, D. (2023b). Valladolid y el servicio de cortes a inicios del siglo XVI. Evolución y gestión. In R. Lanza García (Ed.), *Los dineros de la corona. Finanzas y cambio fiscal en la monarquía hispánica (siglos XVI-XVII)* (pp. 23–51). Comares.

Casado Alonso, H. (2007). Comercio textil, crédito al consumo y ventas al fiado en las ferias de Medina del Campo en la primera mitad del siglo XVI. In S. de Dios de Dios, J. Infante Miguel-Motta, R. Robledo Hernández, & E. Torijano Pérez (Eds.), *Historia de la propiedad. Crédito y garantía, V Encuentro Interdisciplinar. Salamanca, 31 de mayo-2 de junio* (pp. 127–160). Colegio de Registradores de Madrid, Servicio de Estudios.

Casado Alonso, H. (2010a). Comercio y mercaderes en el valle del Duero (siglos XV y XVI). *Estudios de historia de España, 12*(1), 93–116.

Casado Alonso, H. (2010b). Crédito y comercio en las ferias de Medina del Campo en la primera mitad del siglo XVI. In E. M. García Guerra & G. De Luca (Eds.), *Il mercato del credito in età moderna. Reti e operatori finanziari nello spazio europeo* (pp. 21–48). Franco Angeli.

Casado Alonso, H. (2010c). El Duero oriental a finales de la Edad Media y principios del siglo XVI crecimiento económico y transformaciones. *Biblioteca: estudio e investigación, 25*, 25–37.

Casado Alonso, H. (2015). El seguro marítimo en la Carrera de Indias en la época de Felipe II. In J. J. Iglesias Rodríguez, R. M. Pérez García, & M. F. Fernández Chaves (Eds.), *Comercio y cultura en la Edad Moderna. Actas de la XIII Reunión Científica de la Fundación Española de Historia Moderna. Comunicaciones* (pp. 943–960). Universidad de Sevilla.

Casado Alonso, H. (2017). Comercio y flujos financieros en los negocios de Simón Ruiz. In H. Casado Alonso (Ed.), *Simón Ruiz y el mundo de los negocios en Europa en los siglos XVI y XVII* (pp. 139–163). Ediciones Universidad de Valladolid.

Casado Alonso, H. (2018). Comprar y vender en las ferias de Castilla durante los siglos XV y XVI. In J. Petrowiste & M. Lafuente Gómez (Eds.), *Faire son marché au Moyen Âge: Méditerranée occidentale, XIIIe-XVIe siècles* (pp. 111–132). Casa de Velázquez.

Casado Alonso, H. (2020). Insuring life, insuring debt: Life insurance in sixteenth-century Spain. *Pedralbes: Revista d'Història Moderna, 40*, 75–95.

Casarino, G. (1988). *Maestri e garzoni nella società genovese fra XV e XVI secolo. Profilo e itinerario quantitativo della ricerca*. Prima Cooperativa Grafica Genovese.

Cassandro, M. (1976). Banca e commercio fiorentini alle fiere di Ginevra nel secolo XV. *Rivista Storica Svizzera, XXVI*, 567–611.

Cassandro, M. (1979). *Le fiere di Lione e gli uomini d'affari italiani nel Cinquecento*. Baccini e Chiappi.

Cassandro, M. (1985) Strategia degli affari dei mercanti-banchieri italiani alle fiere internazionali d'Oltralpe (secoli XIV-XVI). In *«Aspetti della vita economica medievale», Atti del Convegno di Studi nel X anniversario della morte di Federigo Melis, Firenze-Pisa-Prato, 10-14 marzo 1984* (pp. 140–150). Università degli Studi di Firenze.

Cassandro, M. (1989). I forestieri a Lione nel '400 e nel '500: la nazione fiorentina. In G. Rossetti (Ed.), *Dentro la città, Stranieri e realtà urbane nell'Europa dei secoli XII-XV* (pp. 163–175). GISEM, Liguori.

Cassandro, M. (1994). Le élites internazionali a Ginevra e Lione nei secoli XV-XVI. In M. del Treppo (Ed.), *Sistema di rapporti ed élites economiche in Europa (secoli XII-XVII)* (pp. 231–248). Liguori.

Cassandro, M. (1996). Economia e politica nelle città di fiera: Ginevra e Lione (secoli XIV-XVI). In G. Petti Balbi (Ed.), *Strutture del potere ed élites economiche nelle città europee dei secoli XII-XVI* (pp. 291–310). Liguori.

Catellacci, D. (1881). Diario di Felice Brancacci, ambasciatore con Carlo Federighi al Cairo per il Comune di Firenze (1422). *Archivio storico italiano, S. IV*(VIII), 157–188.

Cavaciocchi, S. (Ed.). (1993). *La seta in Europa. Secc. XIII-XX, Atti della Ventiquattresima Settimana di studi dell'Istituto Internazionale di Storia Economica «F. Datini» di Prato (Prato, 4-9 maggio 1992)*. Istituto Internazionale di Storia Economica "F. Datini" Prato, Le Monnier.

Ceccarelli, G. (2020). *Risky markets: Marine insurance in Renaissance Florence*. Brill.

Cessi, R. (1917). Note per la storia delle Società di commercio nel Medioevo in Italia. *Rivista italiana di Scienze Giuridiche, 59*(fasc. I), 1–140.

Chabod, I. (2012). *Ricostruzione di una famiglia. I Ciurianni di Firenze tra XII e XV secolo, con l'edizione critica del «Libro propio» di Lapo di Valore Ciurianni e successori (1326-1429)*. Le Lettere.

Chauduri, K. N. (1985). *Trade and civilisation in the Indian Ocean. An economic history from the rise of Islam to 1750*. Cambridge University Press.

Chini, E. (1984). *La chiesa dei Santi Michele e Gaetano a Firenze*. Edizioni Cassa di Risparmio di Firenze.

Chorley, P. (2003). Rascie and the Florentine cloth industry during the sixteenth century. *The Journal of European Economic History, XXXII*(3), 487–527.

Ciappelli, G. (1995). *Una famiglia e le ricordanze; i Castellani di Firenze nel Tre-Quattrocento*. Olschki.

Cioranescu, A. (1972) La aventura americana de los hermanos Silva. In *Anuario de Estudios Atlánticos*, 18, Patronato de la "Casa de Colón", Madrid-Las Palmas de Gran Canaria (pp. 277–304).

Cipolla, C. M. (1969). *Literacy and development in the west*. Penguin.

Cipolla, C. M. (2002). *Istruzione e sviluppo, Il declino dell'analfabetismo nel mondo occidentale*. Il Mulino.

Clutton-Brock, J. (1987). *A natural history of domesticated mammals*. Cambridge University Press.

Conte, G. (1988-1989). *La holding della famiglia Capponi,1485-1516. (Con trascrizione del libro segreto paghonazzo segnato *, 1485-1516)* [Degree thesis], Università degli Studi di Florence, Facoltà di Economia e Commercio, Istituto di Storia Economica, a.a.

Corona Pérez, E. (Ed.). (2022). *Trata atlántica y esclavitud en Sevilla (ca. 1500-1650)*. Universidad de Sevilla.

Cotrugli, B. (1990). In U. Tucci (Ed.), *Il libro dell'arte di mercatura*. Arsenale Editrice.

Crabb, A. (2000). *The Strozzi of Florence. Widowhood and family solidarity in the Renaissance*. University of Michigan Press.

Cruz Barney, O. (1998). *El riesgo en el comercio hispano-indiano. Préstamos y seguros marítimos durante los siglos XVI a XIX*. Universidad Nacional Autónoma de México.

Curtin, P. D. (1984). *Cross-cultural trade in world history*. Cambridge University Press.

da Cunha Pinheiro, L. (2012). A produção açucareira em São Tomé ao longo de Quinhentos. In *Actas do Colóquio Internacional São Tomé e Príncipe numa perspectiva interdisciplinar, diacrónica e sincrónica* (pp. 27–46). Instituto Universitário de Lisboa.

DaCosta Kaufmann, T. (1995). *Court, cloister, city. The art and culture of Central Europe, 1450–1800* (pp. 23–49). University of Chicago Press.

Danna, R. (2019). Una scienza per la rinascita. Note su Paolo dell'Abaco e la matematica abacista fiorentina. *Rinascimento, 59*, 245–269.

De La Roncière, C. (1987). La vita privata dei notabili toscani alle soglie del Rinascimento. In P. Ariès & G. Duby (Eds.), *La vita privata dal Feudalesimo al Rinascimento* (pp. 130–251). Bari.

De La Rosa Olivera, L. (1959). Don Pedro Fernández de Lugo prepara la expedición a Santa Marta. In *Anuario de Estudios Atlánticos*, 5, Patronato de la "Casa de Colón", Madrid-Las Palmas de Gran Canaria (pp. 399–433).

De Luca, A., Nuovo, F., Piseri, F. 2021. La formazione del mercante. Scuole libri cultura economica a Milano nel Rinascimento. Milano: Editoriale Delfino.

de Luxán Meléndez, S., & Viña, A. (2009). *La Empresa Azucarera en Canaria. Siglos XV-XX*. Destilerías Arehucas.

De Mercado, T. (1523–1575). *Suma de tratos y contratos*. Retrieved June 25, 2024, from https://www.cervantesvirtual.com/obra-visor/suma-de-tratos-y-contratos%2D%2D0/html/feec322c-82b1-11df-acc7-002185ce6064_4.html#I_51

De Molina, L. (1597). *De Iustitia et Iure*, Cuenca, Tomo II, col. 496, B.

de Ory Lozano, E. (1993). *Colón, Cádiz y el descubrimiento de América*. S.L. Rústica Editorial.

de Osma, G. J. (1908). *Los maestros alfareros de Manises, Paterna y Valencia. Contratos y ordenanzas de los siglos XIV, XV y XVI*. Instituto de Valencia de D. Juan. (edición facsímil, Valencia, Librerías París-Valencia, 1996).

De Roover, R. (1953). *L'evolution de la lettre de change (XIVe-XVIIIe sieclès)*. Librairie Armand Colin.

De Roover, R. (1970). *Il Banco Medici. Dalle origini al declino (1397–1494)*. La Nuova Italia.

del Corazza, B. (1991). In R. Gentile (Ed.), *Diario Fiorentino (1405-1439)*. De Rubeis.

Del Punta, I. (2011). *Lucca e il commercio della seta nel Medioevo*. Pacini Editore.

Del Punta, I., & Rosati, M. L. (2017). *Lucca una città di seta. Produzione, commercio e diffusione dei tessuti lucchesi nel tardo Medioevo*. Pacini-Fazzi.

Del Treppo, M. (Ed.). (1994). *Sistema di rapporti ed élites economiche in Europa (secoli XII-XVII)*. GISEM, Liguori.

Delzant, J. B. (2013). Per l'onore della città, per l'onore del signore. Circolazione di modelli politici e di artisti tra le signorie cittadine dell'Italia centrale (secolo XV). In I. Lori Sanfilippo & S. Maddalo (Eds.), *Civiltà urbana e committenze artistiche al tempo del Maestro di Offida (secoli XIV–XV). Atti del convegno (Ascoli Piceno, Palazzo dei Capitani, 1-3 dicembre 2011)* (pp. 13–37). Istituto Storico per il Medioevo.

Denucé, J. (Ed.). (1934). *Inventaire des Affaitadi banquiers italiens à Anvers de l'année 1568*. Éditions de «Sikkel».

DePrano, M. (2018). *Art patronage, family and gender in Renaissance Florence*. Cambridge University Press.

Dini, B. (1978). Aspetti del commercio di esportazione dei panni di lana e dei drappi di seta fiorentini in Costantinopoli, negli anni 1522–1531. In *Studi in memoria di Federigo Melis*, Giannini, 5 vols., IV (pp. 1–54).

Dini, B. (1987). Una manifattura di battiloro nel Quattrocento. In *Tecnica e società nell'Italia dei secolo XII-XVI, Atti dell'undicesimo Convegno Internazionale di studio tenuto a Pistoia nei giorni 28-31 ottobre 1984* (pp. 83–111). Centro Italiano di Studi di Storia e d'Arte Pistoia, Editografica.

Dini, B. (1993). L'industria serica in Italia. In S. Cavaciocchi (Ed.), *La seta in Europa. Secc. XIII-XX, Atti della "Venticinquesima Settimana di Studi" 4-9 maggio 1992* (pp. 91–123). Istituto Internazionale di Storia Economica "F. Datini" Prato, Le Monnier.

Dini, B. (2000). I battilori fiorentini del Quattrocento. In *Medioevo, Mezzogiorno, Mediterraneo: studi in onore di Mario Del Treppo* (pp. 139–161). Naples.

Dini, B. (2006). I mercanti banchieri italiani e le fiere di Ginevra e Lione. In F. Salvestrini (Ed.), *L'Italia alla fine del Medioevo. I caratteri originali nel quadro europeo* (Vol. I, pp. 433–456). Centro di Studi sulla civiltà del tardo Medioevo San Miniato, FUP.

Doucet, R. (1933). Le Grand Parti de Lyon au XVIe siècle. *Revue Historique, CLXXI*(3), 473–513.

Doucet, R. (1934). Le Grand Parti de Lyon au XVIe siècle (suite et fin). *Revue Historique, CLXXII*(1), 1–41.

Duby, G. (1987). La vita privata nelle famiglie aristocratiche della Francia feudale. In P. Ariès & G. Duby (Eds.), *La vita privata dal Rinascimento all'Illuminismo* (pp. 37–71). Bari.

Edler De Roover, F. (1993). *Le sete lucchesi*. Istituto Storico Lucchese.

Edler De Roover, F. (1999). *L'arte della seta a Firenze nei secoli XIV e XV*. Leo S. Olschki.

Elliot, J. H. (1982). *La Spagna imperiale: 1469-1716*. Il Mulino.

Fábregas García, A. (2001). Estrategía de los mercaderes toscanos y genoveses en el Reino de Granada a través de la correspondencia Datini. *Serta Antiqua e Mediaevalia, 5*, 259–302.

Favier, J. (1990). *L'oro e le spezie. L'uomo di affari dal Medioevo al Rinascimento*. Garzanti.

Fernández Chaves, M. F., et al. (Eds.). (2019). *Mercaderes y redes mercantiles en la Península Ibérica. Siglos XV-XVIII*. Universidad de Sevilla.

Fernández de Béthencourt, F. (1878-1879). *Nobiliario y blasón de Canarias. Diccionario histórico, biográfico, genealógico y hèraldico*, Imprenta isleña, Santa Cruz de Tenerife , Tomo I. https://bibliotecadigital.jcyl.es/es/catalogo_imagenes/grupo.do?path=10130529

Fernández-Armesto, F. (1997). *Las Islas Canarias después de la conquista. La creación de una Sociedad Colonial a principios del siglo XVI*. Ediciones del Cabildo Insular de Gran Canaria.

Fierli, G. (n.d.) *Della societa chiamata accomandita e di altre materie mercantili secondo le leggi, e statuti veglianti in Toscana*, Antonio Brazzini, Florence 1803 text available at https://archive.org/details/bub_gb_uKVuath84WQC/mode/2up

Figliuolo, B. (2013). Mercanti fiorentini e il loro spazio economico: un modello di organizzazione capitalistica. *Archivio Storico Italiano, 638*, 639–664.

Figliuolo, B., Bocchi, A., & Passera, L. (2020). *Ragioni di mercatura. Un rotolo pergamenaceo fiorentino trecentesco di argomento commerciale*. Forum Edizioni.

Findlen, P. (2004). Ereditare un museo. Collezionismo, strategie familiari e pratiche culturali nell'Italia del XVI secolo. *Quaderni Storici, 39*(115), 45–81.

Florido del Corral, D. (2005). *Evolución histórica y cultural de las almadrabas en el litoral atlántico meridional (siglos XVI-XX)*, Barcelona.

Fornell Fernández, F. J. (2011). Los Fonte, un ejemplo del comercio gaditano con Canarias durante el siglo XVI. *Trocadero, 23*, 165–173.

Fossi, G. (1992). Grandi casati, uomini illustri e committenti. In L. Berti (Ed.), *La Chiesa di Santa Maria del Carmine a Firenze* (pp. 313–342). Cassa di Risparmio di Firenze.

Franceschi, F. (1993). *Oltre il «Tumulto». I lavoratori fiorentini dell'Arte della Lana fra Tre e Quattrocento*. Olschki.

Franceschi, F. (1996). Les enfants au travail dans la manufacture textile florentine des XIVe et XVe siècles. *Médiévales, 30*, 69–82.

Franceschi, F. (1999). La bottega come spazio di sociabilità. In F. Franceschi & G. Fossi (Eds.), *Arti fiorentine. La grande storia dell'Artigianato, Vol. II, Il Quattrocento* (pp. 64–83). Giunti.

Franceschi, F. (2014). In I. Lori Sanfilippo & A. Rigon (Eds.), *I giovani, l'apprendistato, il lavoro, in I giovani nel Medioevo. Ideali e pratiche di vita. Atti del Convegno di studio (Ascoli Piceno, 29 novembre-1 dicembre 2012)* (pp. 122–143). Istituto Storico Italiano per il Medioevo.

Franceschi, F. (2016). Woollen luxury cloth in late medieval Italy. In B. Lambert & K. A. Wilson (Eds.), *Europe's rich fabric. The consumption, commercialisation, and production of luxury textiles in Italy, the low countries and neighbouring territories (fourteenth-sixteenth centuries)* (pp. 181–204). Ashgate.

Franceschi, F. (2020). Big business for firms and states: Silk manufacturing in Renaissance Italy. *Business History Review, 94*(1), 95–123.

Franci, R., & Toti Rigatelli, L. (1981). La trattatistica matematica del Rinascimento senese. *Atti dell'Accademia delle Scienze di Siena detta de' Fisiocritici, XIV*(13), 1–71.

Franco Silva, A. (1995). *La Isla de León en la Baja Edad Media*, Excmo. Ayuntamiento de San Fernando-Fundación Municipal de Cultura.

Frangioni, L. (2002). *Chiedere e ottenere. L'approvvigionamento di prodotti di successo della bottega Datini di Avignone nel XIV secolo*. Opus Libri.

Frattarelli Fischer, L. (2018). *L'Arcano del mare. Un porto nella prima età globale: Livorno*. Pacini.

Fusaro, M. (2003). Les Anglais et les Grecs. Un réseau de coopération commerciale en Méditerranée vénitienne. *Annales, Histoire, Sciences Sociales, 58*(3), 605–625.

Fusaro, M. (2012). Cooperating mercantile networks in the early modern Mediterranean. *Economic History Review, 65*(2), 701–718.

Fusaro, M. (2018). The Greeks of Venice, 1498–1600: Immigration, settlement, and integration. *Renaissance Quarterly, 71*(2), 716–717.

Gaeta Bertelà, G. (1997). *La Tribuna di Ferdinando I de' Medici. Inventari 1589–1631*. Panini Editore.

Gambín García, M. (2014). Sevillanos y andaluces en la colonización Canaria y en la conquista de América. In E. Acosta Guerrero (Ed.), *XX Coloquio de Historia Canario-Americana* (pp. 246–261). Cabildo Insular de Gran Canaria.

García Bernal, J. J., Guillaume Alonso, A., Pérez, B., & Zerari-Penin, M. (2020). Del Mediterráneo al Atlántico. Mercaderes en las urbes (Siglos XVI-XVII). *Studia historica. Historia moderna, 42*(2), 13–19.

García y Sanz, A. (1994). El seguro marítimo en España en los siglos XV y XVI. In F. Ballesteros Caballero, H. Casado Alonso, A. C. Ibáñez Pérez, & S. Escolar Díez (Eds.), *Actas del V centenario del Consulado de Burgos* (pp. 445–498). Diputación Provincial de Burgos.

García-Baquero, A. (1991). *Comercio y burguesía mercantil en el Cádiz de la Carrera de Indias*. Diputación Provincial de Huelva.

Garzella, G., & Salvatori, E. (Eds.). (2007). *"Un filo rosso" studi antichi e nuove ricerche sulle orme di Gabriella Rossetti in occasione dei suoi settanta anni*. ETS.

Garzón Pareja, M. (1975). El riesgo en el comercio de Indias. *Revista de Indias, 35*, 187–191.

Garzoni, T. (1996). In P. Chierchi & B. Collina (Eds.), *La piazza universale di tutte le professioni del mondo*. Einaudi.

Gascon, R. (1956). Nationalisme économique et géographie des foires, la querelle des foires de Lyon, 1484–1494. *Cahiers d'Histoire, III*, 253–287.

Gascon, R. (1960). Un siècle du commerce des épices à Lyon, fin XVe - fin XVIe siècle. *Annales. Économies, Sociétés, Civilisations, XV*, 638–666.

Gascon, R. (1971). *Grand commerce et vie urbaine au XVIe siècle. Lyon et ses marchands (environs de 1520 –environs de 1580)*. SEVPEN.

Geisseler, D., & Horwath, W. R. (2016). *Pistachio Production in California*. https://apps1.cdfa.ca.gov/FertilizerResearch/docs/Pistachio_Production_CA.pdf

Gentil Da Silva, J. (1956). *Stratégie des affaires à Lisbonne entra 1595 et 1607. Lettres marchandes des Rodrigues d'Evora et Veiga*. A. Colin.

Gil, J. (1988). Los armadores de Sebastian Caboto: un ingles entre italianos. In *Anuario de Estudios-Americanos* (Vol. XLV, pp. 3–65). Escuela de Estudios Hispano-Americanos.

Gil, J. (2004). Los mercaderes florentinos en Sevilla. In A. D'Ascenzo (Ed.), *Mundus Novus. Amerigo Vespucci e i metodi della ricerca storico-geografica, Atti del Convegno Internazionale di Studi, Roma-Firenze 27-30 novembre 2002* (pp. 101–141). Società Geografica Italiana.

Ginori Lisci, L. (1985). *I palazzi di Firenze nella storia e nell'arte*. Giunti.

Giusti, G. (Ed.). (2014). *La Galleria degli arazzi. Fragilità della bellezza*. Giunti.

Goldthwaite, R. A. (1968). *Private wealth in Renaissance Florence. A study of four families*. Princeton University Press.

Goldthwaite, R. A. (1972). Schools and teachers of commercial arithmetic in Renaissance Florence. *Journal of European Economic History, I*, 418–433.

Goldthwaite, R. A. (1984). *La costruzione della Firenze rinascimentale. Una storia economica e sociale*. Il Mulino.

Goldthwaite, R. A. (1995). *Ricchezza e domanda nel mercato dell'arte in Italia dal Trecento al Seicento. La cultura materiale e le origini del consumismo*. Unicopli.

Goldthwaite, R. A. (1997). Local banking in Renaissance Florence. *The Journal of European Economic History, 14*, 5–56.

Goldthwaite, R. A. (2013). *L'economia della Firenze rinascimentale*. Il Mulino.

Gómez Camacho, F. (1985) La teoría monetaria de los doctores españoles del siglo XVI. *Moneda y Crédito Revista de Economía*, (172), 55–92.

González Arévalo, R. (2010). Florentinos entre Cádiz y Sevilla en los siglos XIV y XV. In E. Aznar Vallejo & R. J. González Zalacaín (Eds.), *De mar a mar. Los puertos castellanos en la Baja Edad Media* (pp. 273–307). Universidad de La Laguna.

González Arévalo, R., 2018. Hermanas. Relaciones entre la península ibérica y la península itálica, de la Edad Media a la Moderna. eHumanista: Journal of Iberian Studies 38.

González Arévalo, R. (2023). Privilegios, franquicias y consulados. Naciones italianas y diplomacia mercantil en la Castilla bajomedieval. In J. Á. Solórzano Telechea, D. Ditchburn, & M. Álvarez Fernández (Eds.), *Políticas y estrategias socio-económicas en la ciudad medieval atlántica* (pp. 83–133). Instituto de Estudios Riojanos.

Grafton, A. (1990). Introduction: Notes from underground on cultural transmission. In A. Grafton & A. Blair (Eds.), *The transmission of culture in early modern Europe* (pp. 1–7). University of Pennsylvania Press.

Greci, R. (1988). Il contratto di apprendistato nelle corporazioni bolognesi (XIII-XIV sec.). In *Corporazioni e mondo del lavoro nell'Italia padana medievale* (pp. 157–223). CLUEB.

Greci, R., Pinto, G., & Todeschini, G. (2005). La riflessione etica sulle attività economiche. In R. Greci, G. Pinto, & G. Todeschini (Eds.), *Economie urbane ed etica economica nell'Italia medievale* (pp. 151–228). Laterza.

Greer, B. M. (1983). The turning tide. The last significant influence from The Netherlands: Hugo van der Goes and the Florentine painters Ghirlandaio and Botticelli. *Fifteenth Century Studies, VII*, 121–177.

Greif, A. (1989). The organisation of long-distance trade: Reputation and coalitions in the Geniza documents during the eleventh and twelfth centuries. *The Journal of Economic History, 49*(4), 847–882.

Grendi, E. (1968). Traffico portuale, naviglio mercantile e consolati genovesi nel Cinquecento. *Rivista Storica Italiana, LXXX*, 593–629.

Grendler, P. F. (1991). *La scuola nel Rinascimento italiano*. Laterza.

Gribaudi, G. (n.d.). Navigatori, banchieri e mercanti italiani nei documenti degli archivi notarli di Siviglia (secolo XVI). *Bollettino della R. Società geografica italiana, LXXXIII*, 13–22.

Guasch-Tomás, J. L. (2016). Agents of globalisation: An approximation to Santi Federighi's commercial network, c.1620-1643. In M. Herrero & K. Kaps (Eds.), *Merchants and trade networks in the Atlantic and the Mediterranean, 1550-1800. Connectors of commercial maritime systems* (pp. 130–144). Routledge.

Guidi Bruscoli, F. (2000). *Benvenuto Olivieri. I «mercatores» fiorentini e la Camera apostolica nella Roma di Paolo III Farnese (1534-1549)*. Olschki.

Guidi Bruscoli, F. (2011). Circolazione di notizie e andamento dei mercati nel basso Medioevo. In I. Lori Sanfilippo & A. Rigono (Eds.), *Fama e publica vox nel Medioevo, Atti del convegno Internazionale (Ascoli Piceno, 4-5 Dicembre 2009)* (pp. 119–146). Istituto Storico Italiano per il Medioevo.

Guidi Bruscoli, F. (2014). *Bartolomeo Marchionni, «Homem de grossa fazenda» (ca. 1450-1530). Un mercante fiorentino a Lisbona e l'impero portoghese*. Olschki.

Guidi Bruscoli, F. (2015). I mercanti italiani e le lingue straniere. In I. Lori Sanfilippo & G. Pinto (Eds.), *Comunicare nel medioevo. La conoscenza e l'uso delle lingue nei secoli XII-XV, Atti del convegno Internazionale (Ascoli Piceno, 28-20 novembre 2013)* (pp. 103–131). Istituto Storico Italiano per il Medioevo.

Guidi Bruscoli, F. (2016). London and its merchants in the Italian archives, 1380–1530. In M. Allen & M. Davies (Eds.), *Medieval merchants and money. Essays in honour of James L. Bolton* (pp. 113–135). University of London—Institute of Historical Research.

Guidi Bruscoli, F. (2017). Perception, identity and culture: The Italian communities in fifteenth-century London and Southampton revisited. In M. Ormrod, N. McDonald, & C. Taylor (Eds.), *Resident aliens in later medieval England* (pp. 89–104). Brepols.

Guidi Bruscoli, F. (2019). Los mercaderes italianos en Lisboa y los portugueses, siglos XV-XVI. In M. F. Fernández Cháves, R. M. Pérez García, & B. Perez (Eds.), *Mercaderes y redes mercantiles en la península ibérica, siglos XV-XVIII* (pp. 69–85). Editorial Universidad de Sevilla.

Guidi Bruscoli, F., & Spallanzani, M. (2023). *Tessuti di seta tra Firenze e il Levante (ca. 1350–1550). Le fonti.* FUP.

Hayez, J. (2005). Un facteur siennois de Francesco di Marco Datini. Andrea di Bartolomeo di Ghino et sa correspondance (1383-1389). *Bollettino dell'Opera del Vocabolario italiano, 10,* 203–239.

Herlihy, D., & Klapisch-Zuber, C. (1988). *I toscani e le loro famiglie. Uno studio sul catasto fiorentino del 1427.* Il Mulino.

Herrera, R. 2021. "De los ciclos de no espacialización a la era de azúcar: elementos de Historia de Cuba en un largo período (1492–1492) - Parte 1." International Journal of Cuban Studies 12, 2: 183–212.

Hibbert, C. (1990). *Ascesa e caduta di Casa Medici.* Mondadori.

Hoshino, H. (1978) *L'industria laniera fiorentina dal Basso Medioevo all'Età Moderna: abbozzo storico dei secoli XIII-XVII*, Rome.

Hoshino, H. (1980). *L'Arte della lana in Firenze nel basso Medioevo. Il commercio della lana e il mercato dei panni fiorentini nei secoli XIII-XV.* Olschki.

Hoshino, H. (2001a). Alcuni aspetti del commercio dei panni fiorentini nell'Impero Ottomano ai primi del '500. In *Industria tessile e commercio internazionale nella Firenze del Tardo Medioevo* (pp. 125–135). Olschki.

Hoshino, H. (2001b). In F. Franceschi & S. Tognetti (Eds.), *Industria tessile e commercio internazionale nella Firenze del tardo Medioevo.* Olschki.

Howard, D. (2000). *Venice and the east: The impact of the Islamic world on Venetian architecture, 1100–1500.* Yale University Press.

Iacono, G., & Furone, S. E. (1999). *Les marchands banquiers florentins et l'architecture à Lyon au XVI*[e] *siècle.* Publisud.

Iglesia Rodríguez, J. J., et al. (Eds.). (2022). *En torno a la primera globalización: circulaciones y conexiones entre el Atlántico y el Mediterráneo (1492-1824).* Universidad de Sevilla.

Iglesias Rodríguez, J. J. (2009). *El árbol de sinople. Familia y patrimonio entre Andalucía y Toscana en la Edad Moderna.* Universidad de Sevilla.

Iglesias Rodríguez, J. J. (2016). Redes familiares y élites mercantiles internacionales en la Andalucía atlántica moderna (Cádiz, siglos XVI y XVII). In F. Sánchez-Montes, J. Lozano, & A. Jiménez Estrella (Eds.), *Familias, élites y redes de poder cosmopolitas de la Monarquía Hispánica en la Edad Moderna* (pp. 143–170). Editorial Comares.

Iglesias Rodríguez, J. J. (2022). Los Fantoni. Fuentes y metodología para el estudio de la familia y el patrimonio en Toscana y en la Andalucía moderna. *e-Spania, 43*(11), 1–21. https://idus.us.es/bitstream/handle/11441/139834/Iglesias%20Rodriguez%20JJ%20-%20Los_Fantoni_PDF.pdf?sequence=1&isAllowed=y

Iglesias Rodríguez, J. J., García Bernal, J. J., & Melero Muñoz, I. M. (Eds.). (2021). *Ciudades atlánticas del sur de España. La construcción de un mundo nuevo (siglos XVI-XVIII).* Universidad de Sevilla.

Iglesias Rodríguez, J. J., García Bernal, J. J., & Melero Muñoz, I. M. (Eds.). (2022). *Ciudades y puertos de Andalucía en un Atlántico global, siglos XVI-XVIII.* Universidad de Sevilla.

Igual Luis, D. 2014. "Valladolid y sus círculos económicos de relación (1475-1520)." Edad Media, Revista de Historia 15: 97–114.

Innocenti, C. (Ed.). (2000). *Meraviglie tessute della Galleria degli Uffizi. Il restauro di tre arazzi medicei*. Edifir.
Jacks, P., & Caferro, W. (2001). *The Spinelli of Florence. Fortune of a Renaissance Merchant Family*. The Pennsylvania State University Press, University Park.
Jardine, L., & Brotton, J. (2000). *Global interests. Renaissance art between East and West*. Cornell University Press.
Jordan Gschwend, A. (2023). Sartorial elegance at the Lisbon Court. Shopping for luxury fabrics in Florence, Lucca, and Venice. In P. Venturelli (Ed.), *Textile and Fashion-Venice etc. Rintracciare Studiare Divulgare. Per Doretta Davanzo Poli* (pp. 205–214). Palermo University Press.
Kent, F. W. (1977). *Household and lineage in Renaissance Florence. The family life of the Capponi, Ginori and Rucellai*. Princeton University Press.
Ladero Quesada, M. Á. (1987). El banco de Valencia, los genoveses y la saca de moneda de oro castellana. 1500-1503. *Anuario de Estudios Medievales, 17*, 571–594.
Ladero Quesada, M. Á. (1993). Las almadrabas de Andalucía (siglos XIII-XVI). In *Boletín de la Real Academia de la Historia* (pp. 345–354). CXC.
Lains, P., Freire Costa, L., Grafe, R., Herranz-Locán, A., Igual Luis, D., & Vasconcelos Vilar, H. (Eds.). (2024). *An economic history of the Iberian Peninsula, 700-2000*. Cambridge University Press.
Lane, F. C. (1973). *Venice. A maritime republic*. The Johns Hopkins University Press.
Lanfranchi, G. B. (2004). Prestiti alimentari nelle tradizioni greca e romana. In M. Montanari & F. Sabban (Eds.), *Atlante dell'alimentazione e della gastronomia. I, Risorse, scambi, consumi* (pp. 78–86). Utet.
Lang, H. (2015). Credito e insolvenza sovrana. I prestiti alla Corona francese di mercanti-banchieri toscani e tedeschi meridionali (1550–1559). *Annali dell'Istituto Storico Italiano-Germanico in Trento, 41*, 12–38.
Lapeyre, H. (1953). *Simon Ruiz et les «asientos» de Philippe II*. A. Colin.
Lapeyre, H. (1955). *Une famille de marchands, les Ruiz. Contribution à l'étude du commerce entre la France et l'Espagne*. A. Colin.
Lasocki, D., & Prior, R. (2016). *The Bassanos. Venetian musicians and instrument makers in England, 1531-1665*. Routledge.
Levi Pisetzky, R. (1978). *Il costume e la moda nella società italiana*. Giulio Einaudi editore.
Livi, G. (1882). I mercanti di seta lucchesi in Bologna. *Archivio Storico Italiano, IV*(7), 29–55.
Lobo Carrera, M. (1985). Los mercaderes italianos y el comercio azucarero canario en la primera mitad del siglo XVI. In *«Aspetti della vita economica medievale», Atti del Convegno di Studi nel X anniversario della morte di Federigo Melis, Firenze-Pisa-Prato, 10-14 marzo 1984* (pp. 268–282). Università degli Studi di Firenze.
López y Sebastian, L. E., & Del Rio Moreno, J. L. (1992). Comercio y transporte en la economía del azúcar antillano durante el siglo XVI. *Anuario de Estudios Americanos, 49*, 55–87.
López y Sebastian, L. E., & Del Rio Moreno, J. L. (1996). El Azúcar en Canarias y la Española: sistemas de explotacion y efectos en el comercio del siglo XVI. *AULA Revista de Humanidades y Ciencias Sociales, 60*(5–6), 53–77.
Lorenzo Sanz, E. (1986). Los Ruiz Embito en el comercio con Sevilla y América. In E. Lorenzo Sanz (Ed.), *Historia de Medina del Campo y su tierra* (Vol. 2, pp. 393–436). Ayuntamiento de Medina del Campo y Consejería de Educación y Cultura de la Junta de Castilla y León.
Luca, D., Nuovo, A., & Piseri, F. (2021). *La formazione del mercante. Scuole libri cultura economica a Milano nel Rinascimento*. Editoriale Delfino.
Lucas-Dubreton, J. (1985). *La vita quotidiana a Firenze ai tempi dei Medici*. Rizzoli.
Lynch, J. (1989). *España bajo los Asturias/1. Imperio y absolutismo (1516-1598)*. Ediciones Península.
MacGregor, A. (2001). The collection-history of the Botti Madonna. In *Andrea del Sarto. The Botti Madonna, Catalogo e Appendice preparati in occasione dell'esposizione del quadro presso la Galleria Doria Pamphilj* (pp. 43–53). Courtauld Institute of Art.
Magalhães Godinho, V. (1969). *L'économie de l'empire portugais aux XVe et XVIe siècles*. SEVPEN.

Malanima, P. (2018). Italy in the Renaissance: A leading economy in the European context, 1350–1550. *Economic History Review, 71*(1), 3–30.
Malanima, P., Riccardi, I., & di Firenze. (1977). *Una famiglia e un patrimonio nella Toscana dei Medici*. Olschki.
Mandich, G. (1986). Fiere cambiarie concorrenti (genovesi, fiorentine, veneziane) nel 1622-1652. In A. De Maddalena & H. Kellenbenz (Eds.), *La repubblica internazionale del denaro tra XV e XVII secolo* (pp. 123–151). Istituto trentino di cultura, Il Mulino.
Manikowski, A. (1993). Il secolo della seta. Conseguenza del boom della seta nel Seicento per le trasformazioni sociali e politiche in Europa. In S. Cavaciocchi (Ed.), *La seta in Europa. Secc. XIII-XX, Atti della "Ventiquattresima Settimana di Studi" 4-9 maggio 1992* (pp. 839–853). Istituto Internazionale di Storia Economica "F. Datini" Prato, Le Monnier.
Marsilio, C. (2011). La lunga avventura delle fiere di cambio: da Lione a Novi. In A. Sisti & M. Balbi (Eds.), *Libri italiani del Seicento nel fondo antico della Biblioteca Civica di Novi Ligure* (pp. 83–90). Città del silenzio edizioni.
Marsilio, C. (2018). *Exchange fairs and the money market in early modern Italy (1630-1650)/Fiere di cambio e mercato monetario nell'Italia di Età Moderna (1630-1650)*. Città del Silenzio.
Martelli, F., & Galasso, C. (2007). *Istruzioni agli ambasciatori e inviati medicei in Spagna e nell' "Italia spagnola" (1536-1648) II 1587-1648* (pp. 223–230). Ministero per i beni e le attività culturali, Direzione Generale per gli Archivi.
Martín Acosta, E. (2004). Don Alonso Fernández de Lugo, III adelantado de las Islas Canarias, conquistador de Santa Marta y San Borondón. In F. Morales Padrón (Ed.), *XV Coloquio de Historia Canario-Americana* (pp. 500–512). Cabildo Insular de Gran Canaria.
Martini, A. (1976). *Manuale di metrologia, ossia misure, pesi e monete in uso attualmente e anticamente presso tutti i popoli*. Editrice E.R.A.
Massa, P. (1974). *Un'impresa serica genovese della prima del Cinquecento*. Giuffrè.
Massa, P. (1981). *La "Fabbrica" dei velluti genovesi. Da Genova a Zoagli*. Scheiwiller.
Mathews, K. R., Orvietani Busch, S., & Bruni, S. (Eds.). (2022). *A companion to medieval pisa*. Brill.
Matringe, N. (2016). *La Banque en Renaissance. Les Salviati et la place de Lyon au milieu du XVIe siècle*. Presses Universitaires de Rennes.
Mazzei, R. (1991). *Pisa Medicea. L'economia cittadina da Ferdinando I a Cosimo III*. Olschki.
Mazzei, R. (1996). In margine all'attività di un mercante pisano a Siviglia nella seconda metà del Cinquecento: curiosità del Nuovo Mondo inviate a Ferdinando I dei Medici. In *Toscana e Spagna nel secolo XVI. Miscellanea di studi storici* (pp. 309–321). ETS.
McLean, P. D. (2007). *The art network. Strategic interaction and patronage in Renaissance Florence*. Duke University Press.
Melani, I. (2011) *«Di qua» e «di là da' monti». Sguardi italiani sulla Francia e sui francesi tra XV e XVI secolo* (Vol. I). FUP.
Meli, P., & Tognetti, S. (2006). *Il principe e il mercante nella toscana del Quattrocento. Il Magnifico Signore di Piombino Jacopo III Appiani e le aziende Maschiani di Pisa*. Olschki.
Melis, F. (1962). *Aspetti della vita economica medievale (studi nell'Archivio Datini di Prato)*. Monte dei Paschi di Siena.
Melis, F. (1965–1966). Tracce di una storia economica di Firenze e della Toscana in generale dal 1252 al 1550. In B. Dini (Ed.), *Università degli Studi di Firenze, Facoltà di Economia e Commercio*. Istituto di Storia Economica.
Melis, F. (1972). *Documenti per la Storia Economica dei secoli XIII-XVI, con una nota di Paleografia Commerciale a cura di Elena Cecchi*. Istituto Internazionale di Storia Economica "F. Datini" Prato, Leo S. Olschki.
Melis, F. (1975a). *Origini e sviluppi delle assicurazioni in Italia (secoli XIV-XVI), Le fonti*. Istituto Nazionale delle Assicurazioni.
Melis, F. (1975b). Sulle fonti tipiche della storia economica; per una particolare tecnica di lavoro dello storico (relativamente ai secoli XII-XVII). *Rassegna Economica, XXXIX*(2), 307–332.

Melis, F. (1976). Gli italiani e l'apertura delle vie atlantiche. In *Mercaderes Italianos en España. Siglos XIV-XVI. (Investigaciones sobre su correspondencia y su contabilidad)* (pp. 169–175). Universidad de Sevilla.
Melis, F. (1984a). Industria, commercio e credito (secoli XIV-XVI). In B. Dini (Ed.), *L'economia fiorentina nel Rinascimento* (pp. 31–185). Istituto Internazionale di Storia Economica "F. Datini" Prato, Le Monnier.
Melis, F. (1984b). In L. Frangioni (Ed.), *I trasporti e le comunicazioni nel Medioevo*. Istituto Internazionale di Storia Economica "F. Datini" Prato, Le Monnier.
Melis, F. (1984c). Il mercante. In B. Dini (Ed.), *L'economia fiorentina del Rinascimento* (pp. 187–202). Istituto Internazionale di Storia Economica "F. Datini" Prato, Le Monnier.
Melis, F. (1984d). In B. Dini (Ed.), *L'economia fiorentina del Rinascimento*. Istituto Internazionale di Storia Economica "F. Datini" Prato, Le Monnier.
Melis, F. (1984e). In M. Spallanzani (Ed.), *La banca pisana e le origini della banca moderna*. Istituto Internazionale di Storia Economica "F. Datini" Prato, Le Monnier.
Melis, F. (1984f). La grande conquista trecentesca del "credito di esercizio" e la tipologia dei suoi strumenti fino al XVI secolo. In M. Spallanzani (Ed.), *La banca pisana e le origini della banca moderna* (pp. 307–324). Istituto Internazionale di Storia Economica "F. Datini" Prato, Le Monnier.
Melis, F. (1984g). Sulla realtà dell'assicurazione nei trasporti marittimi (secoli XIV-XV). In L. Frangioni (Ed.), *I trasporti e le comunicazioni nel Medioevo* (pp. 225–235). Istituto Internazionale di Storia Economica "F. Datini" Prato, Le Monnier.
Melis, F. (1984h). Werner Sombart e i problemi della navigazione nel Medioevo. In L. Frangioni (Ed.), *I trasporti e le comunicazioni nel Medioevo* (pp. 3–68). Istituto Internazionale di Storia Economica "F. Datini" Prato, Le Monnier.
Melis, F. (1989). Uno sguardo al mercato die panni di lana a Pisa nella seconda metà del Trecento. In B. Dini (Ed.), *Industria e commercio nella Toscana Medievale* (pp. 108–156). Istituto Internazionale di Storia Economica "F. Datini" Prato, Le Monnier.
Melis, F. (1990a). In L. Frangioni (Ed.), *I mercanti italiani nell'Europa medievale e rinascimentale*. Istituto Internazionale di Storia Economica "F. Datini" Prato, Le Monnier.
Melis, F. (1990b). Il commercio transatlantico di una compagnia fiorentina stabilita a Siviglia a pochi anni dalle imprese di Cortes e Pizarro. In L. Frangioni (Ed.), *I mercanti italiani nell'Europa medievale e rinascimentale* (pp. 45–134). Le Monnier.
Melis, F. (1991a). In M. Spallanzani (Ed.), *L'azienda nel Medioevo*. Istituto Internazionale di Storia Economica "F. Datini" Prato, Le Monnier.
Melis, F. (1991b). Le società commerciali a Firenze dalla seconda metà del XIV al XVI secolo. In M. Spallanzani (Ed.), *L'azienda nel Medioevo* (pp. 161–178). Istituto Internazionale di Storia Economica "F. Datini" Prato, Le Monnier.
Melón Jiménez, M. Á. (2015). La trastienda del gran comercio. "Fraudes tolerados o no entendidos" en el Reino de Sevilla a finales del antiguo régimen. In J. J. Iglesias, R. M. Pérez, & M. F. Fernández (Eds.), *Comercio y cultura en la edad moderna en Comercio y cultura en la Edad Moderna* (pp. 801–814). Universidad de Seville.
Meserve, M. (2008). *Empires of Islam in Renaissance historical thought*. Harvard University Press.
Mignone, G. (2022). *Le regole dei mercanti. Introduzione al diritto commerciale*. Università degli Studi di Torino.
Molà, L. (2000). *The silk industry in Renaissance Venice*. The Johns Hopkins University Press.
Molà, L. (2016). A luxury industry: The production of Italian silks 1400–1600. In B. Lambert & K. A. Wilson (Eds.), *Europe's rich fabric. The consumption, commercialisation, and production of luxury textiles in Italy, the low countries and neighbouring territories (fourteenth-sixteenth centuries)* (pp. 205–234). Ashgate.
Molà, L., Mueller, R. C., & Zanier, C. (Eds.). (2000). *La seta in Italia dal Medioevo al Seicento. Dal baco al drappo*. Marsilio.
Molho, A., & Ramanda Curto, D. (2003). Les réseaux marchands à l'époque moderne. *Annales. Histoire, Sciences Sociales, 58*(3), 569–580.

Morales Padrón, F. (1989). *Historia de Sevilla. La ciudad del Quinientos*. Universidad de Sevilla.
Moscadelli, S. (1991). Maestri d'abaco a Siena tra Medioevo e Rinascimento. In *L'Università di Siena: 750 anni di storia* (pp. 207–216). Monte dei Paschi di Siena.
Muccini, U. (1990). *Il Salone dei Cinquecento in Palazzo Vecchio*. Le Lettere.
Munro, J. H. (2012). The rise, expansion, and decline of the Italian wool-based cloth industries, 1100–1730: A study in international competition, transaction costs, and comparative advantage. *Studies in Medieval and Renaissance History, 9*, 45–207.
Nigro, G. (1994). *Il tempo liberato. Festa e svago nella città di Francesco Datini*. Istituto Internazionale di Storia Economica "F. Datini" Prato.
Nigro, G. (2008). L'economia. In V. Baldacci (Ed.), *Eccellenza, Innovazione, Creatività nella Storia della Toscana* (pp. 25–38). Edizioni dell'Assemblea.
Nigro, G. (2010a). Il mercante e la sua ricchezza. In G. Nigro (Ed.), *Francesco di Marco Datini. L'uomo il mercante* (pp. 81–104). Fondazione Istituto Internazionale di Storia Economica "F. Datini" Prato, FUP.
Nigro, G. (2010b). In G. Nigro (Ed.), *La compagnia del Banco, Francesco di Marco Datini. L'uomo il mercante* (pp. 525–536). Fondazione Istituto Internazionale di Storia Economica "F. Datini" Prato, FUP.
Nigro, G. (2020). Alle origini del fattore Italia: lavoro e produzione nelle botteghe fiorentine del Rinascimento. In A. Furió (Ed.), *En torno a la economía mediterránea medieval. Estudios dedicados a Paulino Iradiel* (pp. 41–51). PUV.
Nigro, G. (2024). Tra diuturno affanno e consolazione: il tempo del non lavoro nel Basso Medioevo. In G. Mari, F. Ammannati, S. Brogi, T. Faitini, A. Fermani, F. Seghezzi, & A. Tonarelli (Eds.), *Idee di lavoro e di ozio per la nostra civiltà* (pp. 397–405). FUP.
Nigro, G., & Spallanzani, M. (2006). Intrecci mediterranei tra economia e arte. In *Intrecci Mediterranei. Il tessuto come dizionario di rapporti economici, culturali e sociali*. Museo del Tessuto.
Nowak, R. M. (1991). *Walker's mammals of the word*. The Johns Hopkins University Press.
Nuti, G. (1978) Livorno, il porto e la città nell'età medicea. In *Atti del Convegno "Livorno e il Mediterraneo nell'età medicea"*, Livorno 23-25 September 1977 (pp. 330–345). U. Bastogi Editore.
Nuttall, P. (2004). *From Flanders to Florence. The impact of Netherlandish painting, 1400–1500*. Yale University Press.
Ongaro, G. M. (1992). New documents on the Bassano family. *Early Music, 20*(3), 409–413.
Orlandi, A. (1998). Zucchero e cocciniglia dal Nuovo Mondo, due esempi di precoce diffusione. In S. Cavaciocchi (Ed.), *Prodotti e tecniche d'Oltremare nelle economie europee. Secc. XIII-XVIII, Atti della "Ventinovesima Settimana di Studi" 14–19 aprile 1997* (pp. 477–487). Istituto Internazionale di Storia Economica "F. Datini" Prato, Le Monnier.
Orlandi, A. (2002). *Le Grand Parti. Fiorentini a Lione e il debito pubblico francese nel XVI secolo*. Olschki.
Orlandi, A. (2007a). Affaires et petites vanités. Un marchand florentin à Lyon au XVIe siècle. In A. Burkardt (Ed.), *Commerce, voyage et expérience religieuse, XVIe-XVIIIe siècles, Colloque international, Lyon, 25–26–27 mars 2004* (pp. 341–357). Presses Universitaires de Rennes.
Orlandi, A. (2007b). Oro e monete da Costantinopoli a Firenze in alcuni documenti toscani (secoli XV-XVI). In S. Cavaciocchi (Ed.), *Relazioni economiche tra Europa e Mondo Islamico. Secc. XIII-XVIII, Europe's economic relations with the Islamic world 13th-18th centuries, Atti della "Trentottesima Settimana di Studi", 1-5 maggio 2006* (pp. 981–1004). Istituto Internazionale di Storia Economica "F. Datini" Prato Le Monnier.
Orlandi, A. (2008). *Mercanzie e denaro: la corrispondenza datiniana tra Valenza e Maiorca (1395-1398)*. Universitat de València.
Orlandi, A. (2010a). 'A man from Prato in the Maestrazgo. Tuccio di Gennaio', wool merchant. In G. Nigro (Ed.), *Francesco di Marco Datini. The man the merchant* (pp. 377–383). Fondazione Istituto Internazionale di Storia Economica "F. Datini" Prato, FUP.

Orlandi, A. (2010b). Note su affari e devozione nei documenti di alcuni mercanti fiorentini (1450-1550). *Storia Economica, 3*(13), 319–344.

Orlandi, A. (2012a). *«Ora diremo di Napoli». I traffici dell'area campana nei manuali di commercio*. Firenze University Press.

Orlandi, A. (2012b). Les précurseurs des voyageurs et représentants de commerce parmi les hommes d'affaires toscans de la Renaissance (fin XIVe-début XVIe siècle). *Entreprises et Histoire, 66*, 22–36.

Orlandi, A. (2013). Fiorentini alla ricerca del Nuovo Mondo. In M. Azzari & L. Rombai (Eds.), *Amerigo Vespucci e i mercanti viaggiatori fiorentini del Cinquecento* (pp. 131–156). Firenze University Press.

Orlandi, A. (2014a). Dall'Andalusia al Nuovo Mondo: affari e viaggi di mercanti toscani nel Cinquecento. In G. Pinto, L. Rombai, & C. Tripodi (Eds.), *Vespucci, Firenze e le Americhe. Atti del Convegno Internazionale, Firenze 22–24 novembre 2012* (pp. 63–86). Olschki.

Orlandi, A. (2014b). Impalpabili e trasparenti: i veli bolognesi nella documentazione datiniana. In M. G. Muzzarelli, M. G. Nico Ottaviani, & G. Zarri (Eds.), *Il velo in area mediterranea fra storia e simbolo. Tardo Medioevo-prima Età moderna* (pp. 307–324). Il Mulino.

Orlandi, A. (2014c). Networks and models of the commercial penetration of the late Medieval Mediterranean. Revisiting the case of Datini. In A. Caracausi & C. Jeggle (Eds.), *Commercial networks and European cities, 1400-1800* (pp. 81–106). Pickering & Chatto Publishers Ltd.

Orlandi, A. (2016a). Le prestazioni di una holding tardo medievale rilette attraverso alcune teorie di management e la Social Network Analysis. In *Innovare nella Storia Economica: Temi, Metodi, Fonti, Rome 10-11 ottobre 2014* (pp. 117–148). Fondazione Istituto Internazionale di Storia Economica "F. Datini" Prato.

Orlandi, A. (2016b). Tuscan merchants in Andalusia: A historiographical debate. *European Review of History. Revue Européenne d'Histoire, 23*(3), 347–366.

Orlandi, A. (2017a). Tradizione e innovazione nel capitalismo toscano tardo trecentesco. *Storia Economica, 20*(2), 395–410.

Orlandi, A. (2017b). Tuscan merchants in Andalusia: A historiographical debate. In C. Brilli & M. Herrero Sánchez (Eds.), *Italian merchants in the early-modern Spanish monarchy: Business relations, identities and political resources* (pp. 13–32). Routledge.

Orlandi, A. (2018a). Ibiza entre el Mediterráneo, el Atlantico y el Mar del Norte (siglos XIV y XV). *eHumanista, 38*, 48–64.

Orlandi, A. (2018b). Il costo della guerra. La compagnia di Michele Attendolo da Cotignola ad Anghiari. In *Il prezzo della guerra. Italia e Penisola iberica nei secoli XIII-XVI* (pp. 135–162). Associazione Culturale Antonella Salvatico, Centro Internazionale di Ricerca sui Beni Culturali.

Orlandi, A. (2018c). Tra austerità e lusso. Modelli di consumo dei mercanti fiorentini tra XIV e XVI secolo. In J. Petrowiste & M. Lafuente Gómez (Eds.), *Faire son marché au Moyen Âge. Méditerranée occidentale, XIIIe-XVIe siècle* (pp. 31–45). Casa de Velázquez.

Orlandi, A. (2022a). *La ricchezza del debito pubblico dal XII al XXI secolo*. Il Mulino.

Orlandi, A. (2022b). New world villages and cities in the 16th century: Cross-cultural influences between Italy and the Americas. In M. Asenjo González, D. Alonso García, & S. M. Pérez González (Eds.), *Ciudades en expansión. Dinámicas urbanas entre los siglos XIV-XVI* (pp. 331–348). Dykinson, S.L.

Orlandi, A. (2024). Essere mercante: «governare lui et le sue mercantie et denari» (secoli XIV-XVI). In G. Mari, F. Ammannati, S. Brogi, T. Faitini, A. Fermani, F. Seghezzi, & A. Tonarelli (Eds.), *Idee di lavoro e di ozio per la nostra civiltà* (pp. 387–396). FUP.

Orsi Landini, R. (2005a). I singoli capi di abbigliamento. In R. Orsi Landini & B. Niccoli (Eds.), *Moda a Firenze, 1540-1580. Lo stile di Eleonora di Toledo e la sua influenza* (pp. 77–170). Pagliai Polistampa.

Orsi Landini, R. (2005b). Lo stile di Eleonora. In R. Orsi Landini & B. Niccoli (Eds.), *Moda a Firenze, 1540-1580. Lo stile di Eleonora di Toledo e la sua influenza* (pp. 23–45). Pagliai Polistampa.

Otte, E. (1979). Los Sopranis y los Lugos. In F. Morales Padrón (Ed.), *II Coloquio de Historia Canario-Americana (1977)* (Vol. I, pp. 241–259). Ediciones del Excelentísim Cabildo Insular de Gran Canaria.

Otte, E. (1980). Los Botti y los Lugos. In *III Coloquio de Historia Canario-Americana (1978)* (Vol. I, pp. 47–86). Ediciones del Excelentísimo Cabildo insular de Gran Canaria.

Otte, E. (1982). Canarias: plaza bancaria europea en el siglo XVI. In *IV Coloquio de Historia Canario-Americana, 1980* (Vol. I, pp. 157–173). Ediciones del Excelentísimo Cabildo Insular de Gran Canaria.

Otte, E. (1986). Il ruolo dei Genovesi nella Spagna del XV e XVI secolo. In A. De Maddalena & H. Kellenbenz (Eds.), *La repubblica internazionale del denaro tra XV e XVII secolo. Istituto trentino di cultura* (pp. 17–56). Il Mulino.

Otte, E. (1992). Sevilla y Valencia a fines de la Edad Media. In *Lluís de Santàngel i el seu temps (Congrés Internacional. Valencia, 1987)* (pp. 283–297). Ayuntamiento de Valencia.

Otte, E. (1996). *Sevilla y sus mercaderes a fines de la Edad Media.* Universidad de Sevilla - Fundación El Monte.

Padgett, J. F. (2010). Open elite? Social mobility, marriage and family in Florence, 1282-1494. *Renaissance Quarterly, 63*, 357–411.

Pallini-Martin, A. (2018). *Banque, négoce et politique. Les Florentins à Lyon au moment des guerres d'Italie.* Classiques Garnier Numérique.

Parigino, G. V. (2009). Il patrimonio di Ferdinando II de' Medici. Una prima ricognizione. *Mediterranea ricerche storiche, VI*(17), 479–516.

Parigino, G. V. (2010). Alcune riflessioni sulla politica patrimoniale di Ferdinando II de' Medici. *Mediterranea-ricerche storiche, VII*(19), 279–294.

Patrone, A. M. N. (1996). *Vivere nella scuola. Insegnare e apprendere nel Piemonte del tardo Medioevo.* Gribaudo.

Paulicelli, E. (2006). Geografia del vestire tra Vecchio e nuovo mondo di Cesare Vecellio. In *Moda e moderno. Dal Medioevo al Rinascimento* (pp. 129–153). Meltemi.

Paulicelli, E. (2014). *Writing fashion in early modern Italy. From sprezzatura to satire.* Ashgate.

Pearson, R. (1982, October 23). W.E. Whitehouse Dies. Pistachio Nut Developer. *The Washington Post.* https://www.washingtonpost.com/archive/local/1982/10/24/we-whitehouse-dies/db64936b-0343-4222-bd7d-14bb43061666/

Pérez de Colosía, M. I., & Sarriá Muñoz, A. (1991). Las almadrabas del duque de Medina Sidonia en Tarifa. *Baetica. Estudios de Arte, Geografía e Historia, 13*, 241–254.

Petti Balbi, G. (1979). *L'insegnamento nella Liguria Medievale: scuole, maestri, libri.* Tilgher.

Petti Balbi, G. (Ed.). (1996). *Strutture del potere ed élites economiche nelle città europee dei secoli XII-XVI.* GISEM, Liguori.

Piccirillo, G. (Ed.). (2006). *La chiesa dei Santi Michele e Gaetano.* Becocci Editore.

Picot, É. (1995). In N. Ordine (Ed.), *Les Italiens en France au XVIe siècle, introduction.* Vecchiarelli.

Pinelli, P. (2010). Le relazioni commerciali tra Firenze e Dubrovnik (XV-XVI secolo). In P. Pinelli (Ed.), *Firenze e Dubrovnik all'epoca di Marino Darsa (1508-1567). Atti della Giornata di Studi Firenze, 31 gennaio 2009* (pp. 43–50). FUP.

Piuz, A. M. (1993). La soie, le luxe et le puovoir dans les doctrines françaises (XVIe-XVIIe s.). In S. Cavaciocchi (Ed.), *La seta in Europa. Secc. XIII-XX, Atti della "Ventiquattresima Settimana di Studi" 4-9 maggio 1992* (pp. 817–837). Istituto Internazionale di Storia Economica "F. Datini" Prato, Le Monnier.

Plebani, E. (2002). *I Tornabuoni. Una famiglia fiorentina alla fine del Medioevo.* Franco Angeli.

Poettering, J. (2019). *Migrating merchants: Trade, nation, and religion in seventeenth-century Hamburg and Portugal.* De Gruyter Oldenbourg.

Point-Waquet, F. (1978). Les Botti. Fortunes et culture d'une famille florentine (1550-1621), Mélanges de l'École Française de Rome. *Moyen Age Temps Modernes, 90*(2), 689–712.

Polidori Calamandrei, E. (1973). *Le vesti delle donne fiorentine nel Quattrocento.* Multigrafica Editrice.

Poloni, A. (2018). Banchieri del re. La monarchia angioina e le compagnie toscane da Carlo I a Roberto I. In S. Morelli (Ed.), *Périphéries financières angevines-Periferie finanziarie angioine* (pp. 1–36). Publications de l'École Française de Rome. https://books.openedition.or/efr/3568

Poloni, A. (2019). Un lungo Trecento: economia e mobilità sociale a Pisa nel XIV secolo. In S. Collavini & G. Petralia (Eds.), *La mobilità sociale nel Medioevo italiano. 4: Cambiamento economico e dinamiche sociali (secoli XI-XV)* (pp. 163–205). Viella.

Pommier, E. (2006). *L'invention de l'art dans l'Italie de la Renaissance*. Gallinard.

Prajda, K. (2022). Mercanti come tramite degli scambi culturali nella Firenze del primo Rinascimento: Il caso del Regno d'Ungheria. *I Tatti Studies in the Italian Renaissance, 25*(2), 279–308.

Quilliet, F. (1825) *Les arts italiens en Espagne ou Histoire des artistes italiens qui contribuerent a embellir les Castilles*. Ange Ajani. https://books.google.it/books?id=ZrL9n3dhQ5oC&printsec=frontcover&hl=it&source=gbs_ge_summary_r&cad=0#v=onepage&q&f=false

Ragghianti, C. L. (1974). *Critica d'arte, 20*. Vallecchi.

Rau, V. (1971). O açúcar de S. Tomé no segundo quartel do século XVI. In *Elementos do História de Ilha de S. Tomé (Em comemoração do V Centenário do Descobrimento)* (pp. 7–69). Centro de Estudos de Matinha.

Ricci, G. (2002). *Ossessione turca. In una retrovia cristiana dell'Europa moderna*. Il Mulino.

Riddick, M. (n.d.). *Pietro Torrigiani. Discovery of a St. Anthony in Wood*. https://renbronze.files.wordpress.com/2020/05/pietro-torrigiani-_-a-saint-anthony-in-wood-1.pdf

Ríos Toledan, D. (2019). In J. Córdoba Toro & P. González Zambrano (Eds.), *El mundo de la pesca en la Andalucía atlántica a fines de la Edad Media, Pensando Andalucía. Una visión transdisciplinar* (pp. 214–227). Diputación de Cádiz.

Rodríguez González, R. (1995). *Mercaderes castellanos del Siglo de Oro*. Secretariado de publicaciones, Universidad de Valladolid.

Rodríguez Morel, G. (n.d.) The sugar economy of Española in the sixteenth century. In *Tropical Babylons* (pp. 85–114).

Romano, R. (1974). La storia economica. Dal secolo XIV al Settecento. In R. Romano & C. Vivanti (Eds.,) *Storia d'Italia. Dalla caduta dell'Impero romano al secolo XVIII*, 6 vols, II (pp. 1813–1934). Giulio Einaudi editore Turin.

Rossetti, G. (Ed.). (1989). *Dentro la città. Stranieri e realtà urbane nell'Europa dei secoli XII-XV*. GISEM, Liguori.

Ruffatti, A. (1996–1998). Italian musicians at the Tudor Court —Were they really Jews? *Jewish Historical Studies, 3*, 1–14.

Ruffatti, A. (1998). La famiglia Piva-Bassano nei documenti negli Archivi di Bassano del Grappa. *Musica e Storia, 6*(2), 349–368.

Ruiz Martín, F. (1965). *Lettres marchandes échangées entre Florence et Medina del Campo*. S.E.V.P.E.N.

Rumeu De Armas, A. (1976). *Cádiz, metrópoli del comercio con África en los siglos XV y XVI*. Dante.

Salvestrini, F. (2017). *Il carisma della magnificenza. L'abate vallombrosano Biagio Milanesi e la tradizione benedettina nell'Italia del Rinascimento con l'edizione critica del Memoriale dell'abate Biagio Milanesi*. Viella.

Sapori, A. (1956). Dalla «compagnia» alla «holding». *Rivista delle società, 1*, 72–84.

Sapori, A. (1970). *Libro giallo della Compagnia dei Covoni*. Cisalpino.

Sayous, A. E. (1975). *Els mètodes comercials a la Barcelona medieval*. Editorial Base.

Schwartz, B. S. (2004). *Tropical Babylons. Sugar and the making of the Atlantic world, 1450-1680*. Chapel Hill.

Spallacci, G. (2017). *I rapporti commerciali tra le città delle due sponde adriatiche nella documentazione dell'archivio di Ancona tra 1345 e 1514*, Dottorato di Ricerca in Storia, Ciclo XXVIII, Alma Mater Studiorum-Università di Bologna, Bologna. http://amsdottorato.unibo.it/7989/1/spallacci_giulia_tesi.pdf

Spallanzani, M. (1986) Maioliche di Valenza e di Montelupo in una casa pisana del 1480. *Faenza, LXXII*(3–4), 164–170.
Spallanzani, M. (2006). *Maioliche ispano-moresche a Firenze nel Rinascimento*. SPES.
Spallanzani, M. (2007). Maioliche di Montelupo per Costantinopoli (1493). *Faenza, XCIII*, 36–42.
Spallanzani, M. (2010). *Metalli islamici a Firenze nel Rinascimento*. SPES.
Spallanzani, M. (2023). *I fiorentini e il vetro veneziano (ca. 1450-1550). Fonti*. Olschki.
Studnicki-Gizbert, D. (2003). La "nation" portugaise. Réseaux marchands dans l'espace atlantique à l'époque moderne. *Annales. Histoire, Sciences Sociales, 58*(3), 627–648.
Tangheroni, M. (1973). *Politica, commercio, agricoltura a Pisa nel Trecento*. Pacini.
Tangheroni, M. (1992). *Medioevo Tirrenico*. Pacini.
Tanzini, L. (2022). *Cosimo de' Medici. Il banchiere statista padre del Quattrocento fiorentino*. Salerno Editrice.
Tanzini, L., & Tognetti, S. (Eds.). (2012). *«Mercatura è arte». Uomini d'affari toscani in Europa e nel Mediterraneo tardomedievale*. Viella.
Tanzini, L., & Tognetti, S. (Eds.). (2016). *La mobilità sociale nel Medioevo italiano. Competenze, conoscenze e saperi tra professioni e ruoli sociali (secc. XII-XV)*. Viella.
Tassi, F. (1843) *Le opere di Benvenuto Cellini arricchite di note ed illustrazioni*. Prefazione del dott. Società Editrice Fiorentina.
Todeschini, G. (2002). *I mercanti e il tempio. La società cristiana e il circolo virtuoso della ricchezza fra Medioevo ed Età Moderna*. Il Mulino.
Tognetti, S. (1997). L'attività di banca locale di una grande compagnia fiorentina del XV secolo. *Archivio Storico Italiano, CLV*(574), 595–647.
Tognetti, S. (1999). *Il banco Cambini. Affari e mercati di una compagnia mercantile-bancaria nella Firenze del Quattrocento*. Olschki.
Tognetti, S. (2002). *Un'industria di lusso al servizio del grande commercio. Il mercato dei drappi serici e della seta nella Firenze del Quattrocento*. Olschki.
Tognetti, S. (2003). *Da Figline a Firenze. Ascesa economica e politica della famiglia Serristori (secoli XIV-XVI)*. Opus libri.
Tognetti, S. (2007). I drappi di seta. In F. Franceschi, R. A. Goldthwaite, & R. C. Mueller (Eds.), *Il Rinascimento italiano e l'Europa. Vol. 4: Commercio e cultura mercantile* (pp. 143–170). Fondazione Cassamarca.
Tognetti, S. (2008). Cenni sulla presenza dei mercanti-banchieri fiorentini a Famagosta di Cipro nei primi anni del Trecento. *Archivio Storico Italiano, CLXVI*, 53–68.
Tognetti, S. (2009). Gli affari di messer Palla Strozzi (e di suo padre Nofri). Imprenditoria e mecenatismo nella Firenze del primo Rinascimento. *Annali di Storia di Firenze, IV*, 7–88.
Tognetti, S. (Ed.). (2010). *Firenze e Pisa dopo il 1406. La creazione di un nuovo spazio regionale, Atti del convegno di studi (Firenze, 27-28 settembre 2008)*. Olschki.
Tognetti, S. (2013). *I Gondi di Lione. Una banca d'affari fiorentina nella Francia del primo Cinquecento*. Olschki.
Tommaseo, N., & Bellini, E. (1977). *Dizionario della lingua italiana scritta e parlata*. Rizzoli Editore.
Torres Ramírez, B., & Hernández Paolomo, J. (Eds.). (1985). *Presencia italiana en Andalucía siglos XIV-XVII, Actas del I Coloquio Hispano-Italiano*. Escuela de Estudios Hispano-Americanos de Sevilla.
Torres Ramírez, B., & Hernández Paolomo, J. (Eds.). (1989). *Presencia italiana en Andalucia siglos XIV-XVII, Actas del III Coloquio Hispano-Italiano*. Escuela de Estudios Hispano-Americanos de Sevilla.
Tripodi, C. (2010). I fiorentini "quinto elemento dell'universo": L'utilizzazione encomiastica di una tradizione/invenzione. *Archivio Storico Italiano, 168*(3(625)), 491–516. https://www.jstor.org/stable/26214775?seq=1#page_scan_tab_contents
Tripodi, C. (2013). *Gli Spini tra XIV e XV secolo. Il declino di un antico casato fiorentino*. Olschki.
Tripodi, C. (2018). *Prima di Amerigo. I Vespucci da Peretola a Firenze alle Americhe*. Viella.

Trivellato, F. (2003). Juifs de Livourne, Italiens de Lisbonne, Hindous de Goa. Réseaux marchands et échanges interculturels à l'époque moderne. *Annales. Histoire, Sciences Sociales, 58*(3), 581–603.

Trivellato, F. (2009). *The familiarity of strangers. The Sephardic Diaspora, Livorno and Cross-cultural trade in the early modern period.* Yale University Press.

Trivellato, F. (2010). Renaissance Italy and the Muslim Mediterranean in recent historical work. *The Journal of Modern History, LXXXII*, 127–155.

Trivellato, F. (2020). Renaissance Florence and the origins of capitalism: A business history perspective. *Business History Review, 94*, 229–251.

Tumino, M. (2019). Formazione e attività dei giovani mercanti. Fattori, collaboratori e soci nelle aziende di Francesco Datini. *Mélanges de l'École française de Rome, 131-2*, 229–237.

Turpin, A. (2001). The Frame of the Botti Madonna. In *Andrea del Sarto. The Botti Madonna, Catalogo e Appendice preparati in occasione dell'esposizione del quadro presso la Galleria Doria Pamphilj* (pp. 56–69). Courtauld Institute of Art.

Ulivi, E. (2002). Scuole e maestri d'abaco in Italia tra Medioevo e Rinascimento. In E. Giusti & R. Petti (Eds.), *Un ponte sul Mediterraneo. Leonardo Pisano, la scienza araba e la rinascita della matematica in Occidente* (pp. 121–155). Polistampa.

Ulivi, E. (2008). Scuole d'abaco e insegnamento della matematica. In A. Clericuzio & G. Ernst (Eds.), *Il Rinascimento italiano e l'Europa* (Vol. V, pp. 403–420). Le Scienze.

Ulivi, E. (2013). *Gli abacisti fiorentini delle famiglie 'del Maestro Luca', Calandri e Micceri e le loro scuole d'abaco (secc.XIV–XVI).* Olschki.

Ulivi, E. (2021). Abacisti attivi a Firenze al tempo di Dante. *Bollettino di storia delle scienze matematiche, 41*, 135–162.

Vaccari, O. (2007). Il porto di Pisa, un osservatorio mediterraneo nel tardo Medioevo. In F. Cardini & M. L. Ceccarelli Lemut (Eds.), *Quel mar che la terra inghirlanda: in ricordo di Marco Tangheroni* (pp. 781–796). Pacini.

Vaccari, O. (2019). Il sistema integrato Arno-Tirreno: vie d'acqua e infrastrutture a Pisa e a Livorno tra medioevo ed età moderna. In M. L. Ceccarelli Lemut, F. Franceschini, G. Garzella, & O. Vaccari (Eds.), *Vallis Arni - Arno Valley. La Toscana dal fiume al mare: tra eredità storica e prospettive future* (pp. 83–93). Pacini.

Vaccari, O. (2022). The Mediterranean Port System of Pisa: Role, management, and evolution. In K. R. Mathews, S. Orvietani Busch, & S. Bruni (Eds.), *A companion to medieval Pisa* (pp. 337–358). Brill.

Varchi, B. (1803). *Storia fiorentina.* Soc. Tipografica de' Classici Italiani. https://www.digitale-sammlungen.de/en/view/bsb10754828?page=128,129

Varela, C. (1989). Vida cotidiana de los florentinos en la Sevilla del descubrimiento. In B. Torres Ramírez & J. Hernández Paolomo (Eds.), *Presencia italiana en Andalucía siglos XIV-XVII, Actas del III Coloquio Hispano-Italiano* (pp. 11–22). Escuela de Estudios Hispano-Americanos de Sevilla.

Varela, C. (1991). *Colombo e i fiorentini.* Vallecchi.

Vasari, G. (1862). *Le vite de' più eccellenti pittori, scultori e architetti di Giorgio vasari secondo le migliore stampe*, volume unico, Trieste, Sezione letterario-artistica del Loyd austriaco. https://books.google.it/books?id=dnGxfe4YCwcC&printsec=frontcover&hl=it&source=gbs_ge_summary_r&cad=0#v=onepage&q&f=false

Vasari, G. (n.d.) *Ricordanze,* 1527-1573. https://www.memofonte.it/home/files/pdf/vasari_ricordanze.pdf

Vera Morín, M. V. (2018). El acceso a la nobleza como estrategia social en el ámbito mercantil. Los Botti y los Fonte entre Sevilla y Canarias en el siglo XVI. In M. Á. Pérez Samper & J. L. Betrán Moya (Eds.), *Nuevas perspectivas de investigación en Historia Moderna: Economía, Sociedad, Política y Cultura en el Mundo Hispánico* (pp. 150–158). Fundación Española de Historia Moderna. https://bibliotecadigital.jcyl.es/es/catalogo_imagenes/grupo.do?path=10130529

Vera Morín, M. V. (2019). Patrimono familiar, herencia y ascenso social: el caso de la familia Botti en las Islas Canarias del Quinientos. In J. J. Iglesias Rodríguez & I. M. Melero Muñoz (Eds.), *Hacer Historia Moderna. Lúneas actuales y futuras de investigación* (pp. 416–427). Editorial Universidad de Sevilla.

Vieira, A. (2004). Sugar island. The sugar economy of Madeira and the Canaries, 1450–1650. In S. B. Schwartz (Ed.), *Tropical Babylons: Sugar and the making of the Atlantic World, 1450-1680* (pp. 42–84). University of North Carolina Press.

Vieira, A. (2005). Canaviais, açúcar e aguardente na Madeira. Séculos XV a XX. *Revista de Historia Industrial, 27*, 221–224.

Vieira, A. (2017) *As ilhas do Açúcar-A Economia açucareira da Madeira e Canárias nos séculos XV a XVI*, Funchal. Retrieved June 25, 2024, from https://silo.tips/download/as-ilhas-do-aucar-a-economia-aucareira-da-madeira-e-canarias-nos-seculos-xv-e-xv

Vila Vilar, E. (1986). Partecipación de capitales italianos en la rentas de Sevilla en el siglio XVI. In A. Boscolo & B. Torres Ramírez (Eds.), *La presenza italiana in Andalusia nel Basso Medioevo. Atti del secondo convegno, Roma, 25–27 maggio 1984* (pp. 85–102). Cappelli.

Villani, G. (1845). *Cronica...a miglior lezione ridotta coll'aiuto de' testi a penna*, t. III. Sansone Coen, Florence.

Viña Brito, A., & Ronquillo Rubio, M. (2006). El primer ciclo del azúcar en Canaria. Balance historiográfico. In F. Morales Padrón (Ed.), *XVI Coloquio de Historia Canario-Americana* (pp. 1673–1696). consultato il 25 giugno 2024 https://accedacris.ulpgc.es/bitstream/10553/59048/1/8655-Texto%20del%20art%C3%ADculo-9134-1-10-20140506.pdf

Waterer, J. V. (1981) Cuoio. In C. Singer, E. J. Holmyard, A. R. Hall, & T. I. Williams (Eds.), *Storia della tecnologia. Le civiltà mediterranee e il Medioevo circa 700 a.C.-1500 d.C* (5 vols, II, pp. 150–192). Editore Boringhieri.

Weissen, K. (2003). I mercanti italiani e le fiere in Europa centrale alla fine del Medioevo e agli inizi dell'Età Moderna. In P. Lanaro (Ed.), *La pratica dello scambio. Sistemi di fiere, mercanti e città in Europa (1400–1700)* (pp. 161–176). Marsiglio.

Wolfthal, D. (2007). Florentine Bankers, Flemish Friars, and the Patronage of the Portinari Altarpiece. In I. Alexander-Skipnes (Ed.), *Cultural exchange between the low countries and Italy (1400–1600)* (pp. 1–21). Brepols.

Wyatt, M. (2014). *The Cambridge companion to the Italian Renaissance*. Cambridge University Press.

Yun Casalilla, B. (2014). The Spanish Empire, globalization, and cross-cultural consumption in a world context, c. 1400-c. 1750. In B. Aram & B. Yun Casalilla (Eds.), *Global goods and the Spanish Empire, 1492-1824. Circulation, resistance and diversity* (pp. 277–306). Palgrave.

Yun Casalilla, B. (2019). The Peninsular economies and the impact of globalisation (ca. 1494–1700). In F. Bouza, P. Cardim, & A. Feros Carrasco (Eds.), *The Iberian world, 1450-1820* (pp. 189–210). Routledge.

Yun Casalilla, B. (2024). The economic history of Iberia in a wider context, 1500–1800. In P. Lains, L. Freire Costa, R. Grafe, A. Herranz-Locán, D. Igual Luis, & H. Vasconcelos Vilar (Eds.), *An economic history of the Iberian Peninsula, 700-2000* (pp. 443–470). Cambridge University Press.

Zandri, A. M. (2004). *Famiglie storiche toscane. I Capponi*. Polistampa.

Zemon Davis, N. (2006). *Trickster travels. A sixteenth-century Muslim across worlds*. Hill & Wang.

Index

A. Orlandi, *Money, Culture, Beauty. The Botti Family*,
https://doi.org/10.1007/978-3-032-00453-6

MIX
Papier aus verantwortungsvollen Quellen
Paper from responsible sources
FSC® C105338

If you have any concerns about our products,
you can contact us on
ProductSafety@springernature.com

In case Publisher is established outside the EU,
the EU authorized representative is:
Springer Nature Customer Service Center GmbH
Europaplatz 3, 69115 Heidelberg, Germany

Printed by Libri Plureos GmbH
in Hamburg, Germany